THE CURVES SEMINAR AT QUEEN'S

VOLUME IX

BY

ANTHONY V. GERAMITA

QUEEN'S PAPERS IN PURE AND APPLIED MATHEMATICS
NO. 95

QUEEN'S UNIVERSITY

KINGSTON, ONTARIO, CANADA

1993

ISBN 0-88911-655-5

INTRODUCTION TO VOLUME IX

These are the proceedings of the Curves Seminar for the Academic Year 1992-93. It was a year in which we were very pleased to have several long-term visitors. Their participation in the seminars (and suppers!) made the year very memorable and I want to thank them all for their participation. There were: Anna Bigatti (Genoa - September, 1992 to April 1993); Juan Migliore (Notre Dame - January to June 1993), Uwe Nagel (Paderborn; October 1992 to March 1993), Yves Pitteloud (Lausanne; September 1992 to August 1993).

Several of these visitors contributed to the lectures of the seminar, and their names are noted below.

The theme for the year was, roughly speaking, Hilbert functions and resolutions for ideals of points in projective space. There were several papers that resulted from problems raised in the seminar, but we have included only one of these here (the paper by Nagel and Pitteloud).

During the year we also had a visit from Chris Peterson, a doctoral student of Migliore, who gave us an informal talk on the problem he was studying. In the months after his visit, Chris solved several of those problems and I asked him if he'd be kind enough to write these up for inclusion in these Proceedings. He's done so and I am grateful to him for that.

The short note by T. Harima was supposed to have been included in last year's Proceedings but, due to an oversight on my part, that didn't happen. Regular readers of the Curves Seminar will recognize the problem that Harima discusses as one that has come up several times in the published work of my colleague L. Roberts, our frequent visitor M. Roitman (Israel), and myself. My sincere apologies to Harima for my oversight.

Finally my thanks to Ballico, Chiarli, Del Centina, Davis, Gimigliano and Greco for notes that fit in exceedingly well with the continuing philosophy of the seminar -- namely to expose work on the broad interface between commutative algebra and algebraic geometry.

As always, it is expected that the contributed notes will eventually appear as papers in refereed journals. The interested reader should write to the author to inquire about such things.

Anthony V. Geramita
December, 1993
Kingston, Ontario

TABLE OF CONTENTS

II.   Contributed Notes:

THE CURVES SEMINAR

PROCEEDINGS

Contributions by:

Anthony V. Geramita

Juan C. Migliore

Uwe Nagel

Yves Pitteloud

Lecture 1 – Anthony V. Geramita

I would like to give, in this lecture, an overview of the material I want to talk about this year. In this first lecture I will leave many things unproven. The idea is simply to see where the problems come from and where they fit, from a historical point of view, in the study of curves and surfaces.

We shall be interested in closed subschemes $\mathbf{Y} \subseteq \mathbb{P}^n$ i.e. varieties defined by homogeneous ideals $I \subseteq k[x_0, \ldots, x_n]$. In general we shall assume that k is an algebraically closed field, of characteristic zero (letting $k = \mathbb{C}$, the complex numbers, wouldn't be a bad idea – most of the problems I'll eventually talk about don't seem to involve the nature of the field very much). I don't want to worry about arithmetic difficulties or have to comment on them again so I will avoid non-zero characteristic. Such arithmetic considerations appear to be marginal to the issues I'll raise for discussion.

One way to try and understand these topological objects (the subschemes of $\mathbb{P}^n$) is by attaching to them certain invariants - e.g. integers, functions, groups, other topological spaces, etc.- which are invariant under some notion of "equivalence" or isomorphism. The two most usual notions of equivalence I will use are:

i) isomorphism as abstract projective variety;

ii) isomorphism, under linear coordinate change, i.e. as subscheme of
a particular $\mathbb{P}^n$.

Invariants which are attached using this second notion will be referred to as "embedded" invariants. These are the invariants that will usually interest me most. Notice that, by definition, there should be more invariants of this type than those associated to notion i). However, I shall also be interested in the interplay between these "embedded" invariants and other "non-embedded" invariants.

Let me begin by illustrating some of these ideas in the context of projective curves – a case of historical (and continuing) interest.

Let $\mathcal{C}$ denote a projective curve in $\mathbb{P}^n$ which is reduced and irreducible. In this case, the homogeneous ideal in $k[x_0, \ldots, x_n] = R$ associated to $\mathcal{C}$ is a prime ideal of height $n-1$, which I'll denote by $\wp$. We can also further associate to $\mathcal{C}$ both a ring and a field. The ring will be the homogeneous coordinate ring of this embedding of $\mathcal{C}$ in $\mathbb{P}^n$ and the field will be the field of rational functions on $\mathcal{C}$.

1

The *homogeneous coordinate ring* of $\mathcal{C} \subseteq \mathbb{P}^n$ is $A = R/\wp$. The *field of rational functions* on $\mathcal{C}$ is denoted $k(\mathcal{C})$ and (although it has an intrinsic description) can be described by:

$$k(\mathcal{C}) = \{f/g : f \text{ and } g \neq 0 \text{ are homogeneous elements of } A \text{ of the same degree } \}.$$

The ring A is an invariant of the "embedded" variety but not of the abstract variety. (To see this observe that the map $\phi : \mathbb{P}^1 \to \mathbb{P}^3$ given by $\phi[s:t] = [s^4 : s^3 t : st^3 : t^4]$ is an isomorphism of $\mathbb{P}^1$ with its image, a rational curve in $\mathbb{P}^3$ of degree 4. The coordinate ring of $\mathbb{P}^1 \subseteq \mathbb{P}^1$ is $k[x, y]$, while the coordinate ring of the image curve is

$$A = k[x, y, z, w]/\wp \cong k[s^4, s^3 t, st^3, t^4] \subseteq k[s, t]$$

where we now think of s and t as the coordinate functions on $\mathbb{P}^1$. A is not an integrally closed ring ($s^2 t^2$ is not in A but $(s^2 t^2)^2$ is in A) but $k[x, y]$ is integrally closed. Thus the coordinate ring is not an invariant in this case.)

Although far from obvious, the field of rational functions on $\mathcal{C}$, $k(\mathcal{C})$ **IS** an invariant under isomorphism as abstract variety. We see from the description above that this "non-embedded" invariant can be calculated using something which is an embedded invariant.

One geometric feature of $\mathcal{C}$ can be phrased in terms of the field $k(\mathcal{C})$, namely: what can be the disposition of the zeroes and poles of the elements in $k(\mathcal{C})$. E.G. it was well known that it is possible to find a rational function on the projective line which has zeroes and poles of any prescribed multiplicities at any given finite set of points.

Let's look at some examples: consider the two smooth plane curves with defining equations, respectively, $x^2 + y^2 = z^2$ and $y^2 z = x^3 - xz^2$. We sketch, below, an affine piece of each of the two curves.

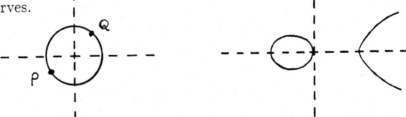

On the circle, let's see (geometrically) how we can make a rational function with a simple zero at P and a simple pole at Q. (sketch: choose another point R, take line **PR** and its equation L_1 and then line **RQ** and its equation L_2 and now consider the rational function with equation L_1/L_2).

2

If we try the same procedure on the cubic curve we run into trouble! In fact, we cannot find such a rational function on a cubic curve, and this points out one of the intrinsic differences between these two curves.

This example leads us to the idea of *linear system*. Let me quickly sketch the definitions and main facts for the case of $\mathcal{C}$ a smooth curve.

We define the group $Div\mathcal{C}$ as the free abelian group on the points of $\mathcal{C}$. If $D \in Div\mathcal{C}$ we write $D = \Sigma n_P P$, where $n_P \in \mathbf{Z}$, $P \in \mathcal{C}$ and $n_P = 0$ for almost all P. We define the *support* of D to be $suppD = \{P \in \mathcal{C} \mid n_P \neq 0\}$ and define the *degree* of D to be $\deg D = \Sigma n_P$.

If f is a rational function on $\mathcal{C}$ we can associate a divisor to f, namely, $div(f) = \Sigma \nu_P(f)P$, where $\nu_P(f)$ is the *order* of the zero or pole of f at P. $div(f)$ is indeed a divisor (called the *principal divisor* associated to f and, in fact, $div(fg) = div(f) + div(g)$. We say that the divisors D and E are *linearly equivalent* if their difference is the divisor of a rational function on $\mathcal{C}$. Since the set of principal divisors is a subgroup, $\mathrm{Pr}(\mathcal{C})$, of the abelian group $Div(\mathcal{C})$ the equivalence classes under linear equivalence are the elements of the group $Div(\mathcal{C})/\mathrm{Pr}(\mathcal{C}) = Cl(\mathcal{C})$, the *divisor class group of the curve* $\mathcal{C}$. We will denote elements of this group by $[D]$ = the divisor class containing the divisor D.

The class $[D]$ is called *effective* if it contains a divisor all of whose coefficients are ≥ 0 (if a divisor D has all of its coefficients ≥ 0 we shall abusively write $D \geq 0$). The set of ALL effective divisors in a divisor class $[D]$ is called the *complete linear system of all effective divisors linearly equivalent to D* (or, more simply, *a complete linear system*).

To see where the word 'linear 'comes from we have to make a few simple remarks: let $[D]$ be an effective divisor class and let

$$\mathcal{L}(D) = \{f \in k(\mathcal{C}) \mid div(f) + D \geq 0\}$$

One shows that $\mathcal{L}(D)$ is a vector subspace of $k(\mathcal{C})$ which (since $\mathcal{C}$ is a projective variety) is finite dimensional as a vector space. The projective space associated to this vector space is, in a simple way, in $1 - 1$ correspondence with the effective divisors in the class $[D]$. In this way, the set of linearly equivalent effective divisors takes on the structure of a finite dimensional projective space, i.e. a linear space. Thus, the complete linear system of effective divisors linearly equivalent to D is a $\mathbb{P}^r$, for some r. One sees in this case that $\dim \mathcal{L}(D) = r + 1$ and we write $\dim \mathcal{L}(D) = \ell(D)$.

Theorem 1.1: *Let D be an effective divisor on C. Then:*

    i) for all $n \gg 0, \ell(nD) = n(\deg D) + 1 - g$ (the number "g" being called the arithmetic genus of C);

    ii) $\deg D + 1 - g \le \ell(D) \le \deg D + 1$.

This theorem gives us some help in knowing when we have discovered all the divisors in a complete linear system and the Riemann-Roch problem is, essentially, trying to figure out, for any divisor D on a curve C, the exact value of $\ell(D)$.

I am not going to enter into a discussion of this very interesting problem right now except to show how to make a modern (homological) connection with these classical notions.

First note that if we have $C \subseteq \mathbb{P}^n$ and we cut C with a hypersurface of $\mathbb{P}^n$ defined by an equation of degree d we obtain a set of $(\deg C)d$ points on C, (counted properly). More precisely we get an effective divisor on C having degree $(\deg C)d$. (I won't go into exactly how that divisor is determined since that would take us a bit far afield. Obviously we want the support of that divisor to be the set of points where the hypersurface meets the curve.) We might as well assume that the hypersurface doesn't contain the curve. I.e. if we look at the homogeneous coordinate ring of the curve in $\mathbb{P}^n$ then we see that it is the homogeneous elements of degree d in that quotient ring which give us hypersurfaces that cut the curve C in distinct divisors. It is not hard to show that any two such divisors are linearly equivalent, so if D is one of those effective divisors on C, and A is the coordinate ring of C in $\mathbb{P}^n$ then $\ell(D) \ge \dim A_d$.

Thus, even though $\ell(D)$ is a non-embedded invariant of the curve C we can get some help in computing it if D is a divisor cut out on $C \subset \mathbb{P}^n$ by a hypersurface of $\mathbb{P}^n$. Of course, it would be wonderful if, for some reason $\ell(D) = \dim A_d$. In that case, we would see the complete linear system as the system of divisors cut out on the curve C by the hypersurfaces of a given degree – a sort of ideal kind of situation!

Theorem 1.2: *(Castelnuovo) Let $C \subseteq \mathbb{P}^n$ be a curve of degree d, then the linear systems cut out on C by the hypersurfaces of degree $\ge d - 2$ are complete. (Recently refined by Gruson, Lazarsfeld and Peskine replacing $d - 2$ by $d - n + 1$.)*

We make the homological connection as follows: $C \leftrightarrow \wp \subseteq R = k[x_o, \ldots, x_n]$, $\wp$ a homogeneous prime ideal with $ht.\wp = n - 1$. By a theorem of Hilbert, $\wp$ has a free resolution by (graded) free R-modules as follows:

$$0 \to F_r \to \cdots \to F_1 \to F_0 \to \wp \to 0 \tag{1.1}$$

where $r \leq n$. The minimal such r we can find is called the *homological dimension* of $\wp$ and, in that case, we write $r = \text{h.dim}_R \wp$.

By a theorem of Auslander-Buchsbaum-Serre (the codimension theorem) we can say more: $r = n$ or $n - 1$; moreover $r = n - 1$ if and only if $\wp$ is a *perfect* ideal if and only if the ring $R/\wp$ is a Cohen-Macaulay ring. (i.e. a ring in which principal ideals are unmixed with respect to height). Moreover, these algebraic conditions are equivalent (for a smooth curve $\mathcal{C}$) to the condition that the linear systems cut out on $\mathcal{C}$ by the hypersurfaces in $\mathbb{P}^n$ of degree d are complete for every $d \geq 1$.

Let me illustrate this with an example: let $\mathcal{C} \subseteq \mathbb{P}^3$ be the rational cubic curve defined as the image of the map from $\mathbb{P}^1$ to $\mathbb{P}^3$, $[s : t] \to [s^3 : s^2 t : st^2 : t^3]$. If we let $k[x, y, z, w]$ be the homogeneous coordinate ring of $\mathbb{P}^3$, then the image curve is defined by the prime ideal $\wp = (yw - z^2, yz - xw, xz - y^2)$. The resolution of $\wp$ is given as follows:

$$0 \to R^2 \xrightarrow{\phi_1} R^3 \xrightarrow{\phi_0} \wp \to 0.$$

If we write vectors in free modules as row vectors, and use the standard bases for the free modules above, then the maps are given, in matrix form, as follows:

$$\phi_1 = \begin{pmatrix} x & y & z \\ y & z & w \end{pmatrix}, \phi_0 = \begin{pmatrix} yw - z^2 \\ yz - xw \\ xz - y^2 \end{pmatrix}$$

Thus, the rational normal curve in $\mathbb{P}^3$ is an example of a Cohen-Macaulay curve in $\mathbb{P}^3$. This means that the linear systems cut out on this curve by the forms in $\mathbb{P}^3$ of degree d are all complete linear systems on this curve.

Lecture 2 – Anthony V. Geramita

Relating information about the projective resolution of the ideal of a projective curve to geometric information about the embedded curve is a relatively new way to look at problems concerning algebraic curves. It was well known that certain information about the curve is encoded in the resolution (e.g. the determination of the genus of the curve can be extracted from the projective resolution). Since I am very interested in this perspective on the interplay between the algebraic and geometric invariants of varieties I will now go into more detail.

So, let R be a graded ring, $R = \oplus R_i, i \geq 0, R_0 = k$ a field (i.e. a ring like the polynomial ring over a field or a quotient of such a ring by a homogeneous ideal) and let $M = \oplus M_i$ be a graded R-module. Each M_i is a vector space over the field k and $R_i M_j \subseteq M_{i+j}$ for all i, j. If we assume (as I will - without comment from now on) that M is a finitely generated R-module and R is a noetherian ring (usually generated as an R_0-algebra by the elements of R_1, i.e. a *standard graded algebra*) then the graded pieces of M are finite dimensional vector spaces.

If M and N are graded R-modules then $M \oplus N$ is easily seen to be graded by: $(M \oplus N)_d = M_d \oplus N_d$.

If $a \in \mathbb{Z}$ we define the graded R-module $M(a)$ as follows:

$$M(a)_i = M_{a+i}.$$

$M(a)$ is called a *shift* of M.

For example: if R is a polynomial ring, then $R(-1)$ is an R-module which is isomorphic to R but begins in degree 1. In fact, both R and $R(-1)$ are free graded R-modules of rank 1 but they have their basis vectors in different places.

If M and N are graded R-modules then a *graded homomorphism* from M to N is an R-module homomorphism which takes homogeneous elements of M to homogeneous elements of N. We say that a *graded homomorphism is of degree d* if $\phi(M_r) \subseteq N_{r+d}$ for all r. Note that if ϕ is a graded homomorphism of degree d from M to N then ϕ defines, in a natural way, a homomorphism of degree 0 from $M(-d)$ to N.

If M and N are graded R-modules we define a graded module called GHom(M,N), where:

$$[\text{GHom}(M, N)]_d = \{\text{graded homomorphisms of degree } d \text{ from } M \text{ to } N\}$$

If M is a finitely generated R-module then $\mathrm{GHom}(M,N)$ is nothing more than the R-module $\mathrm{Hom}(M,N)$ of ALL R-module homomorphisms from M to N.

We can, by using the "shifting" idea, change a free resolution (like (1.1) above) into one in which all the homomorphisms are graded homomorphisms of degree 0.

To see why this is so, let M be a finitely generated graded R-module (R as above). Then M can be generated by a finite number of homogeneous elements. (In fact, by a Nakayama Lemma argument, M can be minimally generated by a set of homogeneous elements.) So, let $f_1, \ldots, f_r$ be such a generating set where $\deg f_i = d_i$. The homomorphism:

$$\phi : R(-d_1) \oplus \ldots \oplus R(-d_r) \to M$$

(defined by taking e_i, a basis of $R(-d_i)$, to f_i) is a homomorphism of degree 0.

Now suppose that for M, as in the previous paragraph, we also have $M \subseteq R(-\ell_1) \oplus \ldots \oplus R(-\ell_t)$. Then $f_i \in M_{d_i}$ means that $f_i = (r_{i,1}, \ldots, r_{i,t})$ where $r_{i,j}$ is a homogeneous polynomial in R of degree $d_i - \ell_j$. Since we can think of ϕ as a homomorphism from R^r to R^t we can, after choosing a basis for each of the modules, use a matrix to describe ϕ. Thinking of R^r as $R(-d_1) \oplus \ldots \oplus R(-d_r)$ and R^t as $R(-\ell_1) \oplus \ldots \oplus R(-\ell_t)$ and choosing the canonical bases for these modules, the matrix for ϕ (an $r \times t$ matrix since, recall, we are thinking of the elements of free modules as row vectors) has ith row $[r_{i,1} \ldots r_{i,t}]$. Our comments above give the degrees of the entries in this matrix.

Let me illustrate this with the example of the rational cubic curve in $\mathbb{P}^3$, which we considered in Lecture 1. Instead of writing the resolution as we did then, namely as:

$$0 \to R^2 \xrightarrow{\phi_1} R^3 \xrightarrow{\phi_0} \wp \to 0$$

we can now rewrite it as:

$$0 \to R(-3)^2 \to R(-2)^3 \to \wp \to 0.$$

Now let I be a homogeneous ideal in R and form a minimal graded free resolution of I (i.e. at each stage we choose a minimal homogeneous generating set for the module of syzygies that arises) to obtain (say):

$$0 \to F_r \to \ldots \to F_1 \to F_0 \to I \to 0 \qquad (2.1)$$

7

Then, from our discussion above, we may write: $F_i = \oplus_{j=1}^{s_i} R(-d_{i,j})$. The numbers $d_{i,j}$ are called the *graded Betti numbers* of I and they form a subtle collection of invariants of I whose full significance is far from being well understood.

If we restrict the resolution (2.1) to degree d and recall (as described above) that all the maps in (2.1) are homogeneous of degree 0, we then get:

$$0 \to (F_r)_d \to \ldots \to (F_1)_d \to (F_0)_d \to I_d \to 0 \qquad (2.2)$$

Since (2.2) is an exact sequence of finite dimensional vector spaces we know that the alternating sum of the dimensions of these spaces is $= 0$. If we know all the graded Betti numbers then we know the dimensions of each of the $(F_i)_d$, since if $R = k[x_0, \ldots, x_n]$ then $\dim R_d = \binom{d+n}{n}$. Consequently we know the dimension of I_d as a vector space.

Thus, $\dim_k I_d$ is a **gross** invariant that can be calculated from the graded Betti numbers. I shall have more to say about this later when I discuss the Hilbert function of the ideal I.

Note also that if we have a free resolution of the ideal I:

$$0 \to F_r \to \ldots \to F_0 \to I \to 0$$

then

$$0 \to F_r \to \ldots \to F_0 \to R \to R/I \to 0$$

is a free resolution of the R-module R/I. Thus, we can detect the graded Betti numbers of I from either of these resolutions.

Castelnuovo Theory - The Method of Hyperplanes

One of several successful ways to study curves in $\mathbb{P}^n$ has become closely associated with the name of one of the towering figures of the school of Italian algebraic geometry of the early decades of the 20th century, Guido Castelnuovo (1865-1952). The simple idea behind this approach is very easy to understand – consider $C \subseteq \mathbb{P}^n$, a reduced and irreducible curve, and let $\mathcal{H}$ be a hyperplane of $\mathbb{P}^n$: cut C with $\mathcal{H}$ and then try to deduce information about C from the resulting subvariety of $\mathcal{H} \cong \mathbb{P}^{n-1}$. (I want to note that this approach has also been used to study varieties bigger than curves. Nevertheless, for simplicity, I shall restrict the discussion to curves.)

Clearly there will be problems with this naive approach – it's impossible to figure out what Jeffery Hall is like by just wandering around on the 3rd floor!! The amazing thing is that, in the hands of Castelnuovo and his school, a great deal could be done with this simple beginning.

So, let's begin by reinterpreting some of the relevant geometric ideas in the language of algebra.

We've already noted that $\mathcal{C} \subseteq \mathbb{P}^n$ corresponds to $\wp \subseteq k[x_0, \ldots, x_n] = R$, where $\wp$ is a prime ideal of height $n - 1$. If $\mathcal{H}$ is a hyperplane of $\mathbb{P}^n$ then $\mathcal{H}$ is the zeroes of a single linear form of R, i.e. an element of R_1, which I'll denote by L. We may as well assume that $\mathcal{C}$ is *non-degenerate*, i.e. that $\mathcal{C}$ is not contained in any $\mathbb{P}^{n-1} \subseteq \mathbb{P}^n$. In algebraic terms, there is no linear form in $\wp$ and, in particular, $L \notin \wp$. Then $\mathcal{C} \cap \mathcal{H}$ corresponds to the ideal $(\wp, L)$ which properly contains $\wp$. Here we come across our first algebraic problem – What can we say about the ideal $(\wp, L)$?

First of all, the only **prime** ideals which contain $(\wp, L)$ are $m = (x_0, \ldots, x_n)$, the unique maximal homogeneous ideal of R, (which corresponds to apparently nothing geometric!) and the prime ideals $\wp_i \leftrightarrow P_i, \{P_i\}$ the points of $\mathcal{C} \cap \mathcal{H}$. By the Nullstellensatz of Hilbert, $\wp_i = (L_{i,1}, \ldots, L_{i,n})$ where the $L_{i,j}$ are (for fixed i) linearly independent linear forms.

To continue in the language of algebra, I need to recall some facts about ideal theory in Noetherian rings. Recall that in a Noetherian ring every ideal, I, has a finite irredundant decomposition into primary ideals: i.e. $I = \mathfrak{q}_1 \cap \ldots \cap \mathfrak{q}_s$, where $\mathfrak{q}_i$ is not contained in $\cap_{j \neq i} \mathfrak{q}_j$ and $\mathfrak{q}_i$ is a $\wp_i$-primary ideal ($\wp_i$ a prime ideal). The $\mathfrak{q}_i$ are called *primary components* of I.

This "pale shadow" of unique factorization of elements in polynomial rings, further tells us that:

> a) the prime ideals $\wp_i$ so enumerated are uniquely determined by I;
> they are called the *associated prime ideals of I*.
>
> b) if we order the $\wp_i$ by inclusion, to obtain a partially ordered set, then the $\mathfrak{q}_i$ corresponding to the minimal $\wp_i$ are also uniquely determined by I. The other $\mathfrak{q}_i$ - the so-called *embedded components of I*, are **not**

uniquely determined by I.

    c) if $\wp$ is any prime ideal which contains I then $\wp$ must contain an associated prime of I.

Let's apply these insights to the ideal $(\wp, L)$ corresponding to $\mathcal{H} \cap \mathcal{C}$. We obtain that $(\wp, L) = \mathfrak{q}_1 \cap \ldots \cap \mathfrak{q}_s \cap \mathfrak{q}$ where $\mathfrak{q}_i$ is $\wp_i$-primary, $\wp_i$ the prime ideal of some point P_i in $\mathbb{P}^n$, and $\mathfrak{q}$ is m-primary. This is the case since we already noted that the $\wp_i$ and m are the only primes which contain $(\wp, L)$. Of course, some of the components might not be there!

So, as a first simple consequence of the decomposition theorem we obtain something geometric – $\mathcal{H}$ and $\mathcal{C}$ meet in at most a finite number of points. In fact, the points where $\mathcal{H}$ and $\mathcal{C}$ meet correspond precisely to the non-maximal primes associated to the ideal $(\wp, L)$.

The fact that there exist **any** non-maximal primes associated to $(\wp, L)$ is another important theorem in commutative algebra - the so-called Principal Ideal Theorem of Krull (which is applied to the principal ideal generated by the class of L in the ring $k[x_o, \ldots, x_n]/\wp$).

There are at least two other important things that have to be discussed when describing the ideal $(\wp, L)$. The first I have in mind comes from trying to understand what the primary ideals $\mathfrak{q}_i$ say about the way that $\mathcal{H}$ and $\mathcal{C}$ meet at P_i and the second concerns whether or not there is a primary component, with associated prime m, in the primary decomposition of $(\wp, L)$.

There is one nice answer to the question of the primary components of $(\wp, L)$ corresponding to points: the ideal $\mathfrak{q}_i$ is exactly $\wp_i$ iff $\mathcal{H}$ and $\mathcal{C}$ meet *transversally* at P_i. So, one might expect that properties of $\mathfrak{q}_i$ will give some measure of the contact of $\mathcal{H}$ and $\mathcal{C}$ at P_i. I will not go into that interesting discussion in this seminar. Nevertheless, there is a lovely theorem of Bertini (dates) (another one of those ubiquitious Italians of the turn of the century) which can be applied to this situation and which says that if $\mathcal{C}$ is reduced and irreducible then the *general* hyperplane meets $\mathcal{C}$ transversally everywhere it meets $\mathcal{C}$.

So, for the *generic* linear form L, the ideal $(\wp, L)$ has primary decompostion: $(\wp, L) = \wp_1 \cap \ldots \cap \wp_s \cap \mathfrak{q}$. It remains only to consider the significance of the primary component $\mathfrak{q}$.

We recall a very general fact about a $\wp$ -primary ideal $\mathfrak{q}$ in a noetherian ring: $\wp^r \subseteq \mathfrak{q}$ for some integer r.

What does this say in the particular case when $\mathfrak{q}$ is m -primary, $m = (x_0, \ldots, x_n) \subseteq R = k[x_0, \ldots, x_n]$?

10

With the usual grading on R, then $R = \oplus_{i \geq 0} R_i$ and $m = \oplus_{i \geq 1} R_i$. It is easy to see that $m^r = \oplus_{i \geq r} R_i$.

It follows that, for $t \geq r$, $(\wp_1 \cap \ldots \cap \wp_s)_t \subseteq \mathfrak{q}_t$, and hence, for degree $t \geq r$, $(\wp_1 \cap \ldots \cap \wp_s \cap \mathfrak{q})_t = (\wp_1 \cap \ldots \cap \wp_s)_t$. As a consequence of this we obtain:

the graded module $M_L = (\wp_1 \cap \ldots \cap \wp_s)/(\wp_1 \cap \ldots \cap \wp_s \cap \mathfrak{q})$ is a finite dimensional vector space since $(M_L)_t = 0$, for all $t \geq r$ (r as above).

Note that I have labelled the module M_L to emphasize its dependence on the linear form L which defined the hypersurface $\mathcal{H}$.

There is an important extremal case to consider: suppose that $M_L = 0$ for some hyperplane $\mathcal{H}$. This is the "wysiwyg" situation: $(\wp, L) = \wp_1 \cap \ldots \cap \wp_s$, i.e. $\mathcal{H}$ cuts $\mathcal{C}$ transversally everywhere it cuts $\mathcal{C}$ and (algebraically) there is no "embedded" component.

In this situation we have a non-trivial fact:

Theorem: $M_L = 0$ for some linear form L iff $M_L = 0$ for every linear form L.

Moreover, in this case, $R/\wp$ is a Cohen-Macaulay ring, i.e.

If $\mathcal{C}$ is a smooth curve in $\mathbb{P}^m$ then: $M_L = 0$ for some L if and only if the linear systems cut out on $\mathcal{C}$ by the curves of degree d, form a complete linear system on $\mathcal{C}$ for every $d, d \geq 1$.

Lecture 3 – Anthony V. Geramita

Let's continue the discussion of the last lecture by looking at some examples of hyperplane sections of curves.

Example 3.1: Let C be the rational cubic curve in $\mathbb{P}^3$ that we studied above. A hyperplane $\mathcal{H}$ in $\mathbb{P}^3$ is defined by an equation $L : ax + by + cz + dw = 0$. Such a hyperplane will meet C exactly when

$$as^3 + bs^2t + cst^2 + dt^3 = 0. \qquad (3.2)$$

I would like to choose L so that $\mathcal{H}$ meets C in exactly 3 distinct points. If we let $a = 1, b = 0, c = -1$, and $d = 0$, i.e. let $\mathcal{H}$ be the hyperplane with defining equation $x - z = 0$, we get that

$$[s : t] \in \{[0 : 1], [1 : 1], [-1 : 1]\}$$

are projective solutions to the homogeneous equation (3.2). We conclude that $\mathcal{H}$ meets C at the points:

$$P_1 = [0 : 0 : 0 : 1], \; P_2 = [1 : 1 : 1 : 1], \; P_3 = [-1 : 1 : -1 : 1],$$

corresponding to the prime ideals:

$$\wp_1 = (x, y, z), \; \wp_2 = (x - w, y - w, z - w), \; \wp_3 = (x + w, y - w, z + w).$$

In Lecture 1 we gave the equations for C. They generate the prime ideal:

$$\wp = (yw - z^2, yz - xw, xz - y^2).$$

Thus, the "algebraic hyperplane section" of C by $\mathcal{H}$ is described by the ideal:

$$(L, \wp) = (x - z, yw - z^2, yz - xw, xz - y^2) = J,$$

while the "geometric hyperplane section" of C is described by the ideal:

$$I = \wp_1 \cap \wp_2 \cap \wp_3 = (x, y, z) \cap (x - w, y - w, z - w) \cap (x + w, y - w, z + w).$$

We know that $J \subseteq I$, but, using the computer algebra programme *Macaulay* (written by Michael Stillman and Dave Bayer) one can show that $J = I$. On the other hand (at

12

least out of solidarity with a member of the seminar!) one can also use the computer programme developed at the University of Genova, called *CoCoA* (and functioning on our MacIntosh computer, and some of our IBM's) to also verify this equality.

(Aside: It is not so easy to just prove this directly! Fortunately both of the programmes, *Macaulay* and *CoCoA,* have a simple macro which allows the computation of the ideal of a set of points in $\mathbb{P}^n$ by just entering the coordinates of the points. There are several ways to then compare I and J. Since $J \subseteq I$, it would be enough to show that both homogeneous ideals have all their graded pieces with the same dimension, alternatively, one could compute the dimensions of the graded pieces of R/J and of R/I and compare. I won't go into this right now, but anyone who would like to play with either of these programmes can have them to play with. They are both in the public domain.)

Example 3.3: In this example I would like to look at the rational quartic curve, $\mathcal{C}$, we discussed in the first lecture and whose ideal was described there as:

$$\wp = (x^3 - w^2 y, wy^2 - x^2 z, y^3 - xz^2).$$

If we intersect $\mathcal{C}$ with the hyperplane $\mathcal{H}$ having defining equation $2x - 5y + 5z - 2w = 0$, then $\mathcal{H}$ meets $\mathcal{C}$ when:

$$[s : t] \in \{[1 : 1], [-1 : 1], [2 : 1], [1 : 2]\},$$

i.e. at the points

$$P_1 = [1 : 1 : 1 : 1], P_2 = [1 : -1 : -1 : 1], P_3 = [16 : 8 : 2 : 1], P_4 = [1 : 2 : 8 : 16],$$

with corresponding prime ideals,

$$\wp_1 = (x - w, y - w, z - w), \wp_2 = (x - w, y + w, z + w),$$

$$\wp_3 = (x - 16w, y - 8w, z - 2w), \wp_4 = (16x - w, 8y - w, 2z - w).$$

The geometric hyperplane section of $\mathcal{C}$ by $\mathcal{H}$ is defined by the ideal

$$I = \wp_1 \cap \wp_2 \cap \wp_3 \cap \wp_4,$$

13

while the "algebraic hyperplane section" is defined by the ideal:

$$(\wp, L) = J = (2x - 5y + 5z - 2w, x^3 - w^2y, wy^2 - x^2z, y^3 - xz^2).$$

It is easy to see, in this case, that J is properly contained in I since, in J, all the quadratic forms have to have $(2x - 5y + 5z - 2w)$ as a factor while it is clear that, for four points in $\mathbb{P}^3$, there are lots of quadratic forms which define quadric hypersurfaces containing the points which do not have a fixed hyperplane in them.

Since the two ideals are not equal the ideal J above must have an embedded component, i.e. a primary component for the homogenous maximal ideal $m = (x, y, z, w)$. (Less obvious, although this can also be computed using *CoCoA* or *Macaulay*, I and J only differ in their quadrics, in fact I/J is a 1-dimensional vector space.)

One thing I have not mentioned so far, but which is important for analysing graded Betti numbers, is a discussion of how the graded Betti numbers behave with respect to hyperplane sections.

Let $R = k[x_0, \ldots, x_n]$ and let I be an ideal of R. There is one case where we can make a good comparison between the graded Betti numbers of I and those of a hyperplane section of the variety described by I, namely the case in which the hyperplane is described by a linear form in R which is not a zero divisor in the ring R/I.

Before going on with this train of thought, we should make a connection between the algebraic property of being a zero-divisor in the ring R/I and some geometric property of the hyperplane with respect to the variety defined by I.

As usual, we must recall another of the very important theorems about ideals in a noetherian ring: if I is an ideal in the noetherian ring R, then the zero divisors in the ring R/I are the union of the associated primes of the zero ideal in R/I.

Since the associated primes of the zero ideal of R/I are in $1 - 1$ correspondence with the prime ideals of R which are associated to I, we see that when we choose our hyperplane, we have to avoid choosing it in any of the associated prime ideals of I, i.e. the hyperplane cannot contain any of the components of the variety defined by I. Unfortunately we have to avoid both physical and "metaphysical" components, i.e. both components corresponding to homogeneous prime ideals which define something and (perhaps) the irrelevant component. We'll see what the difficulty is below.

For now, let me state the exact theorem about the resolutions:

14

Theorem 3.4: *Let I be an ideal in R and suppose that L is a linear form in R that is not a zero divisor in the ring R/I.*

If $S = R/(L)$ and $J = (I, L)/(L)$ then the graded Betti numbers of I are the same as the graded Betti numbers of J.

Notice that with R as above, there is no loss of generality in assuming that $L = x_0$. In that case we can think of $S = k[x_1, \ldots, x_n]$. The ideal J then is determined by setting $x_0 = 0$ in all the elements of I, or equivalently, looking at the ideal generated by the forms obtained by setting $x_0 = 0$ in a set of generators of I.

What does this all say about finding the graded Betti numbers of the ideal of a curve (reduced and irreducible), say in $\mathbb{P}^n$? Such a curve is defined by a prime ideal $\wp$ in R. Since $R/\wp$ is a domain, every non-zero element is not a zero divisor, so it suffices to choose a linear form not in $\wp$ in order to apply the theorem. Let L be such a linear form. We then need to look at the associated prime ideals of $I = (L, \wp)$ if we hope to repeat this process. We know that the associated primes of $(L, \wp)$ can only be of two types: those corresponding to points in $\mathbb{P}^n$ and m. If all associated primes of $(L, \wp)$ were of the first type, then it would be easy to find a linear form not in any of those primes – one would only need to look for a hyperplane which missed the resulting finite set of points. That's easy! But, if the ideal m is associated to $(L, \wp)$ we are doomed. Every linear form is in m and so we cannot proceed.

Let's do this again algebraically: Let L be a linear form not in $\wp$. Then

$$0 \to \wp(-1) \xrightarrow{\cdot L} \wp$$

is exact, since R is a domain. We get $\wp/L\wp$ as cokernel.

Claim: $L\wp = (L) \cap \wp$

> Proof: The containment $\subseteq$ is obvious.
> For the other inclusion, let $F \in (L) \cap \wp$. Then $F = LH$ since $F \in (L)$.
> Since $LH \in \wp$ and $L \notin \wp$, then (since $\wp$ is a prime ideal) we get $H \in \wp$. Thus $F = LH \in L\wp$ as we wanted to show.

So, we have the exact sequence:

$$0 \to \wp(-1) \xrightarrow{\cdot L} \wp \to \wp/((L) \cap \wp) \to 0.$$

15

By one of the fundamental isomorphism theorems,

$$\wp/((L) \cap \wp) \cong (L, \wp)/\wp.$$

Using our earlier notation, we have

$$(L, \wp) = \mathfrak{q}_1 \cap \ldots \cap \mathfrak{q}_s \cap \mathfrak{q}, \ \mathrm{rad}(\mathfrak{q}) = \ m, \ \mathrm{rad}(\mathfrak{q}_i) = \ \wp_i.$$

If we set $M(\mathcal{C}) = \oplus_{d \in \mathbb{Z}} H^1(\mathbb{P}^n, \mathcal{I}_{\mathcal{C}}(d))$ (the so-called *Hartshorne-Rao*, or *deficiency* module of $\mathcal{C}$), then there is a more elaborate exact sequence which takes in many of the special features we have been discussing:

$$0 \ \rightarrow \ \wp(-1) \ \overset{\cdot L}{\rightarrow} \ \wp \ \rightarrow \ (\mathfrak{q}_1 \cap \ldots \cap \mathfrak{q}_s)/(L) \ \rightarrow \ M(\mathcal{C})(-1) \ \overset{\cdot L}{\rightarrow}$$

$$(L, \wp)/(L) \qquad\qquad M_L(\mathcal{C})$$

$$0 \qquad\qquad 0 \qquad\qquad 0 \qquad\qquad 0$$

This exact sequence points out the two ingredients one needs to consider in studying graded Betti numbers for an embedded curve in $\mathbb{P}^n$:

a) the points of the hyperplane section;

b) the module structure of the Hartshorne-Rao module.

Finally, then, we move to one part of this study, the points of the hyperplane section.

The Ideal of a Finite Set of Points in $\mathbb{P}^n$:

Let $\mathbf{X} = \{P_1, \ldots, P_s\}$ be a finite set of points in $\mathbb{P}^n$ and let $P_i \leftrightarrow \wp_i \subseteq R = k[x_0, \ldots, x_n]$. The ideal $I = \wp_1 \cap \ldots \cap \wp_s$ is the ideal of the set of points. The ring $A = R/I$ is the homogeneous coordinate ring of $\mathbf{X} \subseteq \mathbb{P}^n$.

Clearly there is always a linear from L in R which is not a zero divisor in A. Let $B = A/\bar{L}A = (R/I)/(L, I)/I \cong R/(L, I)$.

There is no loss of generality in assuming that $L = x_0$, i.e. that the points are $[p_{i,o} : p_{i,1} : \ldots : p_{i,n}]$ where $p_{i,o} \neq 0$.

Thus, $R/(x_0, I) \cong S/J$ where $S = k[x_1, \ldots, x_n]$ and J is an ideal for which $\text{rad}(J) = (x_1, \ldots, x_n)$. By earlier observations, we must have $J_d = S_d$ for all $d \gg 0$.

One of the simple invariants we shall introduce for the set $\mathbf{X}$ is the *Hilbert function* of $\mathbf{X}$.

Definition 3.5: With the notation above, write $A = \oplus_{i \geq 0} A_i$. The *Hilbert Function* of $\mathbf{X}$ (or of I, or of A) is a function from $\mathbf{N}^{\geq 0}$ to $\mathbf{N}^{\geq 0}$ given by:

$$H_{\mathbf{X}}(d) = H(A, d) := \dim_k A_d.$$

Example 3.6: Let $\mathbf{X} = \{P_1, P_2, P_3\} \subseteq \mathbb{P}^2$, $P_1 = [1 : 0 : 0]$, $P_2 = [0 : 1 : 0]$ and $P_3 = [0 : 0 : 1]$ (the 3 standard reference points of $\mathbb{P}^2$). The corresponding prime ideals are $\wp_1 = (y, z)$, $\wp_2 = (x, z)$ and $\wp_3 = (x, y)$. It is not hard to show that the ideal of $\mathbf{X}$ is $I = \wp_1 \cap \wp_2 \cap \wp_3 = (xy, xz, yz)$. Since I is a monomial ideal, to decide the dimension of $(R/I)_d$ it is enough to figure out the monomials of degree d which are not in I. In fact, it is easy to see that the only monomials of degree d missing from I are x^d, y^d, z^d. It follows that the Hilbert function of $\mathbf{X}$ is:

$$H_{\mathbf{X}}(0) = 1 \text{ and } H_{\mathbf{X}}(d) = 3 \text{ for all } d \geq 1.$$

Example 3.7: Add the point $P_4 = [1 : 1 : 1]$ to the points of Example 3.6 and call the resulting set $\mathbf{X}$. Then $\wp_4 = (x - z, y - z)$. If I is the ideal of this set $\mathbf{X}$ then there are clearly no linear forms in I, so: $H_{\mathbf{X}}(0) = 1$, and $H_{\mathbf{X}}(1) = 3$. From the previous example we know that any quadric which vanishes at the first 3 points of $\mathbf{X}$ must look like: $axy + bxz + cyz$. For this to vanish also at P_4 we must also have $a + b + c = 0$, i.e. there is a 2 dimensional space of quadrics vanishing at $\mathbf{X}$, so $H_{\mathbf{X}}(2) = 4$. It is not difficult to see that imposing to the forms of degree d, that already vanish at the points P_1, P_2, P_3, the additional condition that they vanish at P_4 is exactly one additional condition. It follows that $H_{\mathbf{X}}(d) = 4$ for every $d \geq 3$.

There is another way to do this last example. Notice that $F = z(x - y)$ and $G = y(x - z)$ are in I_2 and are linearly independent. From what we saw above, they must be the generators of I_2 (as a vector space). If we let J be the ideal generated by F and G then $J \subseteq I = \wp_1 \cap \ldots \cap \wp_4$.

To continue this example it is useful to consider the following important theorem of commutative algebra.

Theorem 3.8: *Let* $R = k[x_0, \ldots, x_n]$ *and let* I *be an ideal of* R. *Suppose that* $I = (F_1, \ldots, F_r)$ *then:*

    a) (Krull Principal Ideal Theorem) $\operatorname{ht} I \leq r$;

    b) (Macaulay's Unmixedness Theorem) If $\operatorname{ht} I = r$ *then all the associated prime ideals of* I *have height* r.

We can apply that result to the ideal J above. Since F and G have no common component, $\operatorname{ht} J = 2$. By $b)$ this means that J has only the prime ideals of points as associated prime ideals. It is also obvious that the only points where both F and G vanish are the four points we know. Thus the primes associated to those four points are the only associated primes of J. Finally it is easy to see that F and G meet transversally everwhere they meet. It then follows that $I = J$.

It is a simple exercise to see that the following sequence is exact and gives a free resolution of J:

$$0 \to R(-4) \xrightarrow{(\,G \;\; F\,)} R(-2)^2 \xrightarrow{\begin{pmatrix} F \\ -G \end{pmatrix}} J \to 0$$

Exercise 3.9: Use the exact sequence above to calculate the dimension of J_d and verify that the Hilbert function of J is that which was claimed above.

Lecture 4 – Anthony V. Geramita

We began, in the last lecture, a discussion of the Hilbert function of points in $\mathbb{P}^n$ and I want to continue that discussion.

Throughout this lecture, we shall use $\mathbf{X}$ to denote a set of s distinct points of $\mathbb{P}^n$ and $I_{\mathbf{X}} \subseteq R$, the ideal of those points. Then, recall, $H_{\mathbf{X}}(d) = \dim_k(R/I_{\mathbf{X}})_d$ is, by definition, the Hilbert function of $\mathbf{X}$ (or, as we have mentioned, of $A = R/I_{\mathbf{X}}$).

Lemma 4.1: $H_{\mathbf{X}}(d) \leq s,$ *for all* d.

Proof: Let $M_1, \ldots, M_r,$ $r = \binom{d+n}{n}$, be a basis for the monomials of degree d in R and let $F = \alpha_1 M_1 + \ldots + \alpha_r M_r$ be an arbitrary homogeneous form of degree d. In order that F vanish at P we must substitute the coordinates of P into F and get 0 (note that since F is homogeneous, this will not depend on the choice of coordinates for the point P). Thus, the condition that F vanish at P is a *linear* condition on the coefficients of F.

In order that F vanish at s distinct points, then, we must simultaneously solve s linear equations in the coefficients of F. The matrix of coefficients of this system of linear equations is an $s \times r$ matrix. If we let t be the rank of this matrix then the system of linear equations has $r - t$ independent solutions, i.e. $\dim_k(I_{\mathbf{X}}) = r - t$. Since $H_{\mathbf{X}}(d) = \dim_k R_d - \dim_k(I_{\mathbf{X}})_d$, we get $H_{\mathbf{X}}(d) = t$.

So, for this situation, $H_{\mathbf{X}}(d)$ is nothing more than the rank of the coefficient matrix of the system of equations described above. Since the matrix has size $s \times r$ we get that

$$t \leq \min\{s, r\} \leq s$$

as we wanted to show.

Lemma 4.2: *With the notation above,* $H_{\mathbf{X}}(s-1) = s$.

Proof: Let $H_1, \ldots, H_s$ be hyperplanes of $\mathbb{P}^n$ with the property that H_i contains P_i but H_i does not contain P_j for $i \neq j$. Such hyperplanes exist because k is an infinite field.

Let $L_1, \ldots, L_s$ be linear equations which describe these hyperplanes. Let $F_i = \Pi_{j \neq i} L_j$, $1 \leq i \leq s$. Then $\deg F_i = s - 1$ and $F_i(P_i) \neq 0$ but $F_i(P_j) = 0$ if $i \neq j$. So, $F_1, \ldots, F_s$ are not in $I_{\mathbf{X}}$.

Claim: No linear combination of $F_1, \ldots, F_s$ *(except* 0 *) is in* $I_{\mathbf{X}}$.

19

Proof: Suppose that $F = \alpha_1 F_1 + \ldots + a_s F_s \in I_{\mathbf{X}}$, then, for example, F must vanish at P_1. I.e. $0 = F(P_1) = \alpha_1 F_1(P_1)$, since the other F_i already vanish at P_1. Since $F_1(P_1) \neq 0$ we get that $\alpha_1 = 0$. We continue in this way to show that all the $\alpha_i = 0$.

It follows that the images of the F_i in $(R/I_{\mathbf{X}})_{s-1}$ are linearly independent and so $H_{\mathbf{X}}(s-1) \geq s$. By Lemma 4.1 we are done.

To continue our investigations, we now explore the ring structure of $A = R/I_{\mathbf{X}}$. If L is a linear from which describes a hyperplane in $\mathbb{P}^n$ which misses the points of $\mathbf{X}$ then the image of L in A_1, $\overline{L}$, is **not** a zero-divisor in A.

Observe that multiplication by $\overline{L}$ in A restricts to a multiplication from A_d to A_{d+1}. In fact, this multiplication defines a linear transformation on these vector spaces which, because $\overline{L}$ is not a zero-divisor in A, is $1-1$. A simple consequence of this is:

Lemma 4.3: $H_{\mathbf{X}}(d) \leq H_{\mathbf{X}}(d+1)$ for every integer d.

As an immediate corollary of this we get:

Lemma 4.4: If $H_{\mathbf{X}}(t) = s$ then $H_{\mathbf{X}}(t+1) = s$ also. In particular, $H_{\mathbf{X}}(t) = s$ for all $t \geq s - 1$.

Now, consider the ideal of A generated by $\overline{L}$. It is a homogeneous ideal in this graded ring and so we may ask: what is $\dim_k(\overline{L})_d$? If $\overline{F} \in (\overline{L})_d$ then $\overline{F} = (\overline{LG}), \overline{G} \in A_{d-1}$. Also, since $\overline{L}$ is not a zero-divisor in A we have that $\overline{LG_1} = \overline{LG_2}$ if and only if $\overline{G_1} = \overline{G_2}$. Thus, $\dim_k(\overline{L})_d = \dim_k A_{d-1}$. Note also that this dimension is independent of the linear non-zero-divisor chosen in A_1.

So, if we let $B = A/(\overline{L})$, then B is also a graded ring, and

$$\dim_k B = \dim_k A_d - \dim_k(\overline{L})_d = \dim_k A_d - \dim_k A_{d-1}.$$

Definition 4.5: Let $f : \mathbb{Z} \to \mathbb{Z}$ be a function. We define Δf, the *first difference* of f ("poor man's derivative") by:

$$\Delta f(n) = f(n) - f(n-1).$$

20

Using this language we have shown: if $A = R/I_X$ and $\overline{L}$ is a linear non-zero-divisor in A_1 and $B = A/(\overline{L})$, then

$$H(B,t) = \Delta H(A,t).$$

Recall that the only homogeneous primes of A are m (the irrelevant homogeneous maximal ideal) and the primes which correspond to the points of $\mathbf{X}$. Since $\overline{L}$ is not in any of the primes corresponding to the points of $\mathbf{X}$, the only associated prime of $(\overline{L})$ in A is $\overline{m}$, i.e. in B the only homogeneous prime ideal is the irrelevant maximal ideal, which is then nilpotent. It follows that $H(B,t) = 0$ for all $t \gg 0$.

Moreover, since B is generated, as a k-algebra, by B_1, we see that if $B_t = 0$ then $B_{t+1} = 0$ also.

What are the implications of this for the Hilbert function?

Since $B_t = 0$ if and only if $H_X(t-1) = H_X(t)$ we get: $H_X(t-1) = H_X(t)$ implies that $H_X(d) = H_X(t-1)$ for all $d \geq t-1$. In view of Lemma 4.4 we get:

Lemma 4.6: *If* $H_X(t) = H_X(t+1)$ *for any* t, *then* $H_X(t) = s$.

Example 4.7: Using the results above, it is easy to see that, for a set of 4 points in $\mathbb{P}^2$, the following are the only possible numerical functions which could be the Hilbert function of such a set.

$$
\begin{array}{llllll}
a) & 1 & 2 & 3 & 4 & 4 & \ldots \\
b) & 1 & 2 & 4 & 4 & \ldots \\
c) & 1 & 3 & 4 & 4 & \ldots
\end{array}
$$

We've already seen how $c)$ can be achieved. In case $a)$ and $b)$ we see that the four points would have to be on a line of $\mathbb{P}^2$. (Exercise: show that $a)$ is possible but that $b)$ is not. Try to find all possible Hilbert functions of sets of 5 points in $\mathbb{P}^2$; 6 points; 10 points, ...)

This raises the question: What are all the possible Hilbert functions for sets of points in $\mathbb{P}^n$?

I'm not going to enter into all the details of the answer that was found to this question by L. Roberts, P. Maroscia and me (J. London Math. Soc. (2) 28 (1983) 443-452.) but I want to explain some of it so that we can use these ideas to talk about some still open problems in this area.

The main idea is the old Castelnuovo idea, but this time in a different context. If A is the coordinate ring of a set of points in $\mathbb{P}^n$ and $\overline{L}$ is a linear non-zero-divisor in A then we can take the "hyperplane section" by $\overline{L}$. Unfortunately, as we saw above, the ring associated to this "section" is $B = A/(\overline{L})$, a graded ring with one homogeneous prime ideal which is nilpotent. Not much geometry here! There is, however, a great deal of algebra in this ring that I want to talk about.

There is no loss in assuming that $L = x_0$ and so the ring B is a graded Artinian algebra which is a quotient of $S = k[x_1, \ldots, x_n]$. So, we can ask the following questions:

1) What are the possible Hilbert functions of graded Artinian quotients of S?

2) Which such Artinian quotients can be "lifted" to the ideal of a set of points in $\mathbb{P}^n$?

We'll deal only with the first of these questions now.

So, let $S = k[x_1, \ldots, x_n]$, and let J be a homogeneous ideal in S where $\mathrm{rad}(J) = (x_1, \ldots, x_n) = \eta$. Then $\eta^t \subseteq J$ for some t and so $B = S/J$ is an artinian ring. We can write $B = B_0 \oplus B_1 \oplus \ldots \oplus B_r$, where $B_r \neq 0$. B is then a finite dimensional (graded) vector space over k and $\dim_k B = \sum_{i=0}^r \dim_k B_i = \sum_{i=0}^{\infty} B_i$.

Notice that if A is the homogeneous coordinate ring of a set of s points in $\mathbb{P}^n$ and $B = A/LA$, $L \in A_1$ not a zero-divisor in A, then $\dim_k B = s$.

I now want to explain what we can say about the Hilbert function of rings like B above (in fact for any standard graded k-algebra). One of the more important theorem in this area, and still very difficult to prove, is due to F.S. Macaulay (1862-1937) and was first proved in the early years of this century.

Definition-Proposition 4.8: The *i-binomial expansion* of an integer is defined as follows: let i and h be positive integers, then h can be uniquely written in the form:

$$h = \binom{m_i}{i} + \binom{m_{i-1}}{i-1} + \cdots + \binom{m_j}{j}.$$

where $m_i > m_{i-1} > \ldots > m_j \geq j \geq 1$. This decomposition of h is called the *i-binomial expansion* of h.

To deal with this definition it is convenient to write down Pascal's triangle (but as a rectangle!).

	0	1	2	3	4	
0	1	1	1	1	1	...
1	1	2	3	4	5	...
2	1	3	6	10	15	...
3	1	4	10	20	35	...
4	1	5	15	35	70	...
5	1	6	21	56	126	...
⋮	1	...				

I've numbered the rows (and columns) starting with 0; so the 0th row is

$$1 \quad 1 \quad 1 \quad 1 \quad 1 \quad 1 \quad \ldots$$

and the 0th column also consists entirely of 1's. Note also that the entry in the rth row and sth column is $\binom{r+s}{s}$. Thus, in the sth column we find all the binomial coefficients of the form $\binom{m}{s}$ where $m > s$ (just the sort of thing we are looking for in the s-binomial expansion of a number).

Example 4.9: To illustrate how to use the table, let's find the 4-binomial expansion of 85.

We look in the column labelled 4 for the biggest number ≤ 85. That is 70 and it occurs in the row labelled 4, so $85 = \binom{4+4}{4} + 15$. Now look in the column labelled 3 for the biggest integer ≤ 15. It occurs in the row labelled 2, so $15 = \binom{3+2}{3} + 5$. Now look in the column labelled 2 for the largest integer ≤ 5. It occurs in the row labelled 1, so write $5 = \binom{1+2}{2} + 2$. Now look in the column labelled 1 for the biggest integer ≤ 2, it occurs in the row labelled 1, so $2 = \binom{2}{1} + 0$, and so we stop. We get:

$$85 = \binom{8}{4} + \binom{5}{3} + \binom{3}{2} + \binom{2}{1}.$$

We now define a collection of functions $^{<i>} : \mathbb{Z} \to \mathbb{Z}$ as follows: if $h \in \mathbb{Z}$ has i-binomial expansion as above, then:

$$h^{<i>} = \binom{m_i + 1}{i + 1} + \binom{m_{i-1} + 1}{i} + \cdots + \binom{m_j + 1}{j + 1}$$

23

So, for example, $85^{<4>} = \binom{9}{5} + \binom{6}{4} + \binom{4}{3} + \binom{3}{2} = 148$.

Definition 4.10 : A sequence of non-negative integers $\{c_i : i \geq 0\}$ is called an *O*-sequence ("*O*" is for the letter "oh"), if

$$c_0 = 1 \text{ and}$$

$$c_{i+1} \leq c_i^{<i>}, \text{ for all } i.$$

Theorem 4.11: (Macaulay) *The following are equivalent:*

  a) $\{c_i : i \geq 0\}$ *is an O-sequence;*

  b) $\{c_i : i \geq 0\}$ *is the Hilbert function of a standard graded k-algebra.*

(A modern treatment of Macaulay's famous theorem can be found in the paper of Richard Stanley, *Hilbert Functions of Graded Algebras,* Advances in Math., **28**, 1978, 57-82)

We take a break in the discussion of Macaulay's Theorem to study some special configurations of points in $\mathbb{P}^n$. We shall return to Macaulay's theorem in Lecture 7.

Lecture 5 - Yves Pitteloud

We shall consider, for a while, a very specific class of closed subschemes of $\mathbb{P}^n$, the so called complete intersections.

Definition 5.1: A closed subscheme Y of $\mathbb{P}^n$ defined by an homogeneous ideal I of the polynomial ring $k[x_0, \cdots x_n]$ is a *complete intersection* if the ideal I can be generated by m elements, m the codimension of Y in $\mathbb{P}^n$.

Note that, according to theorem 3.8, one needs at least m elements to generate I, and if I is the ideal of a complete intersection, as above, then all the associated primes of I have height m. Here are some examples of zero dimensional complete intersections in $\mathbb{P}^2$.

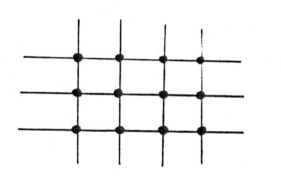 

Two homogeneous polynomials without common factors in $k[x_0, \ldots, x_n]$ define a complete intersection of codimension 2 in $\mathbb{P}^n$. The rational normal curve in $\mathbb{P}^3$ is an example of a non complete intersection. Indeed we saw that a minimal system of generators of its ideal consisted of three quadrics. As a matter of fact, it is a very strong condition for a scheme Y to be a complete intersection.

Let's show now how one can compute the Betti numbers, and thus the Hilbert function, of a complete intersection Y, just by looking at the degree of the generators of the ideal of Y. For that purpose let's recall the definition of the Koszul complex $K(F_1, \ldots, F_m; R)$ (or simply K) associated to a family of homogeneous elements $F_1, \ldots F_m$ in the polynomial ring R (in fact this construction can be done in any ring).

The R-modules $K = (K_i)$ are defined as follows: K_1 is a free R-module with basis, say $e_1, \ldots, e_m$, and the module K_p is equal to the p-th exterior power $\Lambda^p(K_1)$. In other words, for $1 \leq p \leq m$ the module K_p is a free R-module of dimension $\binom{m}{p}$ with basis $e_{i_1} \wedge e_{i_2} \wedge \cdots \wedge e_{i_p}$, with $1 \leq i_1 < i_2 < \cdots < i_p$; the module K_0 is just the ring R and all the others K_i's are zero. The differentials of the Koszul complex $d_p : K_p \to K_{p-1}$ are defined as follows

$$d_p(e_{i_1} \wedge \cdots \wedge e_{i_p}) = \sum_{j=1}^{p} (-1)^{j+1} F_j e_{i_1} \wedge \cdots \wedge \widehat{e_{i_j}} \wedge \cdots \wedge e_{i_p},$$

where the "$\widehat{\ }$" means that we omit the corresponding e_{i_j}. The equality $d_p \circ d_{p+1} = 0$ follows from the definition (after an easy computation), so we have a complex of R-modules.

Examples: Let's write explicitly the Koszul complexes, with the matrices of the differentials, for $m \leq 3$. The basis element $e_{i_1} \wedge \cdots \wedge e_{i_p}$ will be denoted by $e_{i_1 \cdots i_p}$ to save space.

   a) m=1: $0 \longrightarrow Re_1 \xrightarrow{F_1} R \longrightarrow 0.$

   b) m=2: $0 \longrightarrow Re_{12} \xrightarrow{(-F_2 \ \ F_1)} Re_1 \oplus Re_2 \xrightarrow{\begin{pmatrix} F_1 \\ F_2 \end{pmatrix}} R \longrightarrow 0.$

   c) m=3:

$$0 \to Re_{123} \xrightarrow{(F_3 \ \ -F_2 \ \ F_1)} Re_{12} \oplus Re_{13} \oplus Re_{23} \xrightarrow{\begin{pmatrix} -F_2 & F_1 & 0 \\ -F_3 & 0 & F_1 \\ 0 & -F_3 & F_2 \end{pmatrix}}$$

$$Re_1 \oplus Re_2 \oplus Re_3 \xrightarrow{\begin{pmatrix} F_1 \\ F_2 \\ F_3 \end{pmatrix}} R \to 0.$$

One can notice from these examples that these complexes are built up inductively. More precisely, let's denote by $A_{m,p}$ the matrix of the map $d_p : K_p((F_1, \ldots, F_m), R) \to K_{p-1}((F_1, \ldots, F_m), R)$, where we order the basis elements with respect to the "arabic lexicographical order", i.e. the lexicographical order but reading from right to left ($e_{i_1} \wedge \cdots \wedge e_{i_p} \leq e_{j_1} \wedge \cdots \wedge e_{j_p}$ iff there is a k with $i_k < j_k$ and $i_s = j_s$ for $s > k$). The matrix

$A_{m,p}$ is then formed as follows:

$$
\begin{pmatrix}
& A_{n-1,p} & & \vdots & 0 & \\
\cdots\cdots & \cdots\cdots & \cdots\cdots & \vdots & \cdots\cdots & \\
(-1)^{p+1}F_n & & & \vdots & & \\
& \ddots & & \vdots & A_{n-1,p-1} & \\
& & (-1)^{p+1}F_n & \vdots & &
\end{pmatrix}.
$$

The connection between the Koszul complex and the complete intersection subschemes of $\mathbb{P}^n$ is provided by the following two propositions from commutative algebra.

Recall that a sequence of elements $F_1, \ldots, F_m$ in a ring R is said to be a *regular sequence* if F_i is not a zero divisor in $R/(F_1, \ldots, F_{i-1})$ for $i = 1, \ldots, m$.

Proposition 5.2: *Given elements $F_1, \ldots, F_m$ in a commutative ring R which form a regular sequence, then the associated Koszul homology modules $H_i(K(F_1, \ldots, F_m; R))$ satisfy the following equalities*

$$
H_0(K(F_1, \ldots, F_m; R)) \cong R/(F_1, \ldots, F_m) \text{ and } H_i(K(F_1, \ldots, F_m; R)) = 0 \text{ for } i > 0.
$$

Note that the isomorphism concerning $H_0(K(F_1, \ldots, F_m; R))$ is true for an arbitrary family of elements.

Proposition 5.3: *Let $F_1, \ldots, F_m$ be homogeneous polynomials in the polynomial ring $R = k[x_0, \ldots, x_n]$. The following conditions are then equivalent.*

    i) $ht(F_1, \ldots, F_m) = m$,

    ii) $F_1, \ldots, F_m$ *form a regular sequence.*

These two propositions imply that, given a complete intersection Y in $\mathbb{P}^n$ of codimension m, whose homogeneous ideal I can be generated by m polynomials, say $F_1, \ldots, F_m$, a resolution of the coordinate ring R/I of Y is given by the Koszul complex associated to the family of elements $F_1, \ldots, F_m$.

The next step now is to establish that the Koszul complex yields, in fact, a minimal free graded resolution of the coordinate ring R/I. For that purpose we attribute the

27

degree $d_{i_1} + \cdots + d_{i_p}$ to the basis element $e_{i_1} \wedge \cdots \wedge e_{i_p}$ when $p \geq 1$, and the degree 0 to the basis element of $K_0 = R$. In other words, there is an isomorphism of graded modules $R(e_{i_1} \wedge \cdots \wedge e_{i_p}) \cong R(-d_{i_1} - \cdots - d_{i_p})$. It follows from the defining equality $d_p(e_{i_1} \wedge \cdots \wedge e_{i_p}) = \sum_{j=1}^{p}(-1)^{j+1}F_j e_{i_1} \wedge \cdots \wedge \widehat{e_{i_j}} \wedge \cdots \wedge e_{i_p}$ that the maps d_p are then graded maps of degree zero. Moreover (see above) the only entries appearing in the matrices of the maps d_p are zeros or F_i's, in particular there is no invertible element.

In general, a graded free resolution is *minimal* (in the sense of lecture 2) if and only if there is no invertible element in the matrices of the differentials; to see this check that a graded surjection $F \to U$ is *minimal* (i.e induces an isomorphism between F/R^+F and U/R^+U, where $R^+ = \oplus_{i\geq 1}R_i$) iff its kernel is contained in R^+F. Now apply this observation inductively to all syzygies modules.

Let's put all these observations in a proposition.

Proposition 5.4: *Let Y be a complete intersection in $\mathbb{P}^n$ of codimension m. Suppose that $F_1, \ldots, F_m$ are homogeneous polynomials of degree $d_1, \ldots, d_m$ that generate the ideal I of Y. A minimal graded free resolution of the coordinate ring R/I of Y is given by the graded Koszul complex:*

$$0 \to R(-d_1 - \cdots - d_m) \to \cdots \to \oplus_{1 \leq i_1 < \cdots i_p \leq m} R(-d_{i_1} - \cdots - d_{i_p}) \to \cdots$$

$$\cdots \to \oplus_i R(-d_i) \to R \to R/I \to 0$$

In particular, the Betti numbers depend only on the degrees of the polynomials F_i generating I, and the ideal I is always a perfect ideal.

The fact that the ideal I of a complete intersection is always a perfect ideal is a direct consequence of the length of the Koszul resolution in the above proposition (in other words R/I has the "right" homological dimension).

Let us now apply these considerations about the minimal resolution of a complete intersection to get information about the Hilbert fuction of a zero dimensional complete intersection in $\mathbb{P}^n$. More precisely let's consider a set X of points $P_1, \ldots, P_s$ in $\mathbb{P}^n$ which is a complete intersection, i.e. a set of points in $\mathbb{P}^n$ whose ideal can be generated by n homogeneous polynomials $F_1, \ldots, F_n$ of degrees, say $d_1, \ldots, d_n$. It follows then from the discussion about the graded Koszul complex that the Hilbert function $H(X,t)$ satisfies the following equality

$$H(X,t) = H(R,t) - \sum_i H(R,t-d_i) + \sum_{1 \le d_i < d_j \le n} H(R,t-d_i-d_j) - \cdots$$

$$+(-1)^p \sum_{1 \le i_1 < \cdots < i_p \le n} H(R,t-d_{i_1}-\cdots-d_{i_p}) + \cdots + (-1)^n H(R,t-d_1-\cdots-d_n), \quad (*)$$

where $H(R,t)$ denotes the Hilbert function of the polynomial ring $R = k[x_0,\ldots,x_n]$. Given a function $f : \mathbb{N} \to \mathbb{N}$ let us denote by $\Delta_d f$ the function defined by the equality $\Delta_d f(t) = f(t) - f(t-d)$ (The usual difference function Δf corresponds in this notation to $\Delta_1 f$). The above equality can now be rewritten in a more compact form, as follows (check this by induction on m)

$$H(X,t) = \Delta_{d_n} \Delta_{d-n-1} \cdots \Delta_{d_1} H(R,t).$$

For $t \ge 0$ the Hilbert function $H(R,t)$ of the polynomial ring is equal to $\binom{n+t}{n}$. This is a polynomial in t of degree n with leading coefficient $1/n!$. In general, given a polynomial in t of degree k with leading coefficient a, then $\Delta_d g$ is a polynomial in t of degree $k-1$ with leading coefficient kad. Applying this observation inductively yields that for $t \ge d_1 + \cdots + d_n$ the Hilbert function $H(X,t)$ is a polynomial of degree zero with leading coefficients $d_1 d_2 \cdots d_n$. In other words, the Hilbert function of X eventually become equal to $d_1 d_2 \cdots d_n$. But on the other hand we already know that the Hilbert function eventually becomes equal to the number of points involved (here s) so these two numbers have to be equal.

Given a set of points X as above, we have just seen that the Hilbert function $H(X,t)$ eventually will reach the value $d_1 d_2 \cdots d_n$. The next question we want to settle is: What is the smallest integer t for which the first difference, $\Delta H(X,t)$, is equal to zero (this integer is usually denoted by $\sigma(X)$).

Now the formula $(*)$ above implies that $\Delta^n H(X,t)$ is zero for $t \ge d_1 + \cdots + d_n$ while $\Delta^n H(X, d_1 + \cdots d_n - 1) = -1$. This follows from the fact that $\Delta^n H(R, t-d)$ is equal to one when $t \ge d$ and to zero when $t < d$, together with the equality $\sum_{p=0}^{n} \binom{n}{p}(-1)^p = 0$. If we denote by $\sigma(m, X)$ the smallest integer for which $\Delta^m H(X,t)$ is equal to zero ($\sigma(X) = \sigma(1, X)$) it is immediate that $\sigma(m+1, X) = \sigma(m, X) + 1$ for $m \ge 1$. As a consequence of this observation, we obtain that $\sigma(X)$ is equal to $d_1 + d_2 + \cdots d_n - (n-1)$.

29

Note that $\sum_t \Delta^n H(X,t)$ has to vanish since $\Delta^{n-1} H(X,t)$ becomes zero for large t. Also, applying formula (*), we see (after a small computation) that there is an equality $\Delta^n H(X,t) = (-1)^{n+1} \Delta^n H(X, d_1 + \cdots + d_n - 1 - t)$. These two facts imply that there is an equality $\Delta^n H(X,t) = (-1)^n \Delta^{n-1} H(X, d_1 + \cdots + d_n - 2 - t)$. Again the sum $\sum_t \Delta^{n-1} H(X,t)$ has to vanish. Iterating the argument, we obtain that $\Delta H(X,t)$ satisfies the equality

$$\Delta H(X,t) = \Delta H(X, d_1 + \cdots + d_n - n - t).$$

Let's put these observations together into a proposition.

Proposition 5.5: *Let X be a set of distinct points $P_1, \ldots, P_s$ in $\mathbb{P}^n$ whose ideal can be generated by n homogeneous polynomials $F_1, \ldots, F_n$ of degree $d_1, \ldots, d_n$ (i.e. a complete intersection). The following assertions are then true:*

    i) The number of points s is equal to the product $d_1 d_2 \cdots d_n$,

    ii) there is an equality $\sigma(X) = d_1 + d_2 + \cdots d_n - (n-1)$ where $\sigma(X)$ denotes the smallest integer for which the first difference $\Delta H(X,t)$ of the Hilbert function is zero,

    iii) $\Delta H(X,t)$ is symmetric in the following sense:

$$\Delta H(X,t) = \Delta H(X, d_1 + \cdots + d_n - n - t) .$$

Note that the last two equalities in proposition 5.5 can easily be generalized to an r dimensional complete intersection X in $\mathbb{P}^n$, by considering the function $\Delta^{r+1} H(X,t)$ instead of the function $\Delta H(X,t)$. The first equality can be generalized by replacing the number of points s by the degree of X as a subscheme of $\mathbb{P}^n$.

Example 5.6: Let X be a set of points in $\mathbb{P}^2$ and suppose that X is the complete intersection given by two polynomials of degree a, b. The Hilbert function of X is then given by the following formula:

$$H(X,t) = H(R,t) - H(R,t-a) - H(R,t-b) + H(R,t-a-b) ,$$

where R denotes here the polynomial ring $k[x_0, x_1, x_2]$. The first difference function $\Delta H(X,t)$ has then the following form (we suppose that $a < b$)

$$1 \quad 2 \quad \cdots \quad (a-1) \quad a \quad a \quad \cdots \quad a \quad (a-1) \quad \cdots \quad 2 \quad 1 \quad 0 \quad 0 \quad \cdots$$

where the value a is first reached when $t = a - 1$, the value $a - 1$ is reached (for the second time) when $t = b$ and the value 0 is reached first when $t = a + b - 1$. The graph looks like a trapezoid.

Lecture 6 - Yves Pitteloud

In the last lecture we explained how one could compute the Betti numbers and Hilbert functions of complete intersections. A natural question to ask is the following: can this be used to study a wider class of schemes than just the complete intersections?

Consider for instance the rational cubic curve $\mathcal{C}$ whose ideal is $(yw - z^2, yz - xw, xz - y^2)$, where x, y, w, z are coordinates in $\mathbb{P}^3$. As was already mentioned, $\mathcal{C}$ is not a complete intersection. But now take the union $\mathcal{D}$ of $\mathcal{C}$ with the line $\mathcal{L}$ given by the ideal (y, z), itself a complete intersection. The ideal of $\mathcal{C} \cup \mathcal{L}$ is the intersection of the ideals of $\mathcal{C}$ and $\mathcal{L}$

$$(yw - z^2, yz - xw, xz - y^2) \cap (y, z).$$

This ideal can be generated by the polynomials $yw - z^2$ and $xz - y^2$, as one easily checks. In other words, the union of the rational cubic curve $\mathcal{C}$ with the line $\mathcal{L}$ *is* a complete intersection. We say that $\mathcal{C}$ and $\mathcal{L}$ are *linked* by the complete intersection $\mathcal{D}$ (cf below for a precise definition). Is there a relation between the invariants (Betti numbers, Hilbert function,..) of $\mathcal{C}, \mathcal{L}$ and $\mathcal{D}$? If this were the case we could then use the results of the last lecture about complete intersections to get some information about the *non* complete intersection $\mathcal{C}$. The object of this lecture is to answer this question for one of the invariants, the Hilbert function.

Before we state the precise definition of *liaison*, let's consider it through another example, the case of two disjoint set of points X and Y in $\mathbb{P}^n$ whose union Z is a complete intersection (this fact is not relevant in the observations below). The corresponding ideals are denoted by I_X, I_Y and I_Z. Given a polynomial in I_X and a polynomial in I_Y, their product obviously lies in I_Z. Conversely if a polynomial p is such that its product with any element of I_X lie in I_Z then this polynomial has to be in I_Y (to see this, given a point P in Y, take a polynomial in I_X not vanishing on this point, and consider the product of this polynomial with p to conclude that p must vanish at P). If we denote by $(I_Z : I_X)$ the ideal consisting of all the polynomials p with $pI_X \subset I_Z$, the above observations can be put in a more compact form, as follows (note that the second equality is obtained by symmetry)

$$I_Y = (I_Z : I_X) \quad \text{and} \quad I_X = (I_Z : I_Y).$$

Now let's state the definition of liaison, which generalizes the example above.

Definition 6.1: Let I and J be homogeneous ideals in the ring $R = k[x_0, \cdots, x_n]$, and let G be a complete intersection homogeneous ideal (i.e generated by $ht\ G$ elements) contained in the intersection $I \cap J$. We say that I and J are linked by G if the following conditions are satisfied:

$i)$ I and J are equidimensional without embedded component;

$ii)$ $J = (G : I)$ and $I = (G : J)$.

Note that if I, J and G are as above, it follows from the definition that there is an equality $ht\ I = ht\ J = ht\ G$. We say that two subchemes of $\mathbb{P}^n$ are linked by a complete intersection, if the corresponding ideals are linked in the sense of the above definition.

If a disjoint union of two sets of points in $\mathbb{P}^n$ is a complete intersection, then the two sets of points are linked by their union, as the observations above show.

Given a complete intersection ideal G and an unmixed ideal I containing G with $ht\ I = ht\ G$, then I and $(G : I)$ are linked by G.

The following proposition gives another a situation where liaison occurs and provides the connection with the example of the rational cubic curve with which we started the lecture.

Proposition 6.2: *Let G be a complete intersection ideal with irredundant primary decomposition $G = q_1 \cap \cdots \cap q_s \cap q_{s+1} \cap \cdots \cap q_t$; set $I = q_1 \cap \cdots \cap q_s$ and $J = q_{s+1} \cap \cdots \cap q_t$. Then I and J are linked by G.*

Proof: We have to show only the equality $J = (G : I)$, the other will follow by symmetry. The inclusion $J \subset (G : I)$ is obvious, so let x be an element of $(G : I)$. The inclusion $xI \subset G$ implies the inclusion $x(I + J) \subset J$. If x were not in J we would have an inclusion $I + J \subset \wp$ for some $\wp$ in $Ass(A/J)$, which is obviously impossible as I and J have no common component and G is unmixed.

The situation of this proposition describes what we shall call *geometric liaison*. Two subschemes of $\mathbb{P}^n$ are linked *geometrically*, iff they are equidimensional, without common components, and if their union is a complete intersection. For instance the rational cubic curve $\mathcal{C}$ and the line $\mathcal{L}$ of the begining of the lecture are linked geometrically. One can show, with arguments similar to those used in the proof of proposition 6.2, that given

33

two linked schemes, the liaison will be geometric provided that the two schemes have no common components.

Let's see now an example of non geometric liaison. Consider the following ideals in $k[x, y]$:

$$G = (x^2, y^2), \quad I = (x^2, y^2, xy), \quad J = (x, y).$$

Then one can easily check that I and J are linked by G.

Another example of non geometric liaison is given by considering, again, the rational cubic curve $\mathcal{C}$ in $\mathbb{P}^3$ which is linked to itself by the complete intersection defined by the two polynomials $xz - y^2$ and $z(yw - z^2) + w(yz - xw))$. (checked with $CoCoA$; the instruction to give to compute $(G : I)$ is $G : I, \ldots$ who would have thought!).

Hilbert function of linked varieties.

The following theorem, which is taken from the paper of Davis, Geramita and Orecchia, *Gorenstein algebra and the Cayley Bacharach theorem*, *Proceedings of the American Mathematical society*, *volume 93*, *number 4*, *april 1985*, describes a relationship between the Hilbert function of linked varieties. We will not prove it here but rather try to understand how one can use it to compute Hilbert functions, especially in the case of points in $\mathbb{P}^2$.

Theorem 6.3: *Let G be a complete intersection ideal of height r in $R = k[x_0, \ldots, x_n]$, generated by homogeneous polynomials of degree $d_1, \ldots, d_r$. Let I and J be homogeneous perfect ideals linked by G. Then,*

$$\Delta^m H(R/G, t) = \Delta^m H(R/I, t) + \Delta^m H(A/J, \sigma - 1 - t) ,$$

where σ is equal to $d_1 + \cdots + d_r - (r - 1)$ and m is equal to $n + 1 - r$, the dimension of the rings R/G, R/I and R/J.

Remark: a) The integer σ above is the smallest integer where the function $\Delta^m H(R/G)$ becomes zero and there is an equality $\Delta^m H(R/G, t) = \Delta^m(R/G, \sigma - 1 - t)$ (compare last lecture).

b) In the hypothesis of the above theorem, it suffices to suppose that one of the linked ideals I, J is perfect. This will automatically imply that the other one is also perfect. (cf. Peszkine, Szpiro, *Liaisons des variétés algébriques*, Inventiones math. 26 (1974) prop 1.3).

We will now turn our attention to sets of points in $\mathbb{P}^2$ and show, through an example, how Theorem 6.3 can simplify the computations of Hilbert functions. We will use the notation $C.I.(a,b)$ for a complete intersection given by homogeneous polynomials in $k[x_0, x_1, x_2]$ of degree a and b. Let us first restate Theorem 6.3 in that specific situation, taking into account the fact that ideals of points are always perfect ideals.

Theorem 6.4: *Let Z be a set of points in $\mathbb{P}^2$ that is a $C.I.(a,b)$ and let X be a subset of Z. Then,*

$$\Delta H(Z,t) = \Delta H(X,t) + \Delta H(Z \setminus X, a+b-2-t) .$$

Example 6.5: Consider the following set X_1 of points in $\mathbb{P}^2$.

We would like to compute the Hilbert function $H(X_1,t)$. Note that X_1 is a subset of a $C.I.(4,4)$ (see below on the left), where the complement X_2 of X_1 in the $C.I.(4,4)$ is as below on the right.

Now we have that X_2 is a subset of a $C.I.(3,3)$ (see below on the left) where the complement X_3 is as below on the right,

Note that X_3 consists of three points not on a line, so its Hilbert function is: 1 3 3 ...; this implies that its first difference is: 1 2 0 0 ....

The first difference of the Hilbert function of the $C.I.(3,3)$ is: 1 2 3 2 1 0 ... . We apply Theorem 6.4 to compute the function $\Delta H(X_2,t)$:

$$\begin{array}{ccccccc}
1 & 2 & 3 & 2 & 1 & 0 & \\
1 & 2 & 0 & 0 & 0 & 0 & \quad (*) \\
0 & 0 & 3 & 2 & 1 & 0 & \\
\end{array}$$

35

The last row of (*) is the difference of the first two rows and, according to Theorem 6.4, it is the function $\Delta H(X_2, t)$ "written from right to left". In other words, $\Delta H(X_2, t)$ is just: 1 2 3 0 0 ....

We repeat the argument another time, the union $X_2 \cup X_1$ being a $C.I.(4, 4)$ whose first difference function is: 1 2 3 4 3 2 1 0 ...

$$\begin{array}{cccccccc} 1 & 2 & 3 & 4 & 3 & 2 & 1 & 0 \\ 1 & 2 & 3 & 0 & 0 & 0 & 0 & 0 \\ 0 & 0 & 0 & 4 & 3 & 2 & 1 & 0 \end{array}$$

and conclude by theorem 6.4 that $\Delta H(X_1, t)$ is: 1 2 3 4 0 0 .... Finally, we obtain the following Hilbert function $H(X_1, t)$, which shows in particular that the points of X_1 impose linear independant conditions to homogeneous polynomials of any degree

$$1 \ 3 \ 6 \ 10 \ 10 \ \cdots .$$

In fact, from any set of points in $\mathbb{P}^2$, one can obtain (by a finite succession of links) a complete intersection. This is a general fact about arithmetically Cohen-Macaulay varieties of codimension 2 in $\mathbb{P}^n$ (compare Peszkine and Szpiro Theorem 3.2). In other words it is not a coincidence that the method we used to compute the Hilbert function in the above example worked! Note that this may no longer work for points in $\mathbb{P}^n$ when $n \geq 3$.

Let's finally show how two classical results of projective geometry can easily be derived from Theorem 6.4. The first one is the classical *Cayley Bacharach theorem*.

Theorem 6.6: *Let $Z = \{P_1, \ldots, P_9\}$ be the complete intersection of two cubics in $\mathbb{P}^2$. Then any cubic passing through eight of the nine points has to pass through the remaining point.*

Proof: We can assume that the eight points in the theorem are $P_1, \ldots, P_8$. Let's write, below, on a first row the function $\Delta H(Z, t)$, on a second row the function $\Delta H(\{P_9\}, t)$ and on a third row the difference of these two functions:

$$\begin{array}{cccccc} 1 & 2 & 3 & 2 & 1 & 0 \\ 1 & 0 & 0 & 0 & 0 & 0 \\ 0 & 2 & 3 & 2 & 1 & 0. \end{array}$$

36

Theorem 6.4 implies that the last row is $\Delta H(\{P_1, \ldots, P_8\}, t)$ but written from right to left. Now looking at the Hilbert functions, we obtain:

Hilbert function of Z : 1 3 6 8 9 9...

Hilbert function of $\{P_1, \ldots, P_8\}$: 1 3 6 8 8 8....

In particular we deduce from these Hilbert functions that the dimension of the vector space of all cubics through $\{P_1, \ldots, P_8\}$ is the same as the dimension of the vector space of all cubics through $Z = \{P_1, \ldots, P_9\}$. In other words these two vector spaces are equal and the theorem is proved.

Note that there is an analogous theorem for any complete intersection less a point. This follows again from the symmetry of the Hilbert function of complete intersections and from Theorem 6.4.

Another classical application of theorem 6.4 is the following theorem, due to Pascal.

Theorem 6.7: *Given an hexagon whose vertices lie on a conic, then the three points of intersection in $\mathbb{P}^2$ of pairs of line through opposite sides are colinear (compare pictures).*

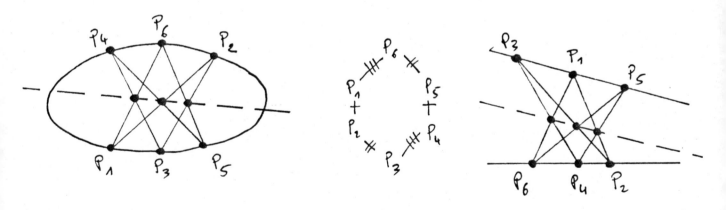

Proof: Let $P_1, \ldots, P_6$ be the vertices of the hexagon, and let P_7, P_8 and P_9 be the three points of intersection. Then $\{P_1, \ldots, P_9\}$ is the complete intersection of the cubic $L_{12}L_{34}L_{56}$ and the cubic $L_{23}L_{45}L_{61}$, where L_{ij} denotes the equation of the line in $\mathbb{P}^2$ through P_i and P_j. The theorem will be a consequence of the following observation:

Let $Z = \{P_1, \ldots, P_9\}$ be the complete intersection of two cubics, and let X be a subset of Z consisting of 3 points. Then the points of X are on a line if and only if remaining 6 points are on a conic.

To prove the observation, note that the Hilbert function of three points is either

$$
\begin{array}{cccccl}
1 & 2 & 3 & 3 & \ldots & \text{if the three points are colinear, or} \\
1 & 3 & 3 & 3 & \ldots & \text{if the three points are not colinear.}
\end{array}
$$

In particular, $\Delta H(X, 2)$ will be non zero if and only if the points of X are colinear, while $\Delta H(X, t)$ will be zero for $t \geq 3$. Now, applying Theorem 6.4 yields that $\Delta H(Z \setminus X, 2)$ is strictly smaller than 3 if and only if the points of X are colinear, while $\Delta H(Z \setminus X, 1) = 2$ and $\Delta H(Z \setminus X, 0) = 1$; this imply that $H(Z \setminus X, 2) < 6$, or in other words the points of $Z \setminus X$ lie on a conic, if and only if the points of X are colinear, so we are done.

Lecture 7 - Anthony V. Geramita

Some remarks about the functions $^{<i>}$.

There is a useful pictorial way to imagine the functions $^{<i>}$ which uses Pascal's "rectangle" above.

If we want to calculate $a^{<i>}$, recall that we must first calculate the i-binomial expansion of a. We'll speak of the summands of that expansion as the *i-binomial factors* of a. Let's think of this expansion as choosing a collection of places in Pascal's rectangle, one place in each of consecutive columns from the one labelled i down to a column labelled $j < i$. Where are these places we have chosen? To get a graphic appreciation of the answer, suppose we are at a chosen place in a fixed column numbered $\ell, (\ell < i)$. Then, if we form a rectangle using that chosen spot as the lower right hand corner, all the other chosen places in the columns labelled $t, t < \ell$, are in (or on the lower perimeter) of that rectangle.

If we now move all the i-binomial factors of "a" exactly one place to the right, we obtain the $(i+1)$-binomial factors of $a^{<i>}$.

This simple observation coupled with Macaulay's theorem has some rather lovely consequences.

Corollary 7.1: *If $\mathcal{S} = \{c_i \mid i \geq 0\}$ is an O-sequence then there is an integer, denoted $j(\mathcal{S})$, such that:*

$$\text{for all } j \geq j(\mathcal{S}), \quad c_{j+1} = c_j^{<j>}.$$

This corollary is clear from the remarks above, for if $c_{i+1} < c_i^{<i>}$ then some $(i+1)$-binomial factor of c_{i+1}, denote it $\binom{*}{\ell}$, is "higher" than the $(i+1)$-binomial factor $\binom{*}{\ell}'$ of $c_i^{<i>}$. This can only happen a finite number of times.

Another immediate corollary of this observation is the following:

Corollary 7.2: *If $\mathcal{S} = \{c_i \mid i \geq 0\}$ is an O-sequence then there is an integer $p(\mathcal{S})$ and a polynomial $H(x) \in \mathbb{Q}[x]$ such that for all $j \geq p(\mathcal{S})$,*

$$c_j = H(j).$$

Proof: Let $j = j(\mathcal{S})$ be as in Corollary 7.1 and write the j-binomial expansion of c_j;

$$c_j = \binom{m_j}{j} + \binom{m_{j-1}}{j-1} + \ldots + \binom{m_{j-r}}{j-r}$$

with $m_j > m_{j-1} > \ldots > m_{j-r} \geq j - r \geq 1$.

Consider the function $H(t) =$

$$\binom{m_j + (t-j)}{t} + \binom{m_{j-1} + (t-j)}{t-1} + \ldots + \binom{m_{j-r} + (t-j)}{t-r}.$$

Because of Corollary 7.1, this function agrees with the original O-sequence for all $t \geq j$. Note also, at least in that range, it can be rewritten

$$\binom{t + (m_j - j)}{m_j - j} + \binom{t + (m_{j-1} - j)}{(m_{j-1} - j) + 1} + \ldots + \binom{t + (m_{j-r} - j)}{(m_{j-r} - j) + r}.$$

Since these summands are each polynomials in t so is their sum, and that finishes the proof of the corollary.

Remark: The function $\binom{t+a}{b} = \frac{(t+a)(t+a-1)\ldots(t+a-b+1)}{b(b-1)\ldots3.2.1}$ is a polynomial of degree "b" whose leading coefficient is $1/b!$.

Vector Subspaces of S = k[x,y]

The first non-trivial artinian algebras to which we shall apply this theorem are the quotients of $S = k[x,y]$ by homogeneous ideals with radical (x,y). So, let J be such an ideal.

Definition 7.3: We define $\alpha(J) = \alpha$ to be the least non-negative integer for which $J_\alpha \neq 0$.

Clearly the Hilbert function of S/J and that of S agree before α. So, $H(S,t) = H(S/J,t) = t + 1$ for every $t < \alpha$. Moreover, $H(S/J,t) < H(S,t)$ for all $t \geq \alpha$. In particular, $H(S/J,\alpha) \leq \alpha$.

Let $F \in J_\alpha$ be a non-zero element. Then $(F) \subseteq J$ and since $S/J \cong (S/(F))/(J/(F))$ we get: $H(S/J,t) = H(S/(F),t) - \dim_k(J/(F))_t$. Since $\deg F = \alpha$ we have that

$$\dim_k(F)_{\alpha+r} = \dim_k S_r.$$

40

So, the Hilbert function of $S/(F)$ is:

$$H(S/(F), t) = \begin{cases} t+1 & \text{if } t \leq \alpha - 1; \\ \alpha & \text{if } t \geq \alpha. \end{cases} \tag{7.4}$$

To continue with this discussion we must verify a simple result about i-binomial expansions.

Lemma 7.5: *Let h be an integer and suppose that $h \leq i$. Then*

$$h^{<i>} = h .$$

Proof: It is easy to see that the i-binomial expansion of h is:

$$h = \binom{i}{i} + \binom{i-1}{i-1} + \ldots + \binom{i-h+1}{i-h+1}.$$

So, $h^{<i>} = \binom{i+1}{i+1} + \binom{i}{i} + \ldots + \binom{i-h+2}{i-h+2} = h$, and we are done. $\square$

Corollary 7.6: *If J is a homogeneous ideal of $S = k[x, y]$, $\text{rad} J = (x, y)$ and $\alpha = \alpha(J)$, then the Hilbert function of J is of the form:*

$$1 \quad 2 \quad 3 \quad \ldots \alpha \quad a_1 \quad a_2 \quad \ldots \quad a_n \quad 0$$

where $\alpha \geq a_1 \geq a_2 \geq \ldots \geq a_n > 0$.

Proof: From equation (7.4) we see that all the $a_i \leq \alpha$ so, in particular, $a_1 \leq \alpha$. By Macaulay's theorem, $a_2 \leq a_1^{<\alpha>}$. By Lemma 7.5 we have that $a_1^{<\alpha>} = a_1$, and so we are done. We can continue by induction and that finishes the proof. $\square$

There is another proof of Corollary 7.6 which does not use Macaulay's theorem. In fact, it only uses some simple linear algebra observations. I would now like to explain this approach, which yields more than Macaulay's theorem in this case. The elementary proofs I am about to give are largely due to Ed Davis (see E.D. Davis, *Complements to a paper of P. Dubreil*, Richerche di Math., Vol. XXXVII, fasc.2, (1988), 347-57). Much more complicated proofs of pieces of this have been cropping up for over a century.

To emphasize the linear algebra aspects of this part of the work I will introduce the following notation and ideas. If V is a subspace of $S_t = (k[x, y])_t$ then the *codimension* of

V, written $codimV$, is the dimension of the vector space S_t/V. If V were the graded piece of an ideal J then $codimV$ would be nothing more than the value of the Hilbert function of S/J in degree t.

Since $\dim S_t = t+1$ we have $codimV = t + 1 - \dim V$.

For homogeneous ideals of the type we are studying in this section, a great deal about the growth of the dimensions of the graded pieces of the ideals (and ultimately the growth of the Hilbert function of these ideals) depends on the degree of the greatest common divisor of the forms in the ideal (of a given degree). More precisely:

Definition 7.7: If $V \subseteq S_t$ as above, then $F \in S_d$ is called a *greatest common divisor of V* (or "gcd " of V) if $F \mid G$ for every $G \in V$ and there is no form of higher degree with this property.

By unique factorization in S, F is uniquely determined up to multiplication by a non-zero constant of k. In view of this fact, we shall abuse the definition and speak of *the* gcd of V and write $F = \gcd(V)$.

Proposition 7.8: *Let $V \subseteq S_t$ be as above and let $F = \gcd(V)$, $\deg F = d$. Then:*

1) $d \leq codimV$
2) $d = 0$ iff $codimS_\ell V = 0$ for all $\ell \geq t - 1$.

Proof: 1). We can write $V = FW$, where W is a subspace of S_{t-d} and $\gcd(W) = 1$. Moreover, $\dim V = \dim W \leq \dim(S_{t-d}) = (t - d) + 1$.

Thus $d \leq (t+1) - \dim V = codimV$, as we wanted to show.

Note: From the proof we see:

$$d = codimV \text{ iff } \dim V = \dim W = \dim(S_{t-d}) \text{ iff } codimW = 0.$$

As for 2): first notice that if $F = \gcd(V)$ then $F = \gcd(S_iV)$ for all $i \geq 0$. Since $\gcd(S_i) = 1$, for any i, we get: $codim(S_\ell V) = 0$ for any $\ell \geq 0$ implies $d = 0$. Thus we have shown that if $codim(S_\ell V) = 0$ for all $\ell \geq t - 1$ then $d = 0$.

For the reverse implication, suppose that $d = 0$. Then we can find F_1, F_2 in V for which $\gcd(F_1, F_2) = 1$. Since two elements in a UFD which have no common factor are always a regular sequence, we can use the results of the previous lecture to say that $H(S/(F_1, F_2), \ell) = 0$ for all $\ell \geq t + t - 1 = 2t - 1$. Put another way, $S_{t-1}(F_1, F_2) =$

42

S_{2t-1}. Since $(F_1, F_2) \subseteq V$ we then obviously have that $S_{t-1}V = S_{2t-1}$ and hence that $codim(S_\ell V) = 0$ for all $\ell \geq t-1$, as we wanted to show. $\square$

The proof of the first part of the next proposition is the promised proof (independent of Macaulay's theorem) of Corollary 7.6. The second part of this proposition is the clever argument of Davis on which almost all the nontrivial results about codimension 2 homogeneous ideals rests.

Proposition 7.9: *Let $V \subseteq S_t$ be as above. Then:*

1) $codim(S_1 V) \leq codimV$;
2) $codim(S_1 V) - codimS_2 V \leq codimV - codimS_1 V$;
3) $codim(S_1 V) = codim(S_2 V) \Leftrightarrow codim(S_t V) = codimV$ *for all* $t \geq 0$.

Proof: Notice immediately that 1) and 2) imply 3) since $S_i V = S_1(S_{i-1}V)$ for all $i > 0$.

Now to the proof of 1). If $F = \gcd(V)$ then $\gcd(xV) = xF$. Since $\gcd(S_1 V) = F$ it follows that $S_1 V \neq xV$. Thus $\dim(S_1 V) \geq \dim(xV) + 1 = \dim V + 1$. Since $\dim(S_{t+1}) = \dim(S_t) + 1$ we are done.

As for 2), suppose $codimV - codimS_1 V = n$. Then

$$\dim(S_1 V) = n + 1 + \dim V. \tag{7.10}$$

So, in order to prove that $codim(S_1 V) - codim(S_2 V) \leq n$ we need to prove that

$$\dim(S_2 V) \leq \dim V + 2n + 2. \tag{7.11}$$

Now $S_1 V = xV + yV$ and so $\dim(S_1 V) = \dim(xV) + \dim(yV) - \dim(xV \cap yV)$. Since $\dim(xV) = \dim(yV) = \dim V$ and from (7.10) we conclude that

$$\dim(V) - \dim(xV \cap yV) = n + 1.$$

It follows that we can choose a subspace U of V, whose dimension is $n + 1$, and with the additional property that $yU \cap xV = (0)$ and $S_1 V = xV + yU$. It follows that $yV \subseteq xV + yU$.

So, $S_2 V = S_1(xV + yU) = xS_1 V + yS_1 U = x^2 V + xyV + yxU + y^2 U$. Since $U \subseteq V$ we have $yxU = xyU \subseteq xyV$, so $S_2 V = x^2 V + xyV + y^2 U$.

But, as we observed above, $yV \subseteq xV + yU$, so

43

$$S_2 V = x^2 V + x(yV) + y^2 U = x^2 V + x(xV + yU) + y^2 U.$$

(We get equality here because everything is contained in $S_2 V$.)

Hence,

$$S_2 V = x^2 V + xyU + y^2 U = x(xV + yU) + y^2 U = x(S_1 V) + y^2 U.$$

Thus $\dim(S_2 V) \leq \dim(x S_1 V) + \dim(y^2 U) = \dim(S_1 V) + \dim U = (n+1+\dim V) + (n+1) = \dim V + 2n + 2$, as we wanted to show. $\square$

We now can prove the most important consequence, for us, of these considerations.

Corollary 7.12: (Castelnuovo Lemma-Gieseker's Lemma)

Let $V \subseteq S_t$, $codim V \neq 0$ and $\gcd(V) = 1$. Then

$$codim(S_1 V) \leq codim V - 1 .$$

Proof: From $7.9, 1)$ we know that $codim V \geq codim(S_1 V)$ in any case. From $7.9, 3)$ we know that if $codim V = codim(S_1 V)$ then $codim V = codim(S_t V)$ for all $t \geq 0$. But, by hypothesis, $codim V \neq 0$ and $7.8, 2)$ tells us that if $\gcd(V) = 1$ then $codim(S_t V) = 0$ eventually. So, we cannot have $codim V = codim(S_1 V)$. The statement in the corollary then follows.$\square$

Remark

After the lecture, I was asked about one of the comments I made in the proof of Proposition 7.8. Let me state the exact result I know to be true.

Proposition: Let $R = k[x_1, \ldots, x_n]$ and let V be a subspace of R_t. Suppose that $\dim V \geq 2$ and that $\gcd(V) = 1$.

If k is an infinite field then we can find F_1, F_2 in V whose gcd is also 1.

(Remark: Leslie Roberts asked to what extent this remark was true if k is a finite field. I use, in this proof, the fact that k is infinite very heavily and that leads me to suspect that the proposition is false if k is a finite field. The proof will also indicate that to find a counterexample when k is finite, one will have to choose V of rather small dimension and t to be rather large. I would be interested to see an example where the proposition failed.)

Proof: The result is obvious (with no restriction on the field), when $\dim(V) = 2$, so we shall proceed by induction on the dimension of V.

Suppose that $\dim(V) = r \geq 3$ and that $F_1, \ldots, F_r$ is a basis for V. Let W be the subspace spanned by the first $r - 1$ members of this basis. If $\gcd(W) = 1$ we are done, by the induction hypothesis. So, we may as well suppose that $\gcd(W) = H$. Clearly H and F_r have $\gcd = 1$ otherwise there would be a common divisor for all the elements in a basis for V, contradicting the fact that $\gcd(V) = 1$.

Now let Q be an irreducible factor of F_r. Let W_Q be the subspace (it is a subspace) of all the elements in W which have Q as a factor. By our comments above, W_Q is a proper subspace of W. We do this for each of the finitely many irreducible factors of F_r and thus obtain a finite number of proper subspaces of W. Since the field k is infinite, the union of these subspaces is not the whole of W, so we can find an element of W which has no irreducible factor in common with F_r. That completes the proof. $\square$

Remark: Notice that if we have an F in V which has only a few irreducible factors and if the dimension of W is large enough, we can find such an element even if the field is finite.

By a dimension count it seems as if a counterexample could come (with a field having two elements) when the dimension of V is 3 and the number of factors of F_3 is at least 8. Probably for lower degree, if one is very, very careful!

We now want to apply our previous observations to study the ideal of a set of points in $\mathbb{P}^2$.

Definition 8.1: Let $\mathbf{X}$ be a set of points in $\mathbb{P}^n$ and let $I = I(\mathbf{X})$ be the ideal of these points in $R = k[x_0, \ldots, x_n]$. Then:

$\beta = \beta(\mathbf{X})$ is the least degree for which there exist two hypersufaces with no common component which contain all the points of $\mathbf{X}$.

Recall that α is the least degree for which $I_\alpha \neq (0)$ and now β is the least degree for which the forms in I_β have no common factor. (In early papers of Dubreil (circa 1930), he called "β" the degree of the "*second*" form in I. In the cases Dubreil was considering, very often there was an irreducible form of degree α through the points and then calling "β" the degree of the second form makes more sense.) Notice also that if L is a linear form that is not a zero divisor in the ring R/I and J is the ideal $(I, L)/L$ in $R/(L)$, then $\alpha(I) = \alpha(J)$ and $\beta(I) = \beta(J)$.

We can thus reinterpret the Castelnuovo Lemma (7.12) for the Hilbert function of a set of points in $\mathbb{P}^2$.

Proposition 8.2: *Let $\mathbf{X}$ be a set of distinct points in $\mathbb{P}^2$. Suppose that $\Delta H(\mathbf{X}, -)$ is the difference function of the Hilbert function of $\mathbf{X}$. If $\beta = \beta(\mathbf{X})$ then:*

$$\text{for } t \geq \beta \text{ we have } \Delta H(\mathbf{X}, t) > \Delta H(\mathbf{X}, t+1) \text{ or } \Delta H(\mathbf{X}, t) = 0.$$

Let's illustrate this proposition with an example.

Example 8.3: Let $\mathbf{X}$ be any set of 10 points with Hilbert function

$$H_{\mathbf{X}} : 1 \quad 3 \quad 6 \quad 8 \quad 10 \quad 10$$

i.e. whose difference function is

$$\Delta H_{\mathbf{X}} : 1 \quad 2 \quad 3 \quad 2 \quad 2 \quad 0$$

From 8.2 we get that $\beta(I(\mathbf{X})) \geq 4$, i.e. the cubics through the 10 points have to have a common factor, and (by 7.8, 1)) that common factor must be of degree $d \leq 2$.

Notice that:

is a set of 10 points with the Hilbert function above and that indeed all the cubics through these 10 points have a common quadratic factor (the product of two linear forms describing the lines between the bottom 5 dots and the next line of 4 dots.)

This raises the question about whether or not it would have been possible to find an example, with the Hilbert function of Example 8.3, for which the gcd of the cubics through the points was only of degree 1. Interestingly enough, the answer is no, and the following proposition of E.D. Davis explains why.

Proposition 8.4: *Let $J \subseteq S = k[x,y]$ be an ideal for which*

$$H(S/J,t) = H(S/J,t+1) = d < \alpha(J).$$

If $G = \gcd(J_t)$ then $\deg G = d$.

Proof: By Proposition 7.8, 1) we know that $g = \deg G \leq d$. Write $J_t = GV$ where V is a subspace of S_{t-g}.

Suppose, first, that V is a proper subspace of S_{t-g}.

Now $\dim V = \dim J_t = t + 1 - d$. By Corollary 7.12 we know (since $\gcd(V) = 1$) that $\dim(S_1 V) \geq 2 + \dim V = t + 3 - d$. Also, $S_1 J_t \subseteq J_{t+1}$.

But, $S_1 J_t = S_1(GV) = G(S_1 V)$ and so $\dim(S_1 J_t) \geq t + 3 - d$. It follows that

$$\dim(S_{t+1}/S_1 J_t) \leq (t+2) - (t+3-d) = d - 1.$$

However, $\dim(S_{t+1}/S_1 J_t) \geq H(S/J, t+1) = d$. This is a contradiction. Hence, we may as well suppose that $V = S_{t-g}$.

In that case, $S_1 J_t = S_1(GV) = G(S_1 V) = GS_{t-g+1}$ and so $\dim(S_1 J_t) = \dim S_{t-g+1} = t - g + 2$. It follows that

$$\dim(S_{t+1}/S_1 J_t) = (t+2) - (t-g+2) = g \geq H(S/J, t+1) = d.$$

47

Since we know $d \leq g$ in any case, we obtain $d = g$. $\square$

Remark: Note also that this proof shows that $S_1 J_t = J_{t+1}$ and so, in this case, J has NO generators in degree $t + 1$ and $G = \gcd(J_{t+1})$ also.

There is a great deal more that can be said about the case of points in $\mathbb{P}^2$. To delve too deeply into proofs of these results, however, would take us a great deal of time. I'm going to try and steer a "middle" (or "muddle"?) course through these beautiful results (mostly due to E.D.Davis) by proving only some things and leaving the rest to the interested reader. In order to have a hope of trying to discern what happens for higher codimension (i.e. for points in $\mathbb{P}^n$ if $n \geq 3$) I believe that we must understand the codimension two case more thoroughly. I will admit to a small fear that the situation in codimension > 2 is so different from that in codimension 2 that "telling" too much about the codimension 2 results will irreparably damage the new reader's intuition. But, this is only a small fear and insufficient to deter me!

Let me illustrate the force of some of Davis' results for sets of points with a very specific Hilbert function.

Example 8.5: Let $\mathbf{X}$ be a set of points in $\mathbb{P}^2$ whose Hilbert function has first difference:

$$1 \ \ 2 \ \ 3 \ \ 4 \ \ 3 \ \ 2 \ \ 2 \ \ 1 \ \ 1 \ \ 0 \ldots$$

It is not hard to show that the following is such a set:

One can apply other results of Davis to assert that any set $\mathbf{X}$ whose Hilbert function has first difference as described above must consist of 19 points: 9 of these points on one line and the remaining 10 points having Hilbert function whose first difference is 1 2 3 2 1 1 0 and consisting of 6 points on a line and 4 off that line, where the four points off that line have Hilbert function whose first difference is: 1 2 1 0.

48

To get some idea where results like those in Example 8.5 come from, let I be the ideal of a set of points in $\mathbb{P}^2$, $R = k[x, y, z]$, and let $\mathcal{G}$ be a form of degree d which is not in I. As we defined in Lecture 6, $(I : \mathcal{G}) = \{F \in R \mid F\mathcal{G} \in I\}$. Then we have an exact sequence of R-modules:

$$0 \to R/(I : \mathcal{G}) \xrightarrow{\phi_1} R/I \xrightarrow{\phi_2} R/(\mathcal{G}, I) \to 0$$

where:

$$\phi_1(F + (I : \mathcal{G})) = F\mathcal{G} + I;$$

and

$$\phi_2(H + I) = H + (\mathcal{G}, I).$$

(I leave all verifications that these are R-module homomorphisms and that the sequence is exact, to the reader.)

Notice that since I is homogeneous and $\mathcal{G}$ is a form of degree d then $I : \mathcal{G}$ and $(\mathcal{G}, I)$ are both homogeneous ideals of R and that ϕ_1 and ϕ_2 are both graded homomorphisms. In fact the exact sequence above can be rewritten:

$$0 \to R/(I : \mathcal{G})(-d) \xrightarrow{\phi_1} R/I \xrightarrow{\phi_2} R/(\mathcal{G}, I) \to 0 \tag{8.6}$$

where all homomorphisms now have degree 0.

We obtain, from (8.6), that:

$$H(R/I, t) = H(R/(\mathcal{G}, I), t) + H(R/(I : \mathcal{G}), t - d).$$

It remains to identify the ideals $(\mathcal{G}, I)$ and $(I : \mathcal{G})$. So, let I be the ideal of the set $\mathbf{X}$ and let $\mathbf{Y} = \{P \in \mathbf{X} \mid \mathcal{G}(P) = 0\}$ and let $\mathbf{Z} = \mathbf{X} \backslash \mathbf{Y}$. Thus $\mathbf{X}$ is the disjoint union of $\mathbf{Z}$ and $\mathbf{Y}$. Write $\mathbf{Z} = \{P_1, \ldots, P_r\}$, $\mathbf{Y} = \{P_{r+1}, \ldots, P_s\}$. Let $P_i \leftrightarrow \wp_i \subseteq k[x, y, z] = R$, then:

Claim: *The ideal of $\mathbf{Z}$ is* $I(\mathbf{Z}) = \wp_1 \cap \ldots \cap \wp_r = (I : \mathcal{G})$.

Proof: If $F \in (I : \mathcal{G})$ then $\mathcal{G}F \in I$ so $\mathcal{G}F$ vanishes at all the points of $\mathbf{X}$. If $P \in \mathbf{Z}$ then $\mathcal{G}(P) \neq 0$ and so $F(P) = 0$, i.e. $(I : \mathcal{G}) \subseteq \wp_1 \cap \ldots \cap \wp_r$.

Conversely, suppose that F vanishes at every point of $\mathbf{Z}$. Then, since $\mathcal{G}$ vanishes at every point of $\mathbf{Y}$ we have that $F\mathcal{G}$ vanishes at

49

every point of **X**, i.e. $F\mathcal{G} \in I$ or, put another way, $F \in (I : \mathcal{G})$, as we wanted to show. $\square$

It is clear that $(\mathcal{G}, I)$ is contained in the ideal of **Y**, but it is not clear when the converse is true. One should not expect $(\mathcal{G}, I)$ to even be a radical ideal (it's not a radical ideal if, for example, $\mathcal{G}$ doesn't vanish at any of the points of **X** – in that case $(I : \mathcal{G}) = I$ and $(\mathcal{G}, I)$ is just some ideal whose radical is (x, y, z) and which, in most cases, contains neither x nor y nor z.) So, the problem is to have some way of deciding when $(\mathcal{G}, I)$ is indeed the ideal of **Y**. This is what Davis did in some cases:

a) if $\mathcal{G} = \gcd(I_t)$ and $\deg \mathcal{G} = d$ and if the ideal $J = (I, L)/L$ in $R/L = S$ satisfies, $H(S/J, t) = d$, then $(\mathcal{G}, I)$ is the ideal of **Y**.

b) we have that a) applies, for instance, if we are in the situation of Proposition 8.4.

So, this explains (a bit) how the work of Davis can sometimes be used to give a decomposition of the Hilbert function of a set of points. It would be interesting to have other results which might show when $(\mathcal{G}, I)$ is the ideal of **Y**.

Example 8.7: Let **X** be a set of points in $\mathbb{P}^2$ whose Hilbert function has first difference: 1 2 3 4 3 2 1 0. Suppose further that the forms in I, the ideal of **X**, of degree 5 have gcd of degree 2 and let $\mathcal{G} = \gcd(I_5)$. Then Davis' theorem says that **X** is the disjoint union of two sets **Y** and **Z**, where **Y** has ideal $(\mathcal{G}, I)$ and is a set of points whose Hilbert function has first difference:1 2 2 2 2 2 1 0 and **Z** has ideal $(I : \mathcal{G})$ and is a set of points whose Hilbert function has first difference 1 2 1 0.

Note that there is no guarantee that a set **X** with this Hilbert function has the decomposition described above, one must have that the gcd of I_5 have degree 2 exactly. The following 16 points have the Hilbert function above but cannot be decomposed into 12 points on a conic and 4 points off the conic.

Notice that for this set of points we have $\beta = 4$.

These examples, and the discussion above, show that (in certain cases) some features of the Hilbert function of a set of points can influence the Hilbert function of subsets of the set of points. This is an important observation and one that I want to pursue, so for the next while I will explain some of these connections.

Before beginning on the theoretical basis for the discussion let's look, in detail, at a particular example.

Example 8.8: Let **X** be the set of points

$$\bullet \quad \bullet \quad \bullet$$
$$\bullet \quad \bullet \quad \bullet$$
$$\bullet \quad \bullet \quad \bullet$$

Since **X** is a $CI(3,3)$, the first difference of the Hilbert function of **X** is: 1 2 3 2 1 0, i.e. $H_{\mathbf{X}}$ is:1 3 6 8 9 9 ...

Since a set consisting of one point always has the same Hilbert function, it follows from the Cayley-Bacharach theorem that every subset of **X** consisting of 8 points always has the same Hilbert function. On the level of difference functions,

8 point subsets have $\Delta H : 1\ \ 2\ \ 3\ \ 2\ \ 0.$

Again, by Cayley-Bacharach and the fact that a 2 point set always has the same Hilbert function, we get:

7 point subsets have $\Delta H : 1\ \ 2\ \ 3\ \ 1\ \ 0.$

Note that in **X** there are two types of 3 point subsets. Those consisting of 3 points on a line (these have $\Delta H : 1\ \ 1\ \ 1\ \ 0\ \ ..$) and those consisting of 3 points not on a line (these have $\Delta H : 1\ \ 2\ \ 0\ \ .$). Thus, by Cayley-Bacharach we have, for 6 point subsets:

$$\Delta H : 1\ \ 2\ \ 2\ \ 1\ \ 0 \text{ (if linked to 3 points on a line)};$$

or,

$$\Delta H : 1\ \ 2\ \ 3\ \ 0 \quad \text{(if linked to 3 points not on a line)}.$$

All four point subsets of **X** have the same Hilbert function, whose first difference is $\Delta H : 1\ \ 2\ \ 1\ \ 0.$ Thus, all 5 point subsets of **X** have the same Hilbert function, namely the Hilbert function whose first difference is 1 2 2 0.

51

In summary, for the set **X** above:

$$H_\mathbf{X} : 1 \quad 3 \quad 6 \quad 8 \quad 9 \quad 9 \quad \ldots .$$

8 pt. subsets	1 3 6 8 8 ..
7 pt. subsets	1 3 6 7 8 ...
6 pt. subsets	1 3 6 6 ... or 1 3 5 6 6 ..
5 pt. subsets	1 3 5 5 ...
4 pt. subsets	1 3 4 4 ...
3 pt. subsets	1 3 3 .. or 1 2 3 3 ..
2 pt. subsets	1 2 2 ..
1 pt. subsets	1 1 ..

Definition 8.9: Let **X** be a set of points with Hilbert function $H_\mathbf{X}$. Let $\mathbf{Y} \subseteq \mathbf{X}$ be a subset consisting of d points. We say that the Hilbert function of $\mathbf{Y}, H_\mathbf{Y}$, is the *truncation of $H_\mathbf{X}$ at d* if:

$$H_\mathbf{Y}(t) = \min\{H_\mathbf{X}(t), d\} \text{ for all t.}$$

Remark: Notice that in Example 8.8 above we have, for every $d \leq 9$, there is at least one subset of d elements whose Hilbert function is the truncation of the Hilbert function of **X** at d. In that example, moreover, not every subset of the same cardinality had the same Hilbert function.

Lecture 9 - Anthony V. Geramita

I now want to begin a more focused discussion of the Hilbert functions of subsets of a given set. The following Lemma and Proposition are taken from the Journal of the London Math. Society paper of Geramita, Maroscia and Roberts referred to earlier.

Lemma 9.1: *Let* $Y \subseteq X$ *be two subvarieties of* $\mathbb{P}^n$. *Then*

    a) $H_Y(t) \leq H_X(t)$ *for any* t.

    b) If P *is a point in* $\mathbb{P}^n$ *not in* Y *then there is an integer d such that:*

$$H_{Y \cup \{P\}}(t) = H_Y(t) \text{ for all } t < d;$$

$$H_{Y \cup \{P\}}(t) = H_Y(t) + 1 \text{ for all } t \geq d.$$

Proof: *a)* Let $I = I(Y)$ and let $J = I(X)$. Since $Y \subseteq X$ we have $J = I(X) \subseteq I(Y) = I$. Hence if $R = k[x_0, \ldots, x_n]$ then there is a surjection $R/J \twoheadrightarrow R/I$. Thus, $H(R/J, t) \geq H(R/I, t)$ for all t, as we wanted to show.

b) Choose $P \notin Y$. Then if $P \leftrightarrow \wp \subseteq R$ we have I is not contained in $\wp$ and so $I + \wp$ is strictly larger than $\wp$. Note also that $R/\wp \cong k[T]$ since $\wp$ is generated by n linearly independent linear forms.

We have the exact sequence

$$0 \to R/(I \cap \wp) \xrightarrow{\phi_1} R/I \oplus R/\wp \xrightarrow{\phi_2} R/(I + \wp) \to 0 \tag{9.2}$$

where $\phi_1(r + I \cap \wp) = (r + I, r + \wp)$ and $\phi_2(r + I, s + \wp) = r - s + (I + \wp)$.

Since $R/(I + \wp) \cong k[T]/(T^d)$ for some integer d, we have (from 9.2) that

$$H(R/I \cap \wp, t) = H(R/I, t) + H(R/\wp, t) - H(R/(I + \wp), t)$$

and that gives the desired result. $\square$

Proposition 9.3: *Let* X *be a subset of* $\mathbb{P}^n$ *with Hilbert function* H_X. *For any* $s \leq | X |$ *there is a subset* Y *of* $X, | Y |= s$, *such that* H_Y *is the truncation of* H_X *at* s.

Proof: We proceed by induction on the cardinality of Y, with the result being obvious when $| Y |= 1$.

So, now suppose that we have proved the result for $r < s$ and let $\mathbf{Y}$ be a subset of $\mathbf{X}$ whose Hilbert function is the truncation of $H_{\mathbf{X}}$ at r, i.e. $H_{\mathbf{Y}}(t) = \min\{H_{\mathbf{X}}(t), r\}$ for all t.

Let e be the least integer for which $H_{\mathbf{Y}}(e) < H_{\mathbf{X}}(e)$, then if $I = I(\mathbf{Y})$ and $J = I(\mathbf{X})$ we have:

$$0 \to I/J \to R/J \to R/I \to 0$$

and since $H(R/I, t) = H(R/J, t)$ for all $t < e$ we have that $(I/J)_t = 0$ for $t < e$. Let F in I represent a non-zero element of $(I/J)_e$, so $F \in I_e$ and $F \notin J$. I.e. F vanishes at all the points of $\mathbf{Y}$ and F does not vanish on some $P \in \mathbf{X}$. Let $\mathbf{Z} = \mathbf{Y} \cup \{P\}$.

Then $H_{\mathbf{Y}}(t) \leq H_{\mathbf{Z}}(t) \leq H_{\mathbf{X}}(t)$ for all t and, since the first and last terms here are equal for all $t < e$, $H_{\mathbf{Y}}(t) = H_{\mathbf{Z}}(t)$ for all $t < e$. Hence, if d is the integer described in Lemma 9.1, b), we must have $d \geq e$. But we have found an F (of degree e) in $I(\mathbf{Y})$ and not in $I(\mathbf{Z})$ and since $I(\mathbf{Y}) \supseteq I(\mathbf{Z})$ we have (again by Lemma 9.1, b)) that $H_{\mathbf{Z}}(e) = H_{\mathbf{Y}}(e) + 1$. Hence for the d of Lemma 9.1, b) we must have $d \leq e$. Thus $d = e$ and so the Hilbert function of $\mathbf{Z}$ is the truncation of $H_{\mathbf{X}}$ at $r + 1$, as we wanted to show. $\square$

Definition 9.4: Let $\mathbf{X}$ be a set of points in $\mathbb{P}^2$. We say that $\mathbf{X}$ has the *Uniform Position Property (UPP) (in the sense of Harris)*, if any two subsets of $\mathbf{X}$ with the same cardinality have the same Hilbert function.

Remark: In view of Proposition 9.3, the only way that a set of points can be in uniform position is if every subset of $\mathbf{X}$ having cardinality d has Hilbert function which is the truncation of $H_{\mathbf{X}}$ at d.

The next proposition shows that if a set $\mathbf{X} \subseteq \mathbb{P}^2$ has UPP then this puts rather strong conditions on the Hilbert function of $\mathbf{X}$.

Proposition 9.5: *Let $\mathbf{X}$ be a set of points in $\mathbb{P}^2$ with UPP and let $\Delta H_{\mathbf{X}}$ be the difference function of the Hilbert function of $\mathbf{X}$. Suppose also that $\alpha = \alpha(\mathbf{X})$. Then, there is an integer $t \geq 0$ such that:*

$$\Delta H_{\mathbf{X}} \text{ is } : 1\ 2\ 3\ \ldots\ \alpha - 1\ \ \alpha\ \ a_1\ \ a_2\ \ldots\ a_t\ \ a_{t+1}\ \ldots\ a_s\ \ 0$$

$$\text{where } \alpha = a_1 = \ldots = a_t > a_{t+1} > \ldots > a_s > 0.$$

Proof: This should be compared with Corollary 7.6. The only difference between the two results is that in this case we are saying that once the Hilbert function begins to decrease it cannot stop doing so. If there were some value $a_r < \alpha$ (for $r > t$) for which $a_r = a_{r+1}$ we would then be in the situation of Proposition 8.4 and obtain a subset of $\mathbf{X}$ whose Hilbert function is not the truncation of $H_{\mathbf{X}}$. That is the contradiction which proves the Proposition. $\square$

Points with the UPP show up rather naturally, as the following result of J. Harris shows.

Theorem 9.6: (Uniform position lemma of Harris) *Let C be a reduced and irreducible curve in $\mathbb{P}^n$ and let $\mathcal{H}$ be a general hyperplane. Then $\mathcal{H} \cap C$ is a set of $\deg C$ points in $\mathcal{H} \cong \mathbb{P}^{n-1}$ which have UPP.*

Remark:

a) This result is not true if the characteristic of the ground field is not zero. J. Rathmann has explored the failure of this theorem in characteristic p and has written a very interesting paper on the subject.

b) Building on the ideas of Harris, S.Diaz and I have recently extended the result above. Without going into great detail we say that a set of points has the *Uniform Resolution Property (URP)* if any two subsets with the same cardinality have all their graded Betti numbers equal. Since the Hilbert function of a variety is determined when we know the resolution of the defining ideal of the variety, this is a stronger property than UPP. We showed that the general hyperplane section of a reduced and irreducible curve (always in characteristic zero) has URP.

We were also able to show that there are sets of points which have UPP but which do not have URP, so the notion of URP is decidedly stronger.

For points in $\mathbb{P}^2$ the possible Hilbert functions of points with UPP and the possible Hilbert functions of points with URP are the same family of Hilbert functions. We have been unable to decide if that is the case in $\mathbb{P}^n$ for $n > 2$.

J. Migliore and I (among others) showed, for $\mathbb{P}^2$, what all the possible resolutions of points with URP can be. We have no ideas, however, what restrictions the URP property imposes on the resolutions of points in higher codimension. Results in this direction would be very interesting.

Results in $\mathbb{P}^n$ for $n > 2$

So far, the most comprehensive results we have about the Hilbert functions of points in $\mathbb{P}^n$ are for $n = 2$. There are, however, some results of a similar nature that are true in $\mathbb{P}^n$ for $n > 2$.

In order to exclude trivial cases, we shall always suppose that our set of points $\mathbf{X}$ in $\mathbb{P}^n$ is *non-degenerate*, i.e. $\mathbf{X}$ is not contained in any hyperplane of $\mathbb{P}^n$. Put another way, $H_{\mathbf{X}}(1) = n + 1$.

So, we are always dealing with at least $n + 1$ points in $\mathbb{P}^n$. It follows, (e.g. by truncation) that we can always find $n+1$ points in $\mathbf{X}$, call then $\mathbf{Y}$, for which $H_{\mathbf{Y}}(t) = n+1$ for all $t \geq 1$. It is easy to see that these points must satisfy: no 3 of them on a line (i.e. on a $\mathbb{P}^1$); no 4 on a $\mathbb{P}^2$; and, more generally, no s of them on a $\mathbb{P}^{s-2}$. They could, without loss of generality be the points labelled $[1 : 0 : \ldots : 0], [0 : 1 : 0 : \ldots : 0], \ldots, [0 : 0 : \ldots : 0 : 1]$.

Our first general theorem is attributed, by P. Maroscia, to G. Castelnuovo.

Theorem 9.7: *Let* $\mathbf{X} = \{P_1, \ldots, P_s\}$ *be distinct points in* $\mathbb{P}^n (s > n \geq 2)$ *with Hilbert function,*

$$H_{\mathbf{X}} : 1 \quad n+1 \quad b_2 \quad \ldots \quad b_{d-1} \quad b_d \quad s \quad s \quad \ldots$$

where d *is the least integer for which* $b_d = s$, *i.e.*

$$\Delta H_{\mathbf{X}} : 1 \quad n \quad c_2 \quad \ldots \quad c_{d-1} \quad c_d \quad 0$$

with $c_d \neq 0$.

If c_j $(j \leq d-1)$ *satisfies* $c_j = n - h$ $(h \geq 1)$ *then there are at least* $n - h + 2$ *points of* $\mathbf{X}$ *in a* $\mathbb{P}^{n-h}$. *In particular the points of* $\mathbf{X}$ *do not have UPP.*

Before beginning a proof of this theorem, let's see what it says in a few cases.

Example 9.8:

a) In case $n = 2$, the theorem speaks of the case where $\Delta H_{\mathbf{X}}(j) = 1$ for some $j < \sigma(\mathbf{X}) - 1$. (recall $\sigma(\mathbf{X})$ is the least integer t for which $\Delta H_{\mathbf{X}}(t) = 0$). By Macaulay's theorem (describing the growth of Hilbert functions) we are thus considering a set of points $\mathbf{X}$ for which $c_t = 1$ for $t \geq j$ (or $c_t = 0$), i.e.

$$\Delta H_{\mathbf{X}} : 1 \quad 2 \quad c_2 \quad \ldots \quad c_j = 1 \quad 1 \quad \ldots \quad 1 \quad 0$$

56

Theorem 9.7 asserts that in this case at least 3 points of $\mathbf{X}$ lie on a line. We have already seen, however, that in the case described above, $\mathbf{X}$ must have $d + 1$ points on a line $(\sigma(\mathbf{X}) = d)$. So, when $n = 2$ this result says **less** than we already knew!

b) In case $n = 3$, the theorem speaks of the case when $\Delta H_{\mathbf{X}}(j) = 1$ or 2 for some $j < \sigma(\mathbf{X}) - 1$.

    i) If $\Delta H_{\mathbf{X}}(j) = 1$, then the theorem tells us that there are at least 3 points on a line of $\mathbb{P}^3$. Note that by Macaulay's growth theorem it would be the case that for $t \geq j$, $\Delta H_{\mathbf{X}}(t) = 1$ (or 0).

    ii) If $\Delta H_{\mathbf{X}}(j) = 2$ then the proposition just tells us that there are at least 4 points on a $\mathbb{P}^2$ (*plane*) $\subseteq \mathbb{P}^3$. Since for $i \geq 2$ we have $2^{<i>} = 2$ we obtain that, for $t \geq j, \Delta H_{\mathbf{X}}(t) = 2, 1$ or 0, and if for some $t > j$, $\Delta H_{\mathbf{X}}(t) = 1$ then $\Delta H_{\mathbf{X}}(t)$ remains at 1 until it becomes 0.

c) In case $n = 4$ the proposition speaks of what happens if $\Delta H_{\mathbf{X}}(j) = 3, 2$ or 1 for some $j < \sigma(\mathbf{X}) - 1$. We've already noted, in b), what the possibilities are if the difference function takes on the value 1 or 2.

    If $\Delta H_{\mathbf{X}}(j) = 3$ and $j \geq 3$ then, by Macaulay's growth theorem, $\Delta H_{\mathbf{X}}(t) \leq 3$ for all $t \geq j$. The theorem says that there are at least 5 points on a $\mathbb{P}^3$ contained in our $\mathbb{P}^4$.

Note that unlike the previous cases, it need not be the case that $\Delta H_{\mathbf{X}}(t) < 4$ for all $t \geq j$. The following difference functions are all the difference functions of points which have 5 points (at least) on a $\mathbb{P}^3$ in $\mathbb{P}^4$.

$$1\ 4\ 3\ 4\ 0\ \cdots$$

$$1\ 4\ 3\ 4\ 5\ 0\ \cdots$$

$$1\ 4\ 3\ 4\ 5\ 6\ 0\ \cdots$$

$$1\ 4\ 3\ 4\ 5\ 4\ 4\ 0\ \cdots$$

$$1\ 4\ 3\ 4\ 5\ 6\ 7\ 0\ \cdots$$

We now return to a proof of the theorem.

Proof: Let $\mathbf{Y}$ be a subset of $\mathbf{X}$ whose Hilbert function is the truncation of $H_{\mathbf{X}}$ at b_j. I.e.

$$H_{\mathbf{Y}} : 1 \quad n+1 \quad b_2 \quad \cdots \quad b_j \quad b_j \quad b_j \quad \cdots$$

Choose a point of $\mathbf{X}$ not in $\mathbf{Y}$ and call it P and let $\mathbf{Z} = \mathbf{Y} \cup \{P\}$, then $\mathbf{Y} \subseteq \mathbf{Z} \subseteq \mathbf{X}$ and so

$$H_{\mathbf{Z}} : 1 \quad n+1 \quad b_2 \quad \cdots \quad b_j \quad b_j+1 \quad b_j+1 \quad \cdots$$

Beginning with P we can build a subset $\mathbf{T} \subseteq \mathbf{Z}$ such that:

a) $P \in \mathbf{T}$;

b) $H_{\mathbf{T}}$ is the truncation of $H_{\mathbf{Z}}$ at b_{j-1} .

We'll write: $\mathbf{T} = \{P, P_1, \ldots, P_{b_{j-1}-1}\}$ and so

$$\mathbf{Z} = \{P, P_1, \ldots, P_{b_{j-1}-1}\} \cup \{P_{b_{j-1}}, \ldots, P_{b_j}\}.$$

The last subset contains $n - h + 1$ elements.

Since $H_{\mathbf{T}}(j - 1) = b_{j-1}$ and $\mathbf{T}$ consists of b_{j-1} elements, we can find an F of degree $j - 1$ which vanishes at all the points of $\mathbf{T}$ except P. Since $n - h < n$ we can find a linear form H which vanishes at the $n - h + 1$ elements $\{P_{b_{j-1}}, \ldots, P_{b_j}\}$. Thus FH vanishes at all the points of $\mathbf{Y}$ and has degree j.

But the forms of degree j which vanish at $\mathbf{Y}$ are the same as the forms of degree j which vanish on all of $\mathbf{X}$. Thus FH vanishes on all of $\mathbf{X}$. But F does not vanish on P so H must vanish on P. Thus H vanishes at $(n - h + 1) + 1$ points.

We can repeat this process for any linear form containing $\{P_{b_{j-1}}, \ldots, P_{b_j}\}$ and that completes the proof. $\square$

There is one unsatisfactory aspect of this result and that is the fact that it does not take into account how many times the difference function dips below n (for points in $\mathbb{P}^n$) and somehow that should be relevant also. Another unsatisfactory aspect of this result is that it does not capture what we know about the situation with respect to linear subspaces in $\mathbb{P}^2$. It would be good to remedy this.

Added Remark:

Spurred on by some of the comments in this lecture, Anna Bigatti, Juan Migliore and I looked much harder at the influence of the UPP on the Hilbert function of a set of points in $\mathbb{P}^n$ when $n \geq 3$. The results of that investigation are contained in the paper by the three of us entitled: Geometric Consequences of Extremal Behaviour in a Theorem of Macaulay.

Lecture 10 - Yves Pitteloud

We would like to understand, in today's lecture, how the vanishing of some syzygies can be reflected in some geometrical condition. Recall that, given a closed subscheme $X \subset \mathbb{P}^n$, with ideal $I \subset R = k[x_0, \ldots, x_n]$, we can consider the minimal graded free resolution

$$0 \longrightarrow \oplus R(-j)^{\alpha_{\bullet,j}} \longrightarrow \cdots \longrightarrow \oplus R(-j)^{\alpha_{1,j}} \longrightarrow R \longrightarrow R/I \longrightarrow 0.$$

Throughout the lecture we will make the assumption that the ideal I contains no linear form, in other words that $\alpha_{1,j} = 0$ for $j \leq 1$. As the resolution is minimal, this will impliy that $\alpha_{i,j} = 0$ for $j \leq i$. We will try to understand the geometric consequences of the vanishing of some $\alpha_{i,i+1}$.

Definition 10.1: We will denote $\alpha_{i,i+1}$ by α_i (sometimes also $\alpha_i(X)$ or $\alpha_i(I)$). The part of the minimal resolution involving only the α_i is called the *2-linear part of the resolution*.

Notice that:

α_1 is the number of linearly independent quadrics in the ideal I ;

α_2 is the number of linearly independent linear relations among these quadrics;

α_3 is the number of linearly independent linear relations among those linear syzygies etc.

If the ideal I has depth at least one, (which is the case if it is a saturated ideal) then α_{n+1} (as well as all the $\alpha_{n+1,j}$) are zero.

The following proposition, taken from a recent paper of Cavaliere-Rossi-Valla [CRV], describes what happens when α_n is non zero.

Theorem 10.2: *Let X be a nondegenerate closed subscheme of $\mathbb{P}^n$. Then $\alpha_n(X) \neq 0$ if and only if X is contained in a $\mathbb{P}^r \cup \mathbb{P}^s$ with $r + s = n - 1$.*

The purpose of this lecture is to understand what happens when α_{n-1} is not zero. The main result is the so-called *Strong Castelnuovo Lemma*, which states that, under some general position hypothesis, $\alpha_{n-1} \neq 0$ if and only if X lies on a rational normal curve.

Let us first recall some properties of rational normal curves that we will be using in the sequel. A rational normal curve is a curve given, after a suitable linear coordinate change, by the embedding

$$
\begin{array}{ccc}
\mathbb{P}^1 & \longrightarrow & \mathbb{P}^n \\
(s,t) & \mapsto & (s^n, s^{n-1}t, \ldots, st^{n-1}, t^n).
\end{array}
$$

The ideal of the rational normal curve in $\mathbb{P}^n$ (parametrized as above) is the ideal of $k[x_0, \ldots, x_n]$ generated by the 2×2 minors of the matrix

$$
\begin{pmatrix}
x_0 & x_1 & x_2 & \cdots & x_{n-1} \\
x_1 & x_2 & x_3 & \cdots & x_n
\end{pmatrix}.
$$

A resolution of the coordinate ring R/I is given by an *Eagon-Northcott complex* as follows:

$$
0 \longrightarrow \oplus_{(n-1)\binom{n}{n}} R(-n) \longrightarrow \cdots \oplus_{2\binom{n}{3}} R(-3) \longrightarrow \oplus_{\binom{n}{2}} R(-2) \longrightarrow R \longrightarrow R/I \longrightarrow 0.
$$

Notice that this resolution consists entirely of its 2-linear part. We call such a resolution *2-linear*.

The following fact will also be useful in the sequel (cf. Griffith Harris, page 530): *$n+3$ points in $\mathbb{P}^n$ in linear general position (i.e no $n+1$ on a hyperplane), lie on exactly one rational normal curve.*

A Computational tool: The Koszul Complex.

Given a graded R-module, M, together with a minimal graded free resolution

$$
0 \longrightarrow \oplus R(-j)^{\alpha_{\bullet,j}} \longrightarrow \cdots \longrightarrow \oplus R(-j)^{\alpha_{1,j}} \longrightarrow \oplus R(-j)^{\alpha_{0,j}} \longrightarrow M \longrightarrow 0,
$$

we have an equality (that follows from the minimality of the resolution)

$$
\alpha_{i,j} = \dim_k Tor_i(M, k)_j.
$$

On the other hand, we can compute the right hand side of the above equality by resolving the R-module k, by means of the Koszul complex on the variables $x_0, \ldots, x_n$ (compare Lecture 6):

$$
0 \longrightarrow R(-n-1) \longrightarrow \cdots \longrightarrow \oplus_{\binom{n+1}{i}} R(-i) \longrightarrow \cdots \oplus_{\binom{n+1}{1}} R(-1) \longrightarrow R \longrightarrow k \longrightarrow 0.
$$

Let V denote the sub-graded-vectorspace R_1 of $k[x_0, \ldots, x_n]$. Wwe can rewrite the above Koszul complex (thanks to the isomorphism $\Lambda^i V \otimes_k R \cong \oplus_{\binom{n+1}{i}} R(-i)$) as follows:

$$0 \longrightarrow \Lambda^{n+1}V \otimes_k R \longrightarrow \cdots \longrightarrow \Lambda^i V \otimes_k R \longrightarrow \cdots \longrightarrow V \otimes_k R \longrightarrow R \longrightarrow k \longrightarrow 0.$$

This implies that $Tor_i^R(M,k)_j$ is the homology of the complex

$$\Lambda^{i+1}V \otimes_k M_{j-i-1} \longrightarrow \Lambda^i V \otimes_k M_{j-i} \longrightarrow \Lambda^{i-1}V \otimes_k M_{j-i+1}$$

where the differential sends the element $e_{l_1} \wedge \cdots \wedge e_{l_i} \otimes m$ of $\Lambda^i V \otimes_k M_{j-i}$ to the element

$$\sum (-1)^k e_{l_1} \wedge \cdots \wedge \widehat{e_{l_k}} \wedge \cdots \wedge e_{l_i} \otimes x_{l_k} m$$

of $\Lambda^{i-1}V \otimes_k M_{j-i+1}$.

In the specific case of an ideal I of R, with $I_1 = 0$, these observations allow us to give a better description of the 2-linear part of the resolution of R/I.

Lemma 10.3: *Let I be as above. Then*

$$\alpha_i(I) = \dim_k \left[(\Lambda^{i-1}V \otimes_k I_2) \cap K_{i-1} \right]$$

where K_{i-1} denotes the kernel of the differential $\Lambda^{i-1}V \otimes_k R_2 \longrightarrow \Lambda^i V \otimes_k R_3$ of the Koszul complex on the variables $x_0, \ldots, x_n$.

Proof: By definition we have $\alpha_i(I) = \dim_k Tor_i^R(R/I,k)_{i+1}$. By dimension shift, the righthand side is isomorphic to $\dim_k Tor_{i-1}^R(I,k)_{i+1}$. By the above observations on the Koszul complex, using the fact that $I_1 = 0$, this latter module is isomorphic to the kernel of $\Lambda^{i-1}V \otimes_k I_2 \longrightarrow \Lambda^{i-2}V \otimes_k I_3$. The assertion now follows from the fact that $\Lambda^{i-1}V \otimes_k I_2$ is a subvectorspace of $\Lambda^{i-1}V \otimes_k R_2$ while $\Lambda^{i-2} \otimes_k I_3$ is a subvectorspace of $\Lambda^{i-2}V \otimes_k R_3$. $\square$

Corollary 10.4: *Given two ideals I, J of R with $I_1 = J_1 = 0$ and with an inclusion $I_2 \subset J_2$, we have $\alpha_i(I) \leq \alpha_i(J)$.*

Corollary 10.5: *If a reduced scheme X in $\mathbb{P}^n$ lies on a rational normal curve, then $\alpha_{n-1}(X) \neq 0$.*

Proof. If X lies on the rational normal curve C, then we have an inclusion $I(C) \subset I(X)$. It follows from the Eagon-Northcott resolution that $\alpha_{n-1}(C) \neq 0$. The assertion is now a consequence of Corollary 10.4. □

There are similar results concerning other $\alpha_i(X)$ in case X lies on some variety of minimal degree (i.e. a variety with degree equal to codimension $+1$), or in the case where X lies on some $\mathbb{P}^r \cup \mathbb{P}^s$. They can be found in [CRV].

The Strong Castelnuovo Lemma

The following theorem provides a partial converse to Corollary 10.5. It was first proved by M. Green in *Koszul cohomology and the geometry of projective varieties*, J. Diff. Geom. 19 (1984).

Theorem 10.6: (Strong Castelnuovo Lemma, SCL) *Let $X \subset \mathbb{P}^n$ be a reduced scheme which contains at least $n+3$ closed points in linear general position. Then $\alpha_{n-1}(X) \neq 0$ if and only if X lies on a rational normal curve.*

The essential ingredient for the proof of the SCL is the following proposition, which, given a 2-linear $(n-2)$-syzygy, examines the quadrics involved. A detailed proof of this proposition can be found in [CRV].

Proposition 10.7: *Let X be a closed subscheme of $\mathbb{P}^n$ which contains at least $n+3$ points in linear general position. Suppose that $\alpha_{n-1}(X) \neq 0$ and let $\alpha = \sum_{|j|=n-2} \epsilon_j \otimes F_j$ (where ϵ_j denotes a basis vector of $\Lambda^{n-2}V$) be a non trivial element of $(\Lambda^{n-2}V \otimes_k I_2) \cap K_{n-2}$ (cf. Corollary 10.3). Then the vector space spanned by the F_j has dimension at least $\binom{n}{2}$.*

We will also need, for the proof of the SCL, the following *vanishing theorem* taken from Eisenbud and Koh, *Some linear syzygy conjectures*, Adv. in Math 1991.. This theorem provides a bound for the length of the linear part of the resolution of a graded R-module.

Theorem 10.8: *Let M be a graded module over the polynomial ring $R = k[x_0, \ldots, x_n]$ (k not necessarily algebraically closed), and suppose that M is torsion free over $R/\wp$ for some absolutely irreducible prime ideal $\wp$. Then $Tor_i(M,k)_{i+j} = 0$ for $j \geq \dim_k M_j$.*

Proof of the SCL: One implication is just Corollary 10.5, so let us see the other implication.

Let I denote the ideal of X; $P_1, \ldots, P_{n+3}$, points of X in linear general position and $\mathcal{C}$ the rational normal curve going through these points.

We want to show first that there is an equality

$$\alpha_{n-1}(P_1, \ldots, P_{n+3}) = \alpha_{n-1}(\mathcal{C}).$$

Let $\wp$ denote the ideal of the rational normal curve $\mathcal{C}$, and let $\wp_i$ denote the ideal of the point P_i. Consider the exact sequence of R-modules

$$0 \longrightarrow \wp_1 \cap \cdots \cap \wp_{n+3}/\wp \longrightarrow R/\wp \longrightarrow R/\wp_1 \cap \cdots \cap \wp_{n+3} \longrightarrow 0.$$

It induces an exact sequence

$$0 \longrightarrow Tor^R_{n-1}(R/\wp, k)_n \longrightarrow Tor^R_{n-1}(R/\wp_1 \cap \cdots \cap \wp_{n+3}, k)_n \longrightarrow$$

$$\longrightarrow Tor_{n-2}(\wp_1 \cap \cdots \cap \wp_{n+3}/\wp, k)_n \longrightarrow 0$$

which will give the equality $\alpha_{n-1}(P_1, \ldots, P_{n+3}) = \alpha_{n-1}(\mathcal{C})$, if we can show that

$$Tor_{n-2}(\wp_1 \cap \cdots \cap \wp_{n+3}/\wp, k)_n = 0.$$

This last statement follows from the vanishing theorem together with the following equalities, where we are using the fact that $n + 3$ points in linear general position impose linearly independent conditions on quadrics:

$$\dim_k [\wp_1 \cap \cdots \cap \wp_{n+3}/\wp]_2 = \binom{n+2}{2} - H(P_1, \cdots, P_{n+3}, 2) - \binom{n}{2}$$

$$= \binom{n+2}{2} - (n+3) - \binom{n}{2} = n - 2.$$

Suppose now that $\alpha_{n-1}(X) \neq 0$ and let $\alpha = \sum_{|j|=n-2} \epsilon_j \otimes F_j$ be a non-trivial syzygy (as in Proposition 10.7). We have the following diagram

$$(\Lambda^{n-2}V \otimes_k \wp_2) \cap K_{n-2} \quad \longrightarrow \quad (\Lambda^{n-2}V \otimes_k [\wp_1 \cap \cdots \cap \wp_{n+3}]_2) \cap K_{n-2}$$

$$\uparrow$$

$$(\Lambda^{n-2}V \otimes_k I_2) \cap K_{n-2}$$

where the vertical arrow is injective, while the horizontal arrow is bijective, thanks to the equality $\alpha_{n-1}(P_1, \ldots, P_{n+3}) = \alpha_{n-1}(\mathcal{C})$.

This diagram implies that the F_j are, in fact, elements of $\wp$. According to Proposition 10.7, the F_j span a vector space of dimension $\geq \binom{n}{2}$. On the other hand we know that $\wp$ is generated by $\wp_2$ and that we have an equality $\dim_k \wp_2 = \binom{n}{2}$. This means that the F_j generates $\wp$, which implies that $\wp$ is contained in I. This concludes the proof of the Strong Castelnuovo Lemma. $\square$

Remark 10.9: The usual Castelnuovo Lemma states that a set X of $s \geq 2n+3$ points in linear general position in $\mathbb{P}^n$ lie on at least $\binom{n}{2}$ linear independant quadrics (in other words the Hilbert function of these points at 2 is $\leq 2n+1$) if and only if these points lie on a rational normal curve. It is fairly easy to check that when $n = 3$, the Strong Castelnuovo Lemma implies the usual Castelnuovo Lemma: using the fact that $H(X, 2) \leq 2n+1$ while $H(X, 3) \geq min(2n+3, 3n+1)$ (as the points are in linear general position), one can manufacture a non trivial linear relation among the quadrics generating the ideals of X. *It doesn't seem obvious at all how to generalize this argument to arbitrary n.*

Notice also that, for a set of $s \geq 2n+3$ points in $\mathbb{P}^n$, Proposition 10.7, together with the usual Castelnuovo Lemma, imply the Strong Castelnuovo Lemma.

Lecture 11 - Uwe Nagel

In the last lecture we saw that the existence of a long linear part in the minimal resolution of the defining ideal of a set of points imposes strong conditions on the points itself. In this lecture we will study the length of the linear part of the resolution in more generality. We follow mainly the paper of D. Eisenbud and J. Koh "Some linear syzygy conjectures", Adv. Math. 90 (1991), $47 - 76$.

We use the following notation: $R = K[x_0, \ldots, x_r]$ and N is a graded R-module. We denote by $[N]_j$ the j-th graded component of N and by $N(i)$ the module with the same underlying module structure as N but grading given by $[N(i)]_j = [N]_{i+j}$ for all integers j. Let M always be a finitely generated graded R-module. Suppose that $[M]_0 \neq 0$ and $[M]_j = 0$ for all $j < 0$. Consider the (unique) minimal free graded resolution of M:

$$\mathcal{F}: \qquad \cdots \longrightarrow \oplus_j R(-e_{1j}) \longrightarrow \oplus_j R(-e_{0j}) \longrightarrow M \longrightarrow 0.$$

Our assumptions imply $e_{ij} \geq i$. Then the *linear part* or the "bottom degree part" of $\mathcal{F}$ is the subcomplex

$$\mathcal{F}_{lin}: \qquad \cdots \longrightarrow F_1 \longrightarrow F_0 \longrightarrow M \longrightarrow 0$$

where $F_i = \oplus_j R(-e_{ij})$ with $e_{ij} = i$. It is called the linear part because the maps between the F_i are given by matrices of linear forms.

Definition 11.1: We say that M has a *k-linear syzygy* if $F_k \neq 0$, i. e. $[Tor_k^R(K, M)]_k \neq 0$.

Note that the linear part, $\mathcal{F}_{lin}$, of the resolution of M depends only on data involved in the multiplication map $[R]_1 \otimes [M]_0 \longrightarrow [M]_1$. Thus the following conjecture makes sense.

Conjecture: (qualitative version) *If M has a k-linear syzygy and no element of $[R]_1$ annihilates any element of $[M]_0$, then rank $[M]_0 > k$.*

In order to state a quantitative version of Conjecture 11.1 we define (for a subspace $\mathcal{R} \subset [M]_0 \otimes [R]_1$):

$$\mathcal{R}_j = \{y \in [M]_0 \otimes [R]_1 \mid \text{rank}(y) \leq j \text{ where } y \text{ is viewed as a linear map } [M]_0^\vee \longrightarrow [R]_1\}.$$

Linear syzygy conjecture 11.2: (Eisenbud - Koh) *If M has a k-linear syzygy, then* $\mathcal{R} := \ker([M]_0 \otimes [R]_1 \longrightarrow [M]_1)$ *satisfies:*

$$if \ rank \ [M]_0 \leq k \quad then \quad \dim \mathcal{R}_1 \geq k \ ,$$

$$if \ rank \ [M]_0 \geq k \quad then \quad \dim \mathcal{R}_{t-k+1} \geq k$$

where $t = rank \ [M]_0$ and dim *denotes the dimension as affine variety.*

This conjecture can be reduced to the case rank $[M]_0 = k$.

In order to understand the conjecture in an easy case let $M = R/I$, that is we consider the case where $t = 1$. Then the linear part of the free resolution of M is the Koszul complex of the linear forms in I. Thus M has a k-linear syzygy iff at least k independent linear forms lie in I iff $\dim \mathcal{R}_1 \geq k$. This shows that the above conjecture is sharp.

The conjecture has been proved if $r \leq 4$.

The most general result bounding the length of the linear part of a resolution is the following. It was first proved by M. Green in a special case and then generalized by D. Eisenbud and J. Koh.

Vanishing Theorem 11.3: *If M is a finitely generated R-module and is torsion free as an S-module, where $S = R/P$ for some (absolutely irreducible) homogeneous prime ideal P with $[P]_1 = 0$, then $[Tor_i^R(K, M)]_i = 0$ for all $i \geq rank[M]_0$.*

Remarks 11.4:
(i) The assumption on torsion freeness can be viewed as a "global" assumption in contrast to the "local" assumption in Conjecture 11.1.
(ii) Since depth $(M) > 0$ there is nothing to prove if rank $[M]_0 > r$. Hence we may assume in the proof that rank $[M]_0 \leq r$. This implies $[M]_j = 0$ for all $j < 0$; otherwise rank $[M]_0 \geq$ rank $[R]_1$ by the assumption on torsion freeness.
(iii) Assuming $[M]_j = 0$ for all $j < 0$ we can apply the theorem to $M^* := [M]_0 R$ in order to obtain the same result but requiring a weaker torsion freeness assumption.
(iv) Later we will apply the theorem to the canonical module of a projective variety. We would like to have a result similar to 11.3 which is applicable to the canonical module of a zero-dimensional projective scheme.

Now we give a first application of the vanishing theorem. We say that a finite set X of points in $\mathbb{P}^r$ is in *generic position* if X has maximal Hilbert function h_X, i. e.

$$h_X(t) = \min\{|X|, \binom{r+t}{t}\} \text{ for all } t$$

where $|X|$ denotes the number of points in the set X.

Corollary 11.5: *Let $X \subset \mathbb{P}^r$ be a set of $\binom{r+e}{r} - p$ points in generic position where $e \geq 2, 0 \leq p < r$. Then the defining ideal $I(X) \subset R$ of X has a graded minimal free resolution of the following shape:*

$$0 \longrightarrow R^{b_{r-1}}(-e-r) \longrightarrow \ldots \longrightarrow R^{b_p}(-e-p-1) \longrightarrow R^{b_{p-1}}(-e-p) \oplus R^{a_{p-1}}(-e-p+1)$$

$$\longrightarrow \ldots \longrightarrow R^{b_0}(-e-1) \oplus R^{a_0}(-e) \longrightarrow I(X) \longrightarrow 0$$

where b_j, a_i are non-negative integers. In particular, X has Cohen-Macaulay type $b_{r-1} = \binom{r+e-1}{e} - p$.

Proof: From the assumption on the Hilbert function of X we get

$$h_X(e) = |X|.$$

This implies $[Tor_i^R(K, I(X)]_j = 0$ for all $j > e + 1 + i$. (This fact will be proved later in a more general context.) Our assumption gives also rank $[I(X)]_e = p$. Thus, applying the vanishing theorem with $P = 0$ we obtain $[Tor_i^R(K, I(X)]_{e+i} = 0$ for all $i \geq p$. $\square$

Proof of Theorem 11.3: (a) By Remark 11.4 we may assume $[M]_j = 0$ for all $j < 0$ and (since P is absolutely irreducible) also that K is algebraically closed.

(b) For $\mathfrak{p} \in \text{Proj}(S)$ we put $\kappa(\mathfrak{p}) = S_{(\mathfrak{p})}/\mathfrak{p}S_{(\mathfrak{p})}$.

To continue with the proof of the theorem we need the following technical Lemma. It is an algebraic translation of the fact that for a global section of a vector bundle to vanish at s general points one requires at least s linear conditions. We now just state the Lemma and we shall prove it after completing the proof of the Theorem.

Lemma 11.6:: *Let $P_i = (x_0, \ldots, \hat{x}_i, \ldots, x_r) \subset R$ for all $i = 0, \ldots, r$ and let $1 \leq s \leq r+1$. Then we have, after making a suitable change of coordinates:*

(i) $P \subset P_i$ for all i,

(ii) for any subset $I \subset \{0, \ldots, r\}$ consisting of s distinct elements of X, there is a K-homomorphism

$$\phi_I : [M]_0 \longrightarrow \oplus_{i \in I} \kappa(P_i)$$

factoring over

$$\alpha_I : [M]_0 \longrightarrow \oplus_{i \in I} M_{(P_i)} / P_i M_{(P_i)}$$

such that ϕ_I is of maximal rank. (Note that $\oplus_{i \in I} \kappa(P_i) \cong K^s$.)

We now continue with the proof of Theorem 11.3.

c) For $I = \{i_1, \ldots, i_s\} \subset \{0, \ldots, r\}$ put $x_I = x_{i_1} \wedge \ldots \wedge x_{i_s}$. Let rank $[M]_0 = t$. It is sufficient to show $[Tor_t^R(K, M)]_t = 0$. Since $[M]_{-1} = 0$, $[Tor_t^R(K, M)]_t$ is the kernel of the Koszul map

$$\psi : \Lambda^t[R]_1 \otimes [M]_0 \longrightarrow \Lambda^{t-1}[R]_1 \otimes [M]_1$$

sending $z = \sum_{|I|=t} x_I \otimes e_I$ to $\sum_I \sum_{j \in I} \pm x_{I-j} \otimes x_j e_I = \sum_{|J|=t-1} x_J \otimes [\sum_{j \notin J} \pm x_j e_{J+j}]$. Let $\psi(z) = 0$. Since the x_J are independent we get, for each J, an equation $\sum_{j \notin J} \pm x_j e_{J+j} = 0$. Collecting all the equations that bear on a fixed t-tuple I, we see for all $j \in I$ that $x_j e_I \in \sum_{i \notin I} x_i M \subset P_j M$. It follows that $\alpha_I(e_I) = \left(\frac{x_j e_I}{x_j} \right)_{j \in I} = 0$. Hence we obtain $e_I \in \ker \phi_I = \{0\}$ by applying Lemma 11.6 with $s = t$. That completes the proof of the Vanishing Theorem modulo the proof of Lemma 11.6.

Lecture 12 - Uwe Nagel

In the last lecture we left open the proof of Lemma 11.6. We now give a proof in some detail because this is the only place where we see the need for the assumptions of the vanishing theorem. Unfortunately the proof is technical but uses only standard facts. This might be a reason why D. Eisenbud and J. Koh gave only a few indications for the proof in their paper. In order to fix the notation we will state this Lemma again (but with a new number!).

Lemma 12.1: *Let* $R = K[x_0, \ldots, x_r]$ *be a polynomial ring over the algebraically closed field* K. *Let* M *be a finitely generated graded* R-module, *torsion free as an* S-*module where* $S = R/P$ *for some homogeneous prime ideal* P *with* $[P]_1 = 0$. *Let* $P_i = (x_0, \ldots, \hat{x}_i, \ldots, x_r) \subset R$ *for all* $i = 0, \ldots, r$ *and let* $1 \leq s \leq r+1$. *Then we have, after a suitable change of coordinates:*

(i) $P \subset P_i$ *for all* i,

(ii) for any subset $I \subset \{0, \ldots, r\}$, *consisting of* s *distinct elements, there is a* K-*homomorphism* $\phi_I : [M]_0 \longrightarrow \oplus_{i \in I} \kappa(P_i)$ *factorizing over*

$$\alpha_I : [M]_0 \longrightarrow \oplus_{i \in I} M_{(P_i)}/P_i M_{(P_i)}$$

such that ϕ_I *is of maximal rank. (Note that* $\oplus_{i \in I} \kappa(P_i) \cong K^s$.)*

Proof: (1) Let $t = \mathrm{rank}[M]_0$. It is sufficient to prove the result if $t \geq s$.

(2) Let $Max(S)$ be $\{\mathfrak{p} \in Proj(S) \mid \mathfrak{p}$ is maximal $\}$ with the topology induced by the Zariski topology of $Proj(S)$. Since K is algebraically closed we get for all $\mathfrak{p} \in Max(S)$ that $\kappa(\mathfrak{p}) \cong K$.

(3) Since S is integral $M_{(0)}$ is a vector space over $S_{(0)}$. Moreover, we have $\frac{m}{1} \neq 0$ in $M_{(0)}$ for all $0 \neq m \in [M]_0$ because M is torsion free as an S-module. Therefore $\frac{m}{1}$ can be extended to a basis of $M_{(0)}$ and mapping any element of $M_{(0)}$ to its coefficient of $\frac{m}{1}$ provides a projection $M_{(0)} \longrightarrow S_{(0)}$. Thus we find, for all $m \neq 0$ in $[M]_0$, an open subset $W_m \subset Max(S)$ such that all $M_{(\mathfrak{p})}$ with $\mathfrak{p} \in W_m$ are free and have the same basis (more carefully, the preimages of the basis elements are the same and always include m) and we get maps

$$[M]_0 \longrightarrow M_{(\mathfrak{p})} \longrightarrow S_{(\mathfrak{p})} \longrightarrow S_{(\mathfrak{p})}/\mathfrak{p} S_{(\mathfrak{p})} = \kappa(\mathfrak{p})$$

69

where the second map is the projection on the coordinate corresponding to the free genera-tor $\frac{m}{1}$. For any $y \in [M]_0$ the image under the composition of the first two maps is denoted by $m(y)$. The composition of all these maps is a homomorphism $\phi_{m,\mathfrak{p}} : [M]_0 \longrightarrow \kappa(\mathfrak{p})$ with $\phi_{m,\mathfrak{p}}(m) = 1$ for all $\mathfrak{p} \in W_m$.

(4) Let $0 \neq m_1 \in [M]_0$ and let $\phi_{1,\mathfrak{p}_1} = \phi_{m_1,\mathfrak{p}_1}$ where $\mathfrak{p}_1 \in W_{m_1} = U_1$. Let $0 \neq m_2 \in \ker \phi_{1,\mathfrak{p}_1}$. Defining $\phi_{2,\mathfrak{p}_2} = \phi_{m_2,\mathfrak{p}_2}$ for some $\mathfrak{p}_2 \in W_{m_2} = U_2$ we get $\phi_{2,\mathfrak{p}_2}(m_2) = 1$. Let $0 \neq m_3 \in \ker \phi_{1,\mathfrak{p}_1} \cap \phi_{2,\mathfrak{p}_2}$. We put $\phi_{3,\mathfrak{p}_3} = \phi_{m_3,\mathfrak{p}_3}$ for some $\mathfrak{p}_3 \in W_{m_3} = U_3$. Repeating this procedure successively we find elements $m_1, \ldots, m_s$ and maps $\phi_1, \ldots, \phi_s$ such that $\bigoplus_{i=1}^{s} \phi_{i,\mathfrak{p}_i} : [M]_0 \longrightarrow \bigoplus_{i=1}^{s} \kappa(\mathfrak{p}_i)$ is surjective.

(5) Let W be $\{\mathfrak{p} \in Proj(S)^s \mid \mathfrak{p} \text{ maximal }\}$ with the topology induced by the Zariski topology of $Proj(S)^s$. We now show:

There is a non-empty open subset $U \subset U_1 \times \ldots \times U_s$ such that for all $(\mathfrak{q}_1, \ldots, \mathfrak{q}_s) \in U$ the map $\bigoplus_{i=1}^{s} \phi_{i,\mathfrak{q}_i} : [M]_0 \longrightarrow \bigoplus_{i=1}^{s} \kappa(\mathfrak{q}_i)$ is surjective, where the $\phi_{i,\mathfrak{q}_i}$ are defined via the elements $m_1, \ldots, m_s$ as chosen in (4).

Let $\{y_1, \ldots, y_t\}$ be a basis of $[M]_0$. Let us denote $\phi_{i,\mathfrak{q}}(y_j)$ by $m_i(y_j)_\mathfrak{q}$. Then the homomorphism $\bigoplus_{i=1}^{s} \phi_{i,\mathfrak{q}_i}$ is given by the matrix

$$
A_{\mathfrak{q}_1 \ldots \mathfrak{q}_s} = \begin{pmatrix} m_1(y_1)_{\mathfrak{q}_1} & \cdots & m_s(y_1)_{\mathfrak{q}_s} \\ \vdots & & \vdots \\ m_1(y_t)_{\mathfrak{q}_1} & \cdots & m_s(y_t)_{\mathfrak{q}_s} \end{pmatrix}.
$$

By (4) $A = A_{\mathfrak{p}_1 \ldots \mathfrak{p}_s}$ has rank s. We may assume that the matrix consisting of the first s rows of A is invertible, i.e. has determinant not zero. Moreover, we have

$$
\sum_{\sigma \in \Pi_s} (-1)^{sgn(\sigma)} m_1(y_{\sigma(1)})_{\mathfrak{q}_1} \cdots m_s(y_{\sigma(s)})_{\mathfrak{q}_s} \neq 0 \text{ iff}
$$

$$
(\mathfrak{q}_1, \ldots, \mathfrak{q}_s) \in D\left(\sum_{\sigma \in \Pi_s} (-1)^{sgn(\sigma)} m_1(y_{\sigma(1)}) \otimes \ldots \otimes m_s(y_{\sigma(s)}) \right) = D \subset W.
$$

Therefore we get, for all $(\mathfrak{q}_1, \ldots, \mathfrak{q}_s) \in U_1 \times \ldots \times U_s \cap D = U$, that rank $A_{\mathfrak{q}_1 \ldots \mathfrak{q}_s} \geq s$. U is non-empty by (4).

(6) Let $\{\pi_I \mid I \subset \{0, \ldots, r\} \text{ with } |I| = s\}$ be the set of projections $Max(S)^{r+1} \longrightarrow Max(S)^s$. Let

70

$$V = \{(Q_0, \ldots, Q_r) \in Max(S)^{r+1} \mid$$

the corresponding points in $\mathbb{P}^r$ are linearly independent $\}$.

Then V is dense and open. Hence the finite intersection of dense subsets

$$U^* = \bigcap_{|I|=s} \pi_I^{-1}(U) \cap V$$

is non-empty. Let $(Q_0, \ldots, Q_r) \in U^*$. Since $[P]_1 = 0$, the Q_i lift to maximal ideals in R. Changing coordinates suitably we may assume $(P_0, \ldots, P_r) \in U^*$. This completes the proof. $\square$

If M is a Cohen-Macaulay module the graded Betti numbers of M are strongly related to the graded Betti numbers of the canonical module of M. We will explain this relationship but first we recall some known results and introduce some notation.

The irrelevant maximal ideal $(x_0, \ldots, x_r)$ of the polynomial ring $R = K[x_0, \ldots, x_r]$ will be denoted by $\mathfrak{m}$. We always assume the R-module M to be finitely generated, graded and of Krull dimension $n + 1$. The local cohomology modules $H^i_\mathfrak{m}(M) = \varinjlim Ext^i_R(R/\mathfrak{m}^t, M)$ are also graded R-modules. The module M is said to be *Cohen-Macaulay* if it has depth $n + 1$. It is well-known that M is Cohen-Macaulay iff $H^i_\mathfrak{m}(M) = 0$ for all $i \neq n + 1$. Let $^\vee = Hom_K(\_, K)$ where K is considered as a graded R-module concentrated in one degree. Then $M^\vee$ is graded by $[M^\vee]_t = Hom_K([M]_{-t}, K)$. Later we will need:

Local duality: *There are isomorphisms of graded R-modules:*

$$H^i_\mathfrak{m}(M)^\vee \cong Ext^{r+1-i}_R(M, R)(-r - 1),$$

$$H^i_\mathfrak{m}(M) \cong Ext^{r+1-i}_R(M, R)^\vee(r + 1).$$

We denote the canonical module $Ext^{r-n}_R(M, R)(-r-1) \cong H^i_\mathfrak{m}(M)^\vee$ of M by ω_M. For an arbitrary R-module M we define its socle, $soc(M)$ to be $0 :_M \mathfrak{m} = \{n \in M \mid n \cdot \mathfrak{m} = 0\}$.

Lemma 12.2: *If M is Cohen-Macaulay of dimension $n + 1$ we have:*

71

(i) $Tor_i^R(K, M)^\vee(-r-1) \cong Tor_{r-n-i}^R(K, \omega_M)$,

(ii) $soc(H_\mathfrak{m}^{n+1}(M)) \cong Tor_{r-n}^R(K, M)(r+1)$.

Proof. We consider the minimal free graded resolution of M

$$0 \longrightarrow \oplus_j R(-e_{r-n,j}) \longrightarrow \dots \longrightarrow \oplus_j R(-e_{0,j}) \longrightarrow M \longrightarrow 0.$$

Applying the functor $Hom_R(\_, R)$ to this sequence we get a complex with i-th homology $Ext_R^i(M, R)$. Since M is Cohen-Macaulay we get, from local duality, that $Ext_R^i(M, R) = 0$ for all $i \neq r - n$. Therefore the sequence

$$0 \longrightarrow \oplus_j R(e_{0,j}) \longrightarrow \dots \longrightarrow \oplus_j R(e_{r-n,j}) \longrightarrow Ext_R^{r-n}(M) \longrightarrow 0.$$

is exact and a minimal free graded resolution of $\omega_M(r+1)$ proving (i)

The second claim follows from the following graded isomorphisms:

$$
\begin{aligned}
soc(H_\mathfrak{m}^{n+1}(M)) &\cong Hom_R(K, H_\mathfrak{M}^{n+1}(M)) \\
&\cong Hom_R(K, Hom_K(Ext_R^{r-n}(M, R), K))(r+1) \\
&\cong Hom_K(K \otimes_R Ext_R^{r-n}(M, R), K)(r+1) \\
&\cong Hom_K(\oplus_j R(e_{r-n,j}), K)(r+1) \quad \text{(by (*))} \\
&\cong \oplus_j R(-e_{r-n,j})(r+1) \\
&\cong Tor_{r-n}^R(K, M)(r+1). \quad \square
\end{aligned}
$$

The first assertion of the above result is well-known. The second claim seems to have been first observed in a recent paper by C. Huneke and B. Ulrich in the case where $\dim(M) = 1$.

Lecture 13 - Uwe Nagel

In this lecture we will use the results of the previous lectures to give an upper bound for the degrees of the defining equations of an arithmetically Cohen-Macaulay variety. A variety in projective r-space is always assumed to be irreducible, reduced and non-degenerate and, to avoid trivialities, of dimension ≥ 1. We use the following notation: R always denotes the polynomial ring $K[x_0, \ldots, x_r]$ over the field K with irrelevant maximal ideal $\mathfrak{m} = (x_0, \ldots, x_r)$. The defining ideal in R of a variety $V \subset \mathbf{P}^r$ is denoted by $I(V)$. The variety V is said to be *arithmetically Cohen-Macaulay* if its homogeneous coordinate ring is Cohen-Macaulay. This is equivalent to the condition $H^i(\mathbf{P}^r, \mathcal{I}_V(t)) = 0$ for all integers t if $0 < i < \dim V$. Note the following relation between local and Serre cohomology:

$$H^i_{\mathfrak{m}}(R/I(V)) \cong \oplus_{t \in \mathbb{Z}} H^i(\mathbf{P}^r, \mathcal{I}_V(t)) \quad \text{for all } i > 0.$$

For positive integers a, b we denote by $\lceil \frac{a}{b} \rceil$ the smallest integer $\geq \frac{a}{b}$. The aim of this lecture is to prove the following result.

Theorem 13.1: *Let $V \subset \mathbf{P}^r_K$ be an arithmetically Cohen-Macaulay variety over an algebraically closed field K, then the defining ideal of V is generated in degree $\leq \left\lceil \frac{\deg V}{\operatorname{codim} V} \right\rceil$.*

This result was proved by Treger under the additional hypothesis that the characteristic of the field K is zero (Theorem 1.1 in "On equations defining arithmetically Cohen-Macaulay varieties. II", Duke Math. J. **48** (1981), 35 - 47). In this case the general position lemma (or even the uniform position lemma of J. Harris) applies and implies that the intersection of the variety V with n general hyperplanes is a set X of d points in linearly general (even uniform) position in their linear span. Treger was able to show that the defining equations of X have degree $\leq \left\lceil \frac{\deg V}{\operatorname{codim} V} \right\rceil$ (In the next lecture I will present generalizations of this result) and this is a bound for the degrees of the defining equations of V as well, due to the Cohen-Macaulay assumption.

However, if $char(K) > 0$ the general position lemma may fail as the following example of J. Rathmann shows.

Example 13.2: Let $p = char(K) > 0$ and let $C \subset \mathbf{P}^r_K$ be a curve defined by $x_0^p - x_1 x_r^{p-1}, x_1^p - x_2 x_r^{p-1}, \ldots$. Then C is a complete intersection of degree p^{r-1} and, as a configuration of points, the general hyperplane section of C looks like an $(r-1)$-dimensional affine space over the finite field with p elements.

73

Proof. Over the affine open subset $x_r \neq 0$, C can be described by the equations $x_0 = t, x_1 = t^p, x_2 = t^{p^2}, \ldots$. If $a_1, \ldots, a_r$ are linearly independent points of C, the points of C in their linear span are given by $a = a_1 + \lambda_2(a_2 - a_1) + \ldots + \lambda_r(a_r - a_1)$ where the λ_i satisfy $\lambda_i^p = \lambda_i$. Indeed, every such point belongs to C by the above parametrization, thus we have found p^{r-1} points of C in the linear span of $a_1, \ldots, a_r$. These are all points of C in the linear span because any hyperplane section of C has degree $p^{r-1} = \deg C$. $\square$

The Theorem above speaks of the degrees of the defining equations of the variety V. Those degrees correspond to the shifts occuring in the minimal free resolution of its homogeneous coordinate ring $R/I(V)$ at the first place. We begin with an upper bound for the shifts occuring in the minimal free resolution of $R/I(V)$ at any place.

We need some notation. For an arbitrary graded R-module N we define

$$e(N) = \sup\{t \in \mathbb{Z} \mid [N]_t \neq 0\}$$

$$i(N) = \inf\{t \in \mathbb{Z} \mid [N]_t \neq 0\}.$$

If N is the zero module we put $e(N) = -\infty$ and $i(N) = \infty$. Let M be a finitely generated graded R-module. The Hilbert function and the Hilbert poynomial of M are denoted by h_M and p_M respectively.

We consider the following invariants of M:

Castelnuovo-Mumford regularity:	$reg(M) = \max\{i + e(H^i_{\mathfrak{m}}(M)) \mid i \in \mathbb{Z}\}$
regularity index:	$r(M) = \min\{t \in \mathbb{Z} \mid h_M(j) = p_M(j) \text{ for all } j \geq t\}$
a-invariant:	$a(M) = -i(\omega_M) = e(H^{\dim M}_{\mathfrak{m}}(M))$.

We have the following relations:

$$a(M) \leq reg(M) - \dim M$$

$$r(M) \leq reg(M) - \operatorname{depth} M + 1.$$

If M is a Cohen-Macaulay module we can say more.

74

Lemma 13.3: *Suppose that M is a Cohen-Macaulay module of dimension $n + 1$. Then the following integers are equal:*

$\quad$ (i) $\ reg(M)$

$\quad$ (ii) $\ a(M) + n + 1$

$\quad$ (iii) $\ r(M) + n$

$\quad$ (iv) $\ \max\{e(Tor_i^R(K, M)) - i \mid i \in \mathbb{Z}\}$

$\quad$ (v) $\ e(Tor_{r-n}^R(K, M)) - (r - n)$.

Proof: Let us denote the numbers in the statement by $A, B, \ldots, E$. Since M is Cohen-Macaulay we have $H_{\mathfrak{m}}^i(M) = 0$ for all $i \neq n + 1$ implying $A = B$. Moreover, it follows that:

$$h_M(t) - p_M(t) = (-1)^{n+1} \mathrm{rank}\, [H_{\mathfrak{m}}^{n+1}(M))]_t.$$

This gives $B = C$.

Lemma 12.2 (ii) provides

$$E = e(Tor_{r-n}^R(K, M)) - (r - n) = e(soc(H_{\mathfrak{m}}^{n+1}(M))) + n + 1$$

$$= e(H_{\mathfrak{m}}^{n+1}(M)) + n + 1 = B.$$

Since (clearly) $D \geq E$, it remains to show that $B \geq D$. Using Lemma 12.2 (i) we obtain

$$0 = [Tor_j^R(K, \omega_M)]_{j+t} = [Tor_{r-n-j}^R(K, M)]_{-t-j+r+1} \quad \text{for all} \quad t < i(\omega_M),$$

thus $e(Tor_{r-n-j}^R(K, M)) \leq -i(\omega_M) - j + r + 1$. It follows that for all integers j:

$$e(Tor_{r-n-j}^R(K, M)) - (r - n - j) \leq a(M) + n + 1 = B$$

completing the proof. $\square$

Remarks 13.4:

(i) The equality $C = D$ was proved in the special case that M is an ideal in R by A. Lorenzini, but with different methods.

(ii) The equality $A = D$ is true even without the Cohen-Macaulay assumtion on M. This is a result of D. Eisenbud and S. Goto. It can be proved along the lines of the above proof using a generalization of Lemma 12.2 (i). Yves Pitteloud will present that generalization in a future lecture.

(iii) Consider a minimal free graded resolution of M:

$$\mathcal{F}: \quad \ldots \longrightarrow \oplus_j R(-e_{1j}) \longrightarrow \oplus_j R(-e_{0j}) \longrightarrow M \longrightarrow 0.$$

Then the Lemma gives $i(M) \leq e_{ij} - i \leq reg(M)$ for all i. We think of the subcomplex of $\mathcal{F}$ described by:

$$\ldots \longrightarrow F_1 \longrightarrow F_0 \longrightarrow M \longrightarrow 0,$$

where $F_i = \oplus_j R(-e_{ij})$ with $e_{ij} - i = reg(M)$ if such e_{ij} exist and is zero otherwise, as the *top degree part* of $\mathcal{F}$. Reversing the directions of the arrows, $\mathcal{F}$ corresponds (if M is Cohen-Macaulay) to the linear part of the resolution of M by Lemma 12.2 (i). We are interested in the length of this top degree part.

Definition 13.5: Let e and $p > 0$ be integers. A finitely generated graded R-module M is said to satisfy $(N_{e,p})$ if

$\quad\quad (i)\ \ reg(M) \leq e + 1$ and

$\quad\quad (ii)\ \ e(Tor_i^R(K, M)) - i \leq e$ for all $i < p$.

A projective scheme $S \subset \mathbf{P}^r$ satisfies $(N_{e,p})$ if its defining ideal $I(S) \subset R$ does. Moreover, we define $reg(S) = reg(I(S))$.

Remarks 13.6:

(i) If M is Cohen-Macaulay then from, Lemma 12.2 (i),we see that M satisfies $(N_{e,p})$ iff $i(\omega_M) \geq n - e$ and if $i(\omega_M) = n - e$ then ω_M has no $(r - n - p + 1)$-linear syzygies.

(ii) Let $X \subset \mathbf{P}^r$ be a 0-dimensional subscheme with homogeneous coordinate ring B. Then:

$$X \text{ satisfies } (N_{e,p}) \text{ iff } h_X(e) = \deg X \text{ and } [Tor_i^R(K, B)]_{i+e} = 0 \text{ for all } i \leq p.$$

This shows that for finite sets, property $(N_{2,p})$ is the same as property (N_p) of Green and Lazarsfeld.

We need one more preparatory result.

Lemma 13.7: *Let M be a graded Cohen-Macaulay module of dimension $n + 1$ and let $\{l_1, \ldots, l_s\} \subset [R]_1$ be a regular M-sequence. Put $f = e(H_{\mathfrak{m}}^{n+1-s}(M/(l_1, \ldots, l_s)M))$. Then we have:*

$$[H_{\mathfrak{m}}^{n+1}(M)]_t \cong \begin{cases} 0 & \text{if } t > f - s \\ [H_{\mathfrak{m}}^{n+1-s}(M/(l_1, \ldots, l_s)M)]_f & \text{if } t = f - s. \end{cases}$$

Proof: Let $l = l_1$. Since l is M-regular, multiplication by l induces an exact sequence

$$0 \longrightarrow M(-1) \longrightarrow M \longrightarrow M/lM \longrightarrow 0.$$

Then the long exact cohomology sequence gives the exact sequence

$$0 \longrightarrow H^n_{\mathfrak{m}}(M/lM) \longrightarrow H^{n+1}_{\mathfrak{m}}(M)(-1) \longrightarrow H^{n+1}_{\mathfrak{m}}(M) \longrightarrow 0.$$

This last proves the Lemma if $s = 1$ because $e(H^{n+1}_{\mathfrak{m}}(M))$ is finite. Induction on s completes the proof. $\square$

We are now in position to prove our main result. Theorem 13.1 is an easy consequence of it.

Theorem 13.8: *Let K be an arbitrary field. Let $V \subset \mathbf{P}^r_K$ be an absolutely integral nondegenerate arithmetically Cohen-Macaulay variety of degree d and dimension n. Let e, p be integers defined by $d - 1 = e(r - n) - p$ where $1 \leq p \leq r - n$. Then V satisfies $(N_{e,p})$.*

Proof: We may assume that K is algebraically closed since local cohomology is compatible with base change. Let $H_1, \ldots, H_n$ be general hyperplanes defined by $l_1, \ldots l_n$. Then, by results of E. Ballico, $X = V \cap H_1 \cap \ldots \cap H_n$ is a set of d points in linear semi-uniform position whose Hilbert function satisfies

$$h_X(t) \geq \min\{d, t(r - n) + 1\} \quad \text{for all } t.$$

Let $A = R/I(V)$ be the coordinate ring of V. Since A is Cohen-Macaulay the coordinate ring of X is $B = A/(l_1, \ldots, l_n)A$ and we get

$$\operatorname{rank}[H^1_{\mathfrak{m}}(B)]_t = d - h_X(t) \leq \max\{0, d - t(r - n) - 1\}.$$

Thus, we obtain from Lemma 13.7 that

$$reg(V) = reg(A) + 1 = e(H^{n+1}_{\mathfrak{m}}(A)) + n + 2 \leq e + 1 \quad \text{and}$$

$$\operatorname{rank}[\omega_A]_{n+1-e} = \operatorname{rank}[H^{n+1}_{\mathfrak{m}}(A)]_{e-1-n} = \operatorname{rank}[H^1_{\mathfrak{m}}(B)]_{e-1} \leq r - n - p.$$

Since the canonical module, ω_A, is torsion free as an A-module we may apply the Vanishing Theorem of Green, Eisenbud and Koh (Theorem 11.3) and get

$$[Tor_i^R(K, \omega_A)]_{n+1-e+i} = 0 \quad \text{for all } i \geq r - n - p.$$

Thus Lemma 12.2 (i) yields

$$[Tor_{r-n-i}^R(K, A)]_{e+r-n-i} = 0 \quad \text{for all } i \geq r - n - p.$$

Hence A satisfies $(N_{e,p+1})$. $\Box$

Remarks 13.9:

(i) The Theorem above implies, in particular, that

$$reg(V) \leq \left\lceil \frac{d-1}{r-n} \right\rceil + 1.$$

Note that this bound remains true if we weaken the Cohen-Macaulay assumption on V to a Buchsbaum assumption on V (as remarked by E. Ballico).

In view of this I want to ask:

Is the claim in Theorem 13.1 true if we assume that V is arithmetically Buchsbaum instead of Cohen-Macaulay?

(ii) Using results of D. Eisenbud and J. Harris on the Hilbert function of points in uniform position, N. V. Trung and G. Valla have shown:

Let $V \subset \mathbf{P}_K^r$ be as in Theorem 13.8. Suppose $char(K) = 0$ and $d > (r - n + 1)^2$. Then the following conditions are equivalent:

(a) $reg(V) = \left\lceil \frac{d-1}{r-n} \right\rceil + 1$

(b) $I(V)$ has a minimal generator of degree $\left\lceil \frac{d}{r-n} \right\rceil$

(c) V lies on a variety of minimal degree and dimension $n + 1$.

It can be shown, using the above techniques and a result of E. Ballico, that this remains true even in positive characteristic if we assume $r - n \geq 5$. *Can this last assumption be dropped?*

Lecture 14 - Uwe Nagel

The results presented in this talk are taken from the preprints "On degree bounds for the syzygies of finite sets of points in $\mathbf{P}^n$" by P. Maroscia, U. Nagel and W. Vogel and "On the minimal free resolution of $r+3$ points in projective r-space" by me. Throughout this talk X will denote a finite set of K-rational points in $\mathbf{P}^r = \mathbf{P}_K^r$, where K is a field. It is always assumed that X spans $\mathbf{P}^r$, i. e., the scheme X is nondegenerate. The number of points in X is denoted by $|X|$. Let me recall some of the definitions I introduced in the last talks with the help of an example. Suppose X, or better its coordinate ring, has a minimal graded free resolution of the following shape:

$$
\begin{array}{ccc}
R(-e-r)^{\gamma_r} & & R(-e-r+1)^{\gamma_{r-1}} \\
\oplus & & \oplus
\end{array}
$$
$$
0 \;\to\; R(-e-r+1)^{\beta_r} \;\to\; R(-e-r+2)^{\beta_{r-1}} \;\to\; R(-e-r+3)^{\beta_{r-2}} \;\to\; \cdots
$$
$$
\to\; R(-e-2)^{\beta_3} \;\to\; R(-e-1)^{\beta_2} \;\to\; R(-e)^{\beta_1} \;\to\; R \;\to\; R/I(X) \;\to\; 0
$$
$$
\begin{array}{ccc}
R(-e)^{\alpha_2} & & R(-e+1)^{\alpha_1} \\
\oplus & & \oplus
\end{array}
$$

where all the occuring α's, β's and γ's are non-negative integers. Suppose further that α_2 and γ_{r-1} are positive.

Recall that we called the subcomplex

$$
0 \longrightarrow R(-e)^{\alpha_2} \longrightarrow R(-e+1)^{\alpha_1} \longrightarrow I(X) \longrightarrow 0
$$

the *linear part* of the resolution of the defining ideal $I(X)$.

The subcomplex

$$
0 \longrightarrow R(-e-r)^{\gamma_r} \longrightarrow R(-e-r+1)^{\gamma_{r-1}} \longrightarrow 0
$$

is what we called the *top degree part* of the above resolution. The property $(N_{e,p})$ is concerned with the length of this "top degree part" complex.

With the help of Lemma 12.3 and Lemma 13.3, the assumption $\gamma_{r-1} > 0$, and the shape of the above resolution, we get:

(i) $\gamma_r > 0$;

(ii) $h_X(e) = |X|, h_X(e-1) = |X| - \gamma_r$;

(iii) X has $(N_{e,r-2})$ but not $(N_{e,r-1})$;

(iv) X has $(N_{e,p})$ forall $p \leq r - 2$.

In general, we have for an arbitrary set, X, of points:

$$X \text{ has } (N_{e+1,r}) \quad \text{iff} \quad h_X(e) = |X|.$$

This information can be improved for many sets of points. The most general result describing sufficient conditions for $(N_{e,p})$ that I know is:

Theorem 14.1: *Let s, p, e be integers with $1 \leq p \leq r$ and $e \geq 2$. Let $|X| = s + r - p$ and consider the following conditions for $i = 1, 2$:*

> (a_1) *There is a subset $X_1 \subseteq X$ consisting of r points which span a hyperplane that does not contain any other point of X.*
>
> (a_2) *There is a subset $X_2 \subseteq X$ of $r + 1$ points spanning $\mathbf{P}^r$ and $h_X(e) = |X|$.*
>
> (b_i) *Any subset $Y \subseteq X$ of s points containing $X \setminus X_i$ satisfies $h_Y(e - 1) = s$.*

Then, if X satisfies (a_i) and (b_i) for some $i \in \{1, 2\}$, then X has property $(N_{e,p})$.

Note that our general assumption, X spans $\mathbf{P}^r$, implies $|X| \geq r + 1$, i.e. $s \geq p + 1$. Furthermore, a subset X_2 as required in (a_2) certainly exists. The essential assumption in case $i = 2$ is that (b_2) is satisfied with the same subset X_2 chosen in (a_2). The condition (b_1) is certainly weaker than (b_2). But, a complete comparison of the different conditions is not clear for me. It seems reasonable that the assumptions (a_1) and (b_1) are independent of the assumptions (a_2) and (b_2).

The assumptions in the theorem imply, in particular, that $h_X(e - 1) \geq |X| - p$. Therefore, it is only applicable if

$$h_X(e - 1) > |X| - r.$$

From Lecture 13 we already know that X satisfies $(N_{e,r})$ if and only if $h_X(e - 1) = |X|$. The Theorem says that it is often possible to improve this information if the inequality above is satisfied.

Before I prove Theorem 14.1, I will first give some of its consequences. In order to be able to apply Theorem 13.1 we need information on the Hilbert function of X and its subsets. Furtunately, lower bounds for the Hilbert functions of interesting classes of sets of points have been studied by many authors and we can use their results. We need some terminology.

Definition 14.2: X is said to be in *linearly general position* if any subset of $r + 1$ points of X is linearly independent.

A result of P. Maroscia (cf. Theorem 9.7) immediately implies the following well-known result.

Lemma 14.3: *If X is in linearly general position then its Hilbert function satisfies:*

$$h_X(t) \geq \min\{|X|, tr + 1\} \quad \text{for all } t.$$

Corollary 14.4: *Let e, p be integers determined by $|X| = er + 1 - p$ where $1 \leq p \leq r$. If X is in linearly general position then X satisfies $(N_{e,p})$.*

Proof: We want to apply Theorem 14.1 with $s = (e - 1)r + 1$. By the assumption of linearly general position, condition (a_1) is clearly satisfied. In order to check (b_1), consider an arbitrary subset $Y \subset X$ consisting of s points. Then Lemma 14.3 gives

$$h_Y(e - 1) \geq \min\{s, (e - 1)r + 1\} = s = |Y|.$$

Thus we obtain $h_Y(e - 1) = s$. Therefore (b_1) is satisfied and Theorem 14.1 yields the claim. $\square$

Note that in the last lecture we proved the same result but with the stronger assumption that X is the general hyperplane section of an arithmetically Cohen-Macaulay integral curve.

Let us recall the following concept (cf. Definition 9.4). X is said to be in *uniform position* if for all subsets $Y \subset X$ and all t we have:

$$h_Y(t) = \min\{|Y|, h_X(t)\}.$$

81

Recall that the importance of this concept stems from the fact that the general hyperplane section of an integral curve over an algebraically closed field of characteristic zero is in uniform position (see Theorem 9.6). Note that uniform position implies linearly general position. Indeed, if $Y \subset X$ is an arbitrary subset of $r+1$ points and $X \subset \mathbf{P}^r$ is in uniform position and nondegenerate, we obtain

$$|Y| \geq h_Y(1) \geq \min\{|Y|, r+1\} = r+1 = |Y|.$$

Thus Y spans $\mathbf{P}^r$ and X is in linearly general position.

Corollary 14.5: *Suppose X is in uniform position in $\mathbf{P}^r$. Let e, p be integers such that $1 \leq p \leq r$ and*
$$h_X(e-1) \geq |X| - (r-p).$$

Then X satisfies $(N_{e,p})$.

Proof: As in the previous proof we need only check condition (b_1) in Theorem 14.1. But the uniform position assumption gives, for all subsets $Y \subset X$ consisting of $s = |X| - (r-p)$ points,
$$|Y| \geq h_Y(e-1) \geq \min\{|Y|, h_X(e-1)\} = s = |Y|.$$

Hence condition (b_1) is also satisfied. $\square$

Remarks 14.6:

(i) We already knew that for any set of points, X, for which $h_X(e-1) = |X|$, the defining ideal of X is generated by forms of degree $\leq e$. This can be improved for points in uniform position. The above result already tells us that if $h_X(e-1) > |X| - r$ then $I(X)$ is generated in degree $\leq e$.

(ii) Let ω_X be the canonical module of the coordinate ring of X. Then Corollary 14.6 is equivalent to the following statement: If $\mathrm{rank}\,[\omega_X]_{-e+1} \leq r-p$ then ω_X has no $(r-p)$-linear syzygies. I would like to have a proof of this result which primarily deals with the canonical module.

Let us now consider a set X for which $h_X(e-1) = |X| - 1$. To such a set a certain integer p can be uniquely attached. With the help of Theorem 14.1 it can be shown that

82

X does not satisfy $(N_{e,p})$ but does satisfy $(N_{e,p-1})$ if $p > 1$. This result allows us to describe the possible Betti numbers of a set of $\binom{r+e-1}{r} + 1$ points in $\mathbf{P}^r$ with maximal Hilbert function. A very special case of this result is:

Proposition 14.7: *Let $|X| = r + 2$ and let*

$$p = \min\{t \in \mathbf{N} \mid t + 2 \text{ points of } X \text{ are linearly dependent }\}.$$

Then X has the following minimal free graded resolution

$$
\begin{array}{ccccccccc}
 & & R(-r-2)^{\beta_r} & & & R(-p-2)^{\beta_p} & & & \\
 & & \oplus & & & \oplus & & & \\
0 & \to & R(-r-1)^{\alpha_r} & \to & \cdots & \to & R(-p-1)^{\alpha_p} & \to & R(-p)^{\alpha_{p-1}} & \to & \cdots \\
\end{array}
$$

$$\to R(-2)^{\alpha_1} \to R \to R/I(X) \to 0$$

where

$$\beta_i = \binom{r-p}{i-p}$$

$$\alpha_i = i\binom{r+1}{i+1} - \binom{r}{i-1} + \binom{r-p}{i-p-1}$$

and we use the convention $\binom{a}{b} := 0$ if $b < a$.

Now we want to prove Theorem 14.1. Unfortunately the proof is computational. The main tool is the Koszul complex.

Proof of Theorem 14.1: (I) Let $i = 1$. We denote by $H \subset \mathbf{P}^r$ the hyperplane spanned by X_1. Then, by a general result of P. Maroscia ("Some problems and results on finite sets of points in $\mathbf{P}^n$", LNM 997 (1983), 290 - 314), we have:

$$
\begin{aligned}
h_X(e) &\geq & h_{X \cap H}(e) + h_{X \setminus (X \cap H)}(e-1) \\
&= & h_{X_1}(e) + h_{X \setminus X_1}(e-1) \\
&= & r + |X \setminus X_1| \quad \text{by } (a_1) \text{ and } (b_1) \\
&= & |X|.
\end{aligned}
$$

Thus we have $h_X(e) = |X|$ in any case. It remains to show that $[\mathrm{Tor}_p^R(R/I(X), K)]_{p+e} = 0$. We prove this by induction on s, simultaneously for $i = 1$ and $i = 2$.

83

(II) Since X spans $\mathbf{P}^r$ we have $s > p$. If $s = p+1$ we get $h_X(1) = |X|$. Thus X even satisfies $(N_{2,r})$. Let $s > k+1$. Changing coordinates suitably we may assume that X contains the coordinate points $P_0, \ldots, P_r$ where $P_1 = (1,0,\ldots,0), P_2 = (0,1,0,\ldots,0),\ldots,P_r = (0,\ldots,0,1)$. If $i = 1$ we may assume $X_1 = \{P_1,\ldots,P_r\}$. Let $i = 2$. We can always find at least two different subsets of X consisting of $r+1$ points and spanning $\mathbf{P}^r$. Thus there is a point P_{r+1} in X such that we may assume $X_2 = \{P_1,\ldots,P_r,P_{r+1}\}$ and P_0 is not contained in X_2. Put $X' = X \setminus \{P_0\}$. Then we have $|X'| > r$ and thus $X' \not\subseteq X_1$. Hence X' spans $\mathbf{P}^r$, in view of condition (a_1). Furthermore we have $X_i \subset X'$ for $i = 1,2$. Therefore the induction hypothesis applies to X' in both cases. Moreover, we have the following isomorphisms

$$I(X')/I(X) \cong I(X')/(I(X') \cap I(P_0)) \cong (I(X') + I(P_0))/I(P_0) \cong R/I(P_0)(-t)$$

where t is the smallest degree of a form vanishing on X' but not on P_0. Since $h_X(e) = |X|$ it follows that $t \le e$. Furthermore we get an exact sequence

$(*)$ $$0 \to R/I(P_0)(-t) \xrightarrow{\varphi'} R/I(X) \to R/I(X') \to 0$$

where $\varphi'(1) = \overline{F}_{P_0}$, the residue class of F_{P_0} in $R/I(X)$ and $F_{P_0} \in [R]_t$ is a form vanishing on X' but not on P_0. A part of the induced long exact sequence in degree $p + e$ reads as follows:

$$[\operatorname{Tor}_p^R(R/I(P_0), K)]_{p+e-t} \xrightarrow{\varphi_t} [\operatorname{Tor}_p^R(R/I(X), K)]_{p+e} \to [\operatorname{Tor}_p^R(R/I(X'), K)]_{p+e}.$$

By the induction hypothesis, the right-hand side of the sequence vanishes. Moreover, the left-hand side is zero iff $t < e$. Hence the assertion is shown if $t < e$. In order to complete the proof it remains to show that the map

$$\varphi := \varphi_e : [\operatorname{Tor}_p^R(R/I(P_0), K)]_p \to [\operatorname{Tor}_p^R(R/I(X), K)]_{p+e}$$

in the above exact sequence is the zero map.

(III) We want to analyze the map φ with the help of the Koszul complex. For convenience we introduce the following notation:

$$\bigwedge^j := \bigwedge^j [R]_1 \quad \text{and} \quad x_I := x_{i_1} \wedge \cdots \wedge x_{i_j} \subset \bigwedge^j \quad \text{if } I = \{i_1,\ldots,i_j\}.$$

The exact sequence (*) induces the commutative diagram

$$
\begin{array}{ccc}
0 & \longrightarrow & \bigwedge^{p+1} \otimes [R/I(X)]_{e-1} \\
\downarrow & & \downarrow \alpha \\
\bigwedge^{p} \otimes K & \overset{\varphi^{*}}{\longrightarrow} & \bigwedge^{p} \otimes [R/I(X)]_{e} \\
\downarrow \gamma & & \downarrow \beta \\
\bigwedge^{p-1} \otimes [R/I(P_0)]_1 & \longrightarrow & \bigwedge^{p-1} \otimes [R/I(X)]_{e+1}
\end{array}
$$

where the vertical maps are Koszul maps. Since the Koszul complex of R with respect to the regular sequence $\{x_0, \ldots, x_r\}$ provides a minimal free resolution of K as R-module, we have $[\mathrm{Tor}_p^R(R/I(X), K)]_{p+e} \cong \ker \beta / \mathrm{im}\, \alpha$. Furthermore, we get that $[\mathrm{Tor}_p^R(R/I(P_0), K)]_p \cong \ker \gamma$ is the K-vector space spanned by $x_I \otimes 1$, where $|I| = p$ and $I \subset \{1, \ldots, r\}$. Using the fact that φ is induced by φ^{*}, where $\varphi^{*}(x_I \otimes 1) = x_I \otimes \varphi'(1) = x_I \otimes \overline{F}_{P_0}$, we see that

$$
\varphi = 0 \quad \text{iff} \quad x_{i_1} \wedge \cdots \wedge x_{i_p} \otimes \overline{F}_{P_0} \in \mathrm{im}\, \alpha \quad \text{for all } \{i_1, \ldots, i_p\} \subset \{1, \ldots, r\}.
$$

(IV) We now show that the right-hand side of the above equivalence is satisfied. This will complete the proof. Without loss of generality it is sufficient to show

$$
(+) \qquad\qquad\qquad x_1 \wedge \cdots \wedge x_p \otimes \overline{F}_{P_0} \in \mathrm{im}\, \alpha
$$

Put $Y := \{X \setminus X_1\} \cup \{P_1, \ldots, P_p\} = \{X \setminus X_2\} \cup \{P_1, \ldots, P_p, P_{r+1}\}$. Then $|Y| = s$, $P_0 \in Y$ and by (b_1) as well as by (b_2) we have $h_Y(e-1) = |Y|$. Thus we find a form $G \in [R]_{e-1}$ vanishing on Y but not on P_0. If follows that Gx_i vanishes on X for $i = 1, \ldots, p$. Therefore we get

$$
\alpha_p(x_0 \wedge x_1 \wedge \cdots \wedge x_k \otimes \overline{G}) = x_1 \wedge \cdots \wedge x_k \otimes \overline{Gx_0}
$$

where Gx_0 has degree e and vanishes on all points of X exept P_0. Hence, up to a scalar multiple, Gx_0 and F_{P_0} coincide modulo $I(X)$ and so $(+)$ is satisfied. $\square$

Lecture 15 - Juan C. Migliore

This lecture is intended to give an introduction to the Lifting Problem. Hence we will begin in arbitrary dimension, and give the basic definitions, tools (such as exact sequences, Hartshorne-Rao modules, etc.) and first results. Only at the end of this lecture will we start looking at points. Because of this, the connection to the theme of this seminar will not be apparent for much of the lecture, but it will start emerging at the end, and it will become much clearer starting with the next talk. To misquote a famous Beatles song,

> You say you want a resolution,
> Well, you know, first I need to sketch the plan.

Let $S = k[X_0, ..., X_n]$ (where k is algebraically closed, characteristic zero). Let S_d be the vector space of homogeneous polynomials in S of degree d. Throughout this lecture $V \subset \mathbb{P}^n$ shall denote a locally Cohen-Macaulay, equidimensional, and non-degenerate subscheme of projective space. Unless specified otherwise, we will assume V has dimension r. For any sheaf $\mathcal{F}$ on $\mathbb{P}^n$, for short we will write $H^i(\mathcal{F})$ for $H^i(\mathbb{P}^n, \mathcal{F})$ and $H_*^i(\mathcal{F})$ for $\bigoplus_{t \in \mathbb{Z}} H^i(\mathbb{P}^n, \mathcal{F}(t))$.

In an earlier lecture, Tony Geramita defined the Hartshorne-Rao module of a curve. We now extend this to a collection of r graded modules associated to our subscheme V.

Definition 15.1: For $1 \leq i \leq r$, $(M^i)(V) = H_*^i(\mathcal{I}_V)$. If $r = 1$ then only one module is defined and we just write $M(V)$. $\square$

These modules are sometimes referred to as the Hartshorne-Rao modules of V, or the HR-modules of V, since Hartshorne and (especially) Rao were the first to make a careful study of these objects and their connection to liaison. However, it should be remarked that in the case of arbitrary codimension it was Schenzel who first showed that these modules are (essentially) invariant in a liaison class; Rao considered only the case of codimension two (but in that context he proved much more). It should also be remarked that Gaeta in the 1940's already knew for th e case of curves in $\mathbb{P}^3$ that (essentially) the dimensions of the graded components of these modules are preserved in a liaison class, but he did not realize that there was a module structure to be considered.

Notice that for finite sets of points we have not defined the Hartshorne-Rao module, although later it will be important to look at the cohomology of the ideal sheaf of a finite set of points. But in our present context, an important fact is that $(M^i)(V)$ is a graded S-module of finite length for $1 \le i \le r$. (This is equivalent to the condition that V be locally Cohen-Macaulay and equidimensional. See for instance Theorem 9 of Schwartau's thesis, "Liaison Addition and Monomial Ideals," or (37.4) of the book by Hermann-Ikeda-Orbanz, "Equimultiplicity and Blowing Up.") Furthermore, V is arithmetically Cohen-Macaulay (aCM) if and only if $(M^i)(V) = 0$ for $1 \le i \le r$.

We want to talk about the "general" hypersurface section of V. What does this mean? For $F \in S_d$ let's temporarily denote by Z_F the subscheme of V cut out by F. (We'll define it precisely in a moment.)

Definition 15.2: We say that the general degree d hypersurface section of V has property (*) if there is a Zariski open subset U of S_d such that Z_F has property (*) for all $F \in U$. $\square$

Examples 15.3:

1. The general degree d hypersurface section of V has dimension $r - 1$ and degree $d \cdot \deg V$. (See for instance Hartshorne, Chapter I.)

2. If $\dim V = 1$ and V is integral then the general hypersurface section of V has the Uniform Position Property (UPP). This is a result of J. Harris.

3. If V is aCM then the general hypersurface section of V is aCM. (This is standard, but in any case we will prove it in Proposition 15.6.)

4. If V is Buchsbaum then the general hypersurface section of V is Buchsbaum. (One can give an inductive definition of this property using Hartshorne-Rao modules: V is said to be *Buchsbaum* if either (a) $\dim V = 0$, or (b) the general hyperplane section of V is Buchsbaum *and* for each $1 \le i \le r$, $(M^i)(V)$ is annihilated by the maximal ideal of S).) So if $d = 1$, this can be taken as part of the definition. For higher d it is not too hard to show using an exact sequence which we will derive shortly, but we will omit the details since this is not directly relevant to our discussion. $\square$

Question: What about the converse of (3) and (4)?

This is the starting point for the Lifting Problem with which we will be concerned in these lectures, particularly in the case of (3). The general Lifting Problem is to describe the properties of the general hyperplane section that lift to properties of the original scheme, particularly when some reasonable hypothesis is added. (For example, the aCM assumption in the converse of (3).)

We will be mainly interested in the case where V is a curve, but first we will take care of the higher dimensional case. In order to proceed, we need to define hypersurface sections carefully and get some first results about them. We would like to define the hypersurface section as a subscheme of $\mathbb{P}^n$ and also as a subscheme of F (thought of as a hypersurface). Hence "define" means to give the saturated ideal of the hypersurface section, either in S or in $S/(F)$.

The natural "guess" is to form the ideal $I_V + (F) \subset S$, or $\frac{I_V+(F)}{(F)} \subset S/(F)$. These aren't quite right: in general we need to take the saturation of these ideals. (In my lecture notes from my talks given at Seoul National University, to appear, there is a discussion of "how far" these ideals are from already being saturated, and it is shown that the failure is measured by a submodule of the first Hartshorne-Rao module.)

So we define the hypersurface section Z of V by F in $\mathbb{P}^n$ to be the scheme with saturated ideal

$$I_Z = \overline{I_V + (F)}, \qquad (3.1)$$

(where "$\overline{I}$" denotes the saturation of the ideal I) and in the hypersurface F we have the saturated ideal

$$I_{Z|F} = \overline{\left(\frac{I_V + (F)}{(F)}\right)} \qquad (3.2)$$

in the ring $S/(F)$. Notice that this does not make any generality assumptions on F. We now make our first generality assumption (which will hold from now on): assume that F does not vanish on any component of V. (This is clearly an open condition.) This gives us the following fact:

$$\frac{I_V + (F)}{(F)} \cong \frac{I_V}{I_V \cap (F)} = \frac{I_V}{F \cdot I_V}.$$

(The isomorphism is a standard one in commutative algebra. The equality was essentially shown by Tony Geramita in Lecture 3.)

As a result, we get two useful exact sequences of sheaves:

$$0 \to \mathcal{O}_{\mathbb{P}^n}(-d) \xrightarrow{\times F} \mathcal{I}_Z \to \mathcal{I}_{Z|F} \to 0 \qquad (*)$$

(from sheafifying $0 \to (F) \to I_V + (F) \to \frac{I_V+(F)}{(F)} \to 0$) and

$$0 \to \mathcal{I}_V(-d) \xrightarrow{\times F} \mathcal{I}_V \to \mathcal{I}_{Z|F} \to 0 \qquad (**)$$

(from sheafifying $0 \to I_V(-d) \xrightarrow{\times F} I_V \to \frac{I_V}{F \cdot I_V} \to 0$).

Lemma 15.4:

(a) $H^i_*(\mathcal{I}_Z) \cong H^i_*(\mathcal{I}_{Z|F})$ for $1 \le i \le n-2$.

(b) *There is a one-to-one correspondence between the minimal generators of $I_{Z|F}$ and those of I_Z other than (possibly) F itself.*

Proof:

Both of these come from the exact sequence (*), taking cohomology. The first comes from the vanishing of the higher cohomology of $\mathcal{O}_{\mathbb{P}^n}$. The second comes from the fact that (*) also gives the short exact sequence

$$0 \to S(-d) \xrightarrow{\times F} I_Z \to I_{Z|F} \to 0$$

from which the result follows immediately. (Notice that in particular F is always an element of I_Z.) $\square$

Lemma 15.5: *In fact, F is a minimal generator of I_Z.*

Proof:

This fact is proved in detail in my Seoul notes (to appear) but the idea behind it is very simple. For the sake of clarity we will give it in a special case: suppose that V is integral (i.e. reduced and irreducible). As we noted in Example 15.3, $\deg Z = d \cdot \deg V$ and $\dim V = r - 1$.

Now suppose that F is not a minimal generator, so $F = \sum X_i F_i$ where $F_i \in (I_Z)_{d-1}$. We claim that $F_i \in I_V$ for all i. Once we prove this we're done since then $F \in I_V$, contradicting the fact that F contains no component of V.

Suppose the claim were false. Then F_i also contains no component of V, so F_i cuts out a hypersurface section Z_i of V of dimension $r - 1$ and degree $(d-1) \cdot \deg V$. But $F_i \in I_Z$ so $I_Z \supset (F_i) + I_V$. Since I_Z is saturated, we get $I_Z \supset I_{Z_i}$. Therefore $Z \subset Z_i$, which is impossible by degree considerations (since they have the same dimension).

If we remove the assumption that V is reduced the same idea works by considering the support of V. If we allow V to be reducible, the same idea works by considering the irreducible components one at a time. We omit the details. $\square$

We now return to the question of whether the converse of Example 15.3 (3) and (4) holds. If $r = 1$ then clearly the answer is "no," since non-aCM and non-Buchsbaum curves exist but any finite set is aCM and Buchsbaum. (The following lecture will be devoted to showing the surprising fact that on the other hand, under some very reasonable assumptions on Z, the answer even for curves is "yes.")

Proposition 15.6: *Let V be a locally Cohen-Macaulay equidimensional closed subscheme of $\mathbb{P}^n$ and let F be a general homogeneous polynomial of degree d cutting out on V a scheme $Z \subset V \subset \mathbb{P}^n$. Assume that $\dim V \geq 2$. Then V is arithmetically Cohen-Macaulay if and only if Z is.*

Proof: Consider the exact sequence in cohomology obtained from (**)

$$... \to H^i(\mathcal{I}_V)(t-d) \xrightarrow{\times F} H^i(\mathcal{I}_V(t)) \to H^i(\mathcal{I}_{Z|F}(t)) \to H^{i+1}(\mathcal{I}_V)(t-d) \xrightarrow{\times F} H^{i+1}(\mathcal{I}_V(t))$$

where $1 \leq i \leq (\dim V) - 1$. Notice that Z has dimension equal to $(\dim V) - 1$. If V is aCM then $(M^i)(V) = 0$ for all $1 \leq i \leq \dim V$ so $H_*^i(\mathcal{I}_{Z|F}) = 0$. But then by Lemma 15.4(a) $H_*^i(\mathcal{I}_Z) = 0$, so Z is aCM.

Conversely, If Z is aCM then $H^i(\mathcal{I}_V)(t-d) \xrightarrow{\times F} H^i(\mathcal{I}_V(t))$ is surjective for all t and $H^{i+1}(\mathcal{I}_V)(t-d) \xrightarrow{\times F} H^{i+1}(\mathcal{I}_V(t))$ is injective for all t. This is impossible unless V is aCM, since $(M^i)(V)$ has finite length. $\square$

Notice that this theorem would not be true without the assumption that V is locally Cohen-Maculay and equidimensional. For example, if V is the union of an aCM surface and a point then the general hypersurface section of V is still aCM. (However, it should be enough to assume that I_V has no associated primes of height n.) We now briefly turn to the question of the converse of (4), the Buchsbaum case. In order to give our counterexample, we need to recall a theorem of Evans and Griffith from *Local cohomology modules for normal domains*, J. London Math. Soc. **22** (1979), 277–284. We give only a special case of that theorem, for our purposes.

Theorem 15.7: *Let (M_1, M_2) be a pair of graded S-modules of finite length. Assume that they are shifted to the right by a suitably large integer. (The same integer for both M_1 and M_2.) Then there is a surface $V \subset \mathbb{P}^n$ with $(M^1)(V) = M_1$ and $(M^2)(V) = M_2$.*

Now let $M_1 = k \oplus k$; by this we mean that M_1 has two components of dimension 1 occurring in consecutive degrees, and the other components are zero. Assume that the multiplication on M_1 induced by a general linear form is an isomorphism between these

90

components. Let $M_2 = 0$. Let V be the surface guaranteed by the theorem of Evans and Griffith. Note that V is not Buchsbaum since M_1 has non-zero multiplication by a linear form. Assume that the components of M_1 occur in degrees r and $r+1$. Let L be a general linear form (in particular not containing any component of V) and let C be the hyperplane section cut out by L. For any integer t we have the exact sequence

$$\ldots \to H^1(\mathcal{I}_V(t-1)) \xrightarrow{\times L} H^1(\mathcal{I}_V(t)) \to H^1(\mathcal{I}_{C|L}(t)) \to 0$$

(where the last "0" is because $M_2 = 0$). Then $M(C) \cong H^1_*(\mathcal{I}_{C|L})$ is the cokernel of the multiplication $\times L : (M^1)(V)(-1) \to (M^1)(V)$, which one can easily check is one-dimensional. Hence C is Buchsbaum while V is not.

This leaves the interesting question of whether there are natural conditions in which the converse of (4) is true, much like the case of the converse of (3) for curves to which we now turn.

Let V be a curve. As noted above, the general hyperplane section of V is always aCM, so the converse to (3) is false since there exist non-aCM curves.

Question: What conditions on the general hypersurface section Z force V to be aCM?

We end this lecture with an example of the sort of theorem that can be proved, from *Hypersurface sections of curves* (to appear in the proceedings of the Ravello conference on zero-schemes, 1992). The next lecture will show the techniques that are used to prove this and will generalize this result.

Theorem 15.8: *Let* $V \subset \mathbb{P}^n$ *be a locally Cohen-Macaulay equidimensional curve. If the general degree* d *hypersurface section* Z *is a complete intersection then* V *is a complete intersection, unless:*
(a) $n = 3$, $d = 1$, V *lies on a quadric surface and has even degree,*
(b) $n = 3$, $d = 1$, $\deg V = 4$ *and* V *does not lie on a quadric surface, or*
(c) $n > 3$, $d = 1$, *and* V *is a double line.*

(It's clear that these are exceptions. What is surprising is that they are the *only* exceptions. Note in particular that if $d \geq 2$ then there are *no* exceptions.)

Hypersurface sections of curves is just the most recent of a series of papers on this general subject. A very special case of this theorem was proved in [**GM1**], and the more general question was asked for curves in $\mathbb{P}^3$ and $d = 1$. This question was answered by

Strano in *A characterization of complete intersection curves in* $\mathbb{P}^3$, Proc. AMS **104** (1988), 711–715. Then Strano's student Re proved the analogous result for curves in $\mathbb{P}^n$ and $d = 1$ in *Sulle sezioni iperpiane di una varietà proiettiva*, Le Matematiche XLII, 211–218. This was re-proved by Huneke and Ulrich in *General hyperplane sections of algebraic varieties*, to appear in J. Alg. Geom., and some generalizations were proved for Gorenstein curves, but always assuming $d = 1$. To our knowledge *Hypersurface sections of curves* is the first work in this direction for $d \geq 2$. It is based on a "translation" of the preparatory results of the paper of Huneke and Ulrich, to allow for higher d, and it follows the same approach.

In the next lecture I will describe this approach. For now, I will simply remark that the proof relies on a careful study of the resolution of I_Z (in general). In particular, if

$$0 \to F_n \to ... \to F_1 \to I_Z \to 0$$

then the general lifting theorem which we will discuss shows that a comparison of F_1 and F_n can yield the conclusion that V must be aCM. In the case of a complete intersection, of course this resolution is completely understood and so one can get the above result as we will see next time.

Lecture 16 - Juan C. Migliore

This is a continuation of the discussion of the Lifting Problem, introduced in Lecture 15. As remarked there, the aim is to describe some ideas and results of my paper *Hypersurface sections of curves*, which in turn is based on the approach of Huneke and Ulrich in *General Hyperplane Sections of Algebraic Varieties*.

We retain the notation from Lecture 15, but for most of this lecture X shall be a locally Cohen-Macaulay equidimensional *curve*, since we ended Lecture 15 with the problem of trying to find conditions on the points of a hypersurface section Z of a curve X which would force X to be aCM. Equivalently, we ask: if X is not aCM, what can be deduced about Z?

One of the goals here is to show how, sometimes, certain properties of the resolution of the points of the hypersurface section can force the curve to be aCM. (See for instance Corollary 16.6.)

We recall an important fact (from Lemmas 15.4 and 15.5): Say the hypersurface which cuts out Z is defined by a homogeneous polynomial F of degree d. Then there is a minimal generating set for I_Z containing F, and the images in $I_{Z|F}$ of these generators other than F form a minimal generating set for $I_{Z|F}$. Loosely, we will express these facts by saying that F is a minimal generator of I_Z, and that the minimal generators of $I_{Z|F}$ are in bijective correspondence with the minimal generators of I_Z other than F. (See also remark 16.3.5.)

It will turn out that an important ingredient in our work is the least degree of a generator of I_Z other than F which does *not* lift to X, and this in turn will be connected to the Hartshorne-Rao module of X. We illustrate this with a simple example.

Example 16.1: In $\mathbb{P}^3$ let $d = \deg F = 2$ and consider smooth curves of degree 4. There are two possibilities for such a curve: either it is a curve X_0 of genus 0 or it is a curve X_1 of genus 1. The former is not aCM and the latter is a complete intersection. The respective hypersurface sections Z_0 and Z_1 both have degree 8. Can we tell from Z_0 and Z_1 which curves they came from? Notice that if we had $d = 1$ then we could *not* distinguish between the hyperplane sections: they are both complete intersections of conics.

Note that in either case $h^0(\mathcal{I}_{Z_i}(1)) = 0$ since otherwise the 8 points of Z_i would lie in a *hyperplane* section of X_i, and a hyperplane section consists only of 4 points.

We first consider X_0. Recall that $h^0(\mathcal{I}_{X_0}(2)) = 1$. We have the exact sequence

$$0 \to H^0(\mathcal{I}_{X_0}) \xrightarrow{\times F} H^0(\mathcal{I}_{X_0}(2)) \to H^0(\mathcal{I}_{Z_0|F}(2)) \to H^1(\mathcal{I}_{X_0}) \to H^1(\mathcal{I}_{X_0}(2))$$

and since the first, fourth and fifth entries are zero we get that $h^0(\mathcal{I}_{Z_0|F}(2)) = 1$ and consequently $h^0(\mathcal{I}_{Z_0}(2)) = 2$. We conclude that the minimal generators of I_{Z_0} in degree 2 are F and one other, which lifts to X_0. On the other hand, we can twist the above exact sequence by one:

$$0 \to H^0(\mathcal{I}_{X_0}(1)) \xrightarrow{\times F} H^0(\mathcal{I}_{X_0}(3)) \to H^0(\mathcal{I}_{Z_0|F}(3)) \to H^1(\mathcal{I}_{X_0}(1)) \to H^1(\mathcal{I}_{X_0}(3))$$

and a similar dimension calculation gives that I_{Z_0} has minimal generators in degree 3, *at least one of which does not lift to X_0* (since $h^1(\mathcal{I}_{X_0}(1)) = 1$).

Turning to X_1, recall that it is a complete intersection, so Z_1 is too. Then $h^0(\mathcal{I}_{Z_1}(2)) = 3$ (these are all the minimal generators of I_{Z_1}) and all generators but F lift to X_1. This is the distinction between X_0 and X_1 on which we shall focus. $\square$

Now recall the notation from Lecture 13: Let M be a finitely generated graded R-module. Then
$$e(N) = \sup\{t \in \mathbb{Z} | M_t \neq 0\}$$
$$i(N) = \inf\{t \in \mathbb{Z} | M_t \neq 0\}$$

The following lemma generalizes the so-called *Socle Lemma* of Huneke and Ulrich. Because of time constraints we will not prove this here.

Lemma 16.2: *Let M be a non-zero finitely generated graded R-module. Let $F \in R_d$ be a general homogeneous polynomial of degree d. Let*

$$0 \to K \to M(-d) \xrightarrow{\times F} M \to C \to 0$$

be exact. If $K \neq 0$ then $i(K) \geq i([0 :_C m^d]) + d$ (where m is the maximal ideal $(X_0, ..., X_n)$). $\square$

We now make a sequence of remarks, leading to our Lifting Theorem.

Remarks 16.3:
16.3.1 Recall from Lecture 15 (Lemma 15.4) that $H^i_*(\mathcal{I}_Z) \cong H^i_*(\mathcal{I}_{Z|F})$ for $1 \leq i \leq n - 2$.

94

16.3.2 Let $M = H^1_*(\mathcal{I}_X)$. M has finite length (hence is finitely generated) since X is locally Cohen-Macaulay and equidimensional. Furthermore, as long as F does not vanish on any component of X there is an exact diagram

$$0 \rightarrow I_X(-d) \xrightarrow{\times F} I_X \rightarrow I_{Z|F} \searrow \nearrow \quad M(-d) \xrightarrow{F} M \rightarrow H^1_*(\mathcal{I}_Z)$$

$$K \qquad\qquad C$$

$$0 \qquad 0 \qquad\qquad 0 \qquad 0$$

Notice that if X is not aCM (but is locally Cohen-Macaulay and equidimensional), $M = H^1_*(\mathcal{I}_X)$ is non-zero and has finite length. Hence for *any* homogeneous polynomial F of degree $d \geq 1$, the kernel of the multiplicaton $M(-d) \rightarrow M$ induced by F is non-zero. (This is because there is a last non-zero component of M.) Hence if F is sufficiently general, both this exact diagram and Lemma 16.2 apply.

16.3.3 From the above diagram it follows that if $K_i = 0$ for some degree i then the entire component $(I_{Z|F})_i$ lifts to I_X.

16.3.4 Let $t = i(\text{soc } H^1_*(\mathcal{I}_Z))$. Then we claim that

$$i([0 :_{H^1_*(\mathcal{I}_Z)} m^d]) \geq t - d + 1.$$

Indeed, suppose that $0 \neq x \in [0 :_{H^1_*(\mathcal{I}_Z)} m^d]_i$ for $i \leq t - d$. Then there exists some polynomial G of degree $\leq d-1$ (possibly constant) such that $Gx \neq 0$ but $Gx \in \text{soc } H^1_*(\mathcal{I}_Z)$. But Gx occurs in degree $i + \deg G \leq i + d - 1 \leq (t - d) + d - 1 = t - 1$, contradicting the definition of t.

16.3.5 Suppose Z has minimal free resolution

$$0 \rightarrow F_n \rightarrow \ldots \rightarrow F_2 \rightarrow F_1 \oplus R(-d) \rightarrow I_Z \rightarrow 0$$

where $R(-d)$ is the summand corresponding to the minimal generator F. Then applying

95

the mapping cone to the exact diagram

$$
\begin{array}{ccccccc}
 & & & & \vdots & & \\
 & & & & F_3 & & \\
 & & & & \downarrow & & \\
 & & 0 & & F_2 & & \\
 & & \downarrow & & \downarrow & & \\
 & & R(-d) & \to & R(-d) \oplus F_1 & & \\
 & & \downarrow & & \downarrow & & \\
0 & \to & R(-d) & \xrightarrow{F} & I_Z & \to & I_{Z|F} \to 0 \\
 & & \downarrow & & \downarrow & & \\
 & & 0 & & 0 & &
\end{array}
$$

gives that the R-module $I_{Z|F}$ has a minimal free resolution

$$ 0 \to F_n \to \ldots \to F_2 \to F_1 \to I_{Z|F} \to 0 $$

This means that we can move between the resolution of I_Z and that of $I_{Z|F}$ depending on which is more convenient.

16.3.6 Recall from Lecture 12: If $F_n = \bigoplus_{i=1}^{b_n} R(-m_i)$ then

$$ \operatorname{soc} H^1_*(\mathcal{I}_{Z|F}) = \operatorname{soc} H^1_*(\mathcal{I}_Z) = \bigoplus_{i=1}^{b_n} k(-m_i + n + 1). $$

(This is also shown in the paper of Huneke and Ulrich.) □

Theorem 16.4 (Main Lifting Theorem): *Let F be a general homogeneous polynomial of degree d (see Remark 16.3.2). Assume that X is not arithmetically Cohen-Macaulay, and let $K \neq 0$ be the kernel of multiplication by F as above. Let $b = i(K)$, the least degree in which $I_{Z|F}$ contains an element which does not lift to X. Then $b + n \geq \min\{m_i\}$.*
Proof:

$$
\begin{aligned}
b = i(K) &\geq i([0 :_C m^d]) + d \quad \text{(by Lemma 16.2)} \\
&\geq i([0 :_{H^1_*(\mathcal{I}_Z)} m^d]) + d \quad \text{(since } C \subset H^1_*(\mathcal{I}_Z)) \\
&\geq i(\operatorname{soc} H^1_*(\mathcal{I}_Z)) - d + 1 + d \quad \text{(by 16.3.4)} \\
&= 1 + \min\{m_i - n - 1\} \quad \text{(by 16.3.6)}
\end{aligned}
$$

from which the result follows. □

Theorem 16.4 already says something about the minimal free resolution of I_Z since it involves the last graded Betti numbers $\{m_i\}$. We now show another connection to the minimal resolution of I_Z. First, observe that I_Z must have a minimal generator in degree b other than (possibly) F. Indeed, from the exact diagram

$$0 \;\to\; I_X(-d) \;\xrightarrow{\;\times F\;}\; I_X \;\xrightarrow{\;r\;}\; I_{Z|F} \;\longrightarrow\; M(-d)$$

$$\searrow \quad \nearrow$$
$$K$$
$$\nearrow \quad \searrow$$
$$0 \qquad\qquad 0$$

we get that

$$K \cong \frac{I_{Z|F}}{\mathrm{Im}(r)}.$$

Hence since K has a minimal generator in degree b, it follows that $I_{Z|F}$ does as well; hence I_Z has a minimal generator in degree b and this generator cannot be F. Now, combining this observation with Theorem 16.4 immediately gives:

Corollary 16.5: *Suppose I_Z has a minimal free resolution*

$$0 \to \bigoplus_{i=1}^{b_n} R(-m_i) \to \dots \to F_2 \to \bigoplus_{i=1}^{b_1-1} R(-a_i) \oplus R(-d) \to I_Z \to 0$$

If $\max\{a_i\} + n < \min\{m_i\}$ then X must be aCM. $\square$

We remark that in the case of curves in $\mathbb{P}^3$, if $d = 1$ then Z is a set of points in the plane. Corollary 16.5 deals with the resolution of I_Z, where Z is being considered as a subscheme of $\mathbb{P}^3$. But one can also consider the resolution of I_Z as an ideal in the ring $S = k[X_0, X_1, X_2]$. In this case it can be shown that Corollary 16.5 translates to the statement that if the entries of the degree matrix of the Hilbert-Burch matrix (see below) are all strictly greater than 2 then X must be aCM.

(We explain the notion of the degree matrix of the Hilbert-Burch matrix. Since Z is arithmetically Cohen-Macaulay and codimension two in $\mathbb{P}^2$, its minimal free resolution has the form

$$0 \to \bigoplus_{j=1}^{r-1} S(-b_j) \xrightarrow{\;\phi\;} \bigoplus_{i=1}^{r} S(-a_i) \to I_Z \to 0$$

97

where ϕ is an $r \times (r-1)$ matrix of homogeneous polynomials. ϕ is called the *Hilbert-Burch matrix* of Z. Associated to it is a matrix of integers $[c_{i,j}]$, where $c_{i,j} = b_j - a_i$. This is called the *degree matrix* associated to ϕ, since if $c_{i,j}$ is positive then it is the degree of the corresponding entry in ϕ.)

We can now discuss the "complete intersection" theorem mentioned at the end of Lecture 15:

Corollary 16.6: *Let X be a non-degenerate locally Cohen-Macaulay equidimensional one-dimensional subscheme of $\mathbb{P}^n$. Let F be a general homogeneous polynomial of degree $d \geq 1$ cutting out a zero-scheme Z on X. Assume that Z is a complete intersection in $\mathbb{P}^n$. Then X is a complete intersection, unless one of the following holds:*
(a) $n = 3, d = 1, X$ lies on a quadric surface and has even degree,
(b) $n = 3, d = 1$, $\deg X = 4$ and X does not lie on a quadric,
(c) $n > 3, d = 1, X$ is a double line (i.e. X has degree 2 and is supported on a line).

Idea of Proof:

Notice that once we prove that X is aCM we are done since in that case $I_Z = I_X + (F)$ (i.e. this ideal is already saturated) and the codimension of Z is one more than that of X. Corollary 16.5 basically says that if $\min\{m_i\}$ is big with respect to the degrees of the minimal generators of Z then X is aCM (hence in this case, a complete intersection). But since Z is a complete intersection, its minimal free resolution is of the form

$$0 \to R(-(\textstyle\sum a_i + d)) \to \dots \to \overset{n-1}{\bigoplus} R(-a_i) \oplus R(-d) \to I_Z \to 0.$$

Theorem 16.4 gives that if X is not aCM then $(\sum a_i) + d \leq b + n$. Now, b is one of the a_i so we get that the sum of the degrees of the generators of I_Z, other than b, is less than or equal to n. But there are $n-1$ of these degrees. Hence this sum is either $n-1$ or n. An analysis of the possibilities for these integers, using the properties of b described above, then gives that the only possible exceptions are the ones given in the theorem. $\square$

We can also give a corollary for higher dimensional subschemes of projective space:

Corollary 16.7: *Let X be a non-degenerate locally Cohen-Macaulay equidimensional subscheme of dimension r in $\mathbb{P}^n$. Let Y be a general complete intersection of codimension r. (This makes sense once you specify the degrees of the generators.) Assume that either* *(a)* deg $Y > 1$, *or*

(b) codim $X \geq 3$ *and* deg $X > 2$.

If Y cuts out a zero-scheme on X which is a complete intersection in $\mathbb{P}^n$ then X must be a complete intersection.

Proof:

This follows from Corollary 16.6. The first condition guarantees that at least one of the hypersurfaces will have degree > 1, while the second condition guarantees that even if all the hypersurfaces are hyperplanes, when you cut down to a curve you do not get any of the exceptions listed in Corollary 16.6. □

Huneke and Ulrich introduced the interesting problem of trying to generalize Corollary 16.6 by assuming that Z is merely arithmetically Gorenstein, rather than a complete intersection. (But they assumed that $d = 1$.) Their main result is that if X is a reduced and connected curve not lying on a quadric hypersurface, and if Z is arithmetically Gorenstein, then X is arithmetically Gorenstein. My paper extended these results somewhat, allowing X to be non-reduced and disconnected. The main extension was to allow higher degree hypersurfaces. However, although a number of partial results and examples are given, a complete picture of exactly which non-aCM curves have Gorenstein hypersurface section (analogous to Corollary 16.6) is not yet achieved. Furthermore, the case of higher Cohen-Macaulay type is wide open.

Lecture 17 - Yves Pitteloud

As usual (!) we will denote by R the polynomial ring $k[x_0, \ldots, x_n]$ over a field k. Recall the following fact which has already been mentionned earlier in the seminar: given a Cohen-Macaulay module M, of dimension, say $m+1$, one can dualize the minimal graded free resolution of M and obtain the minimal free resolution of $Ext_R^{n-m}(M, R)$. In other words, as stated in Lemma 12.2, if we denote by ω_M the R-module $Ext_R^{n-m}(M, R)(-n-1)$, we have an isomorphism for all i and j

$$Tor_i^R(M, k)_{i+j} \cong Tor_{n-m-i}^R(\omega_M, k)_{n+1-i-j}.$$

In what follows, I would like to show how the hypothesis that M is Cohen-Macaulay can be weakened if one is just willing to have the isomorphism above only for certain values of j. The *Duality Theorem* of M. Green (Theorem 2.c.6 in *Koszul Cohomology and the Geometry of Projective Varieties*, J. Differential Geometry 19 (1984)) will follow from our result.

Recall that Green required that his variety be smooth. In contrast, all we will need is that the variety be locally Cohen Macaulay and equidimensional. The main result of this lecture is now the following, where the $H_\mathfrak{m}^q(M)$ are the local cohomology modules, with respect to the irrelevant ideal $\mathfrak{m} = (x_0, \ldots, x_n)$. Recall that they are graded R-modules.

Proposition 17.1: *Let M be a R-module of Krull dimension $m+1$. Let j be an integer such that the following equalities are satisfied, for $q = 0, \ldots, m$,*

$$H_\mathfrak{m}^q(M)_{j-q} = 0 \quad and \quad H_\mathfrak{m}^q(M)_{j-q+1} = 0,$$

and such that all the vector spaces $H_\mathfrak{m}^{m+1}(M)_i$ are finite dimensional. There is then an isomorphism of k-vector spaces, for all i,

$$Tor_i^R(M, k)_{i+j} \cong Tor_{n-m-i}^R(\omega_M, k)_{n+1-i-j}.$$

Remark 17.2: Of course, the hypothesis in Proposition 17.1 includes the case where M is a Cohen-Macaulay module.

Before we get involved with the proof, let's see how we can apply Proposition 17.1 to the Castelnuovo-Mumford regularity, $reg\,M$, of a R-module M; that will be the content of Corollary 17.3. Recall that $reg\,M$ is defined as follows (compare Lecture 12):

$$regM = max\{q + e(H_{\mathfrak{m}}^q(M))|q \in \mathbb{Z}\},$$

where, given a graded R-module N, we denote by $e(N)$ the largest integer j for which N_j is not zero. In other words if j_0 is an integer such that $H_{\mathfrak{m}}^q(M)_{j-q} = 0$ for all $j > j_0$ then j_0 is bigger than $reg\,M$. Using the long exact sequence induced in local cohomology by a non zero divisor on $M/H_{\mathfrak{m}}^0(M)$, it is fairly easy to establish, by induction on the depth of M, the following fact:

> let j be an integer such that $H_{\mathfrak{m}}^q(M)_{j-q} = 0$ for all q and such that $H_{\mathfrak{m}}^0(M)_l$ is zero for all $l \geq j$; then j is bigger than $reg\,M$.

The following result was proved by Eisenbud and Goto in *Linear resolutions and minimal multiplicities*, Journal of Algebra 88 (1984); very roughly speaking, it shows how the local chohomology modules give a bound for the Betti numbers of a graded module (and of course also how the Betti numbers give a bound for the local cohomology modules, but this is clearer, thanks to local duality). As this result follows rather easily from our Proposition 17.1, a proof will be given below.

Corollary 17.3: *Given a graded R-module M, there is an equality*

$$regM = max\{e(Tor_i(M,k) - i|i \in \mathbb{Z}\}.$$

Proof of the Corollary: For the proof, we will use the Local Duality Theorem. Recall that the statement of the Local Duality Theorem is as follows: there is an isormorphism of graded R-modules

$$(H_{\mathfrak{m}}^i(M))^{\vee} \cong Ext_R^{n+1-i}(M,N)(-n+1),$$

where, as in Lecture 12, $(\ )^{\vee}$ denotes the k-dual $Hom_R(\ ,k)$.

Let j_0 be an integer. We have to show that $Tor_i(M,k)_{i+j} = 0$ for all $j > j_0$ if and only if $H_{\mathfrak{m}}^q(M)_{j-q} = 0$ for all $j > j_0$. The "only if" implication will be a fairly straightforward consequence of local duality, while the "if" implication will follow from Proposition 17.1.

Suppose first that we have, for some integer j_0, $Tor_i(M, k)_{i+j} = 0$ for all $j > j_0$. This means that in the minimal graded free resolution of M

$$0 \to \oplus R(-e_{sj}) \to \cdots \to \oplus R(-e_{ij}) \to \cdots \to \oplus R(-e_{0j}) \to M \to 0$$

we have the inequality $e_{ij} \leq i + j_0$. Now applying $Hom_R(\ , R)$ to the resolution we obtain the following complex,

$$0 \to Hom_R(M, R) \to \oplus R(e_{0j}) \to \cdots \to \oplus R(e_{ij}) \to \cdots \to \oplus R(-e_{sj}) \to .$$

As $(\oplus R(e_{ij}))_l$ is zero when $l < -i - j_0$, we deduce that $Ext_R^i(M, R)_l$ is also zero when $l < -i - j_0$. By local duality we have the following isomorphisms

$$Ext_R^i(M, R)_l \cong (H_{\mathfrak{m}}^{n+1-i}(M))_{l+n+1}^{\vee} \cong H_{\mathfrak{m}}^{n+1-i}(M)_{-n-1-l}.$$

Setting $q = n + 1 - i$ and $j = -i - l$ yields the desired conclusion.

Suppose now that $H_{\mathfrak{m}}^q(M)_{j-q} = 0$ for all $j > j_0$; in particular the hypothesis of Proposition 17.1 are satisfied for those j, and hence we have the following isomorphism for all $j > j_0$:

$$Tor_i(M, k)_{i+j} \cong Tor_{n-m-i}(\omega_M, k)_{n+1-i-j}.$$

By local duality the module ω_M is isomorphic to $(H_{\mathfrak{m}}^{m+1}(M))^{\vee}$ and so the hypothesis on the local cohomology imply that $(\omega_M)_l$ is zero for all $l < m + 1 - j_0$; this in turn implies that $Tor_{n-m-i}(\omega_M, k)_l$ is zero for all $l < n + 1 - i - j_0$ which concludes the proof of the corollary. $\square$

For the proof of Proposition 17.1 we will use a spectral sequence argument. In what follows, I would like to quickly recall the basics of spectral sequences needed for the proof. For more details the reader can consult, for instance, Rotman, *Introduction to Homological Algebra*.

A (cohomological) *spectral sequence* can be thought of as a book with an infinite number of pages which usually starts at page 2 (but sometimes at page 1). For each integer r, Page r consists of two things:

first there is a collection of objects, $E_r^{p,q}$, in a fixed abelian category (in our case the abelian category will be the category of graded R-modules), where p and q are integers; we will suppose here, to simplify things, that $E_r^{p,q}$ is zero when p or q is negative (in other words everything takes place in the first quadrant);

second there are a given collection of morphisms $d_r^{p,q} : E_r^{p,q} \to E_r^{p+r,q-r+1}$ (i.e. of bidegree $(r, 1-r)$) such that all the compositions $d_r^{p+r,q-r+1} \circ d_r^{p,q}$ are trivial, (in other words we are dealing with an infinite family of complexes involving all the $E_r^{p,q}$). It helps to draw a picture!

One more condition: the various pages are not totally independent of each other: $E_{r+1}^{p,q}$ must be isomorphic to the quotient $ker\, d_r^{p,q}/Im,\, d_r^{p-r,q+r-1}$; in other words the objects of page $r+1$ are obtained from the objects and morphisms of page r by taking homology. Note that we are NOT requiring that the morphisms $d_{r+1}^{p,q}$ be obtained from the objects and morphisms of Page r. Page r is also called the E_r term of the spectral sequence.

Convergence. Consider a spectral sequence, as above. Note that given a pair (p,q), if r is big enough (in fact bigger than $max(p, q+1)$) then all the morphisms leaving $E_r^{p,q}$ or arriving at $E_r^{p,q}$ will be zero. In other words there is an equality $E_r^{p,q} = E_{r+1}^{p,q} = \cdots$. This common value is denoted by $E_\infty^{p,q}$. The collection of all the $E_\infty^{p,q}$ is the "page ∞" of the spectral sequence, or the E_∞ term.

Now, consider a collection E of objects E^n, $n \geq 0$ (in our case a collection of graded R-modules) each filtered by a *regular* decreasing filtration, in other words there are inclusions

$$0 = F^{p(n)}E^n \subseteq \cdots \subseteq F^{p+1}E^n \in F^p E^n \in \cdots \subseteq F^{q(n)}E^n = E^n.$$

We say that a spectral sequence as above *converges to* E if we have isomorphisms

$$E_\infty^{p,q} \cong F^p E^{p+q}/F^{p+1}E^{p+q}.$$

In other words, the line $p+q = n$ on page ∞ contains precisely the various composition factors of E^n with respect to the considered filtration (again, it will help to draw a picture). This whole story is usually written in the more compact form

$$E_2^{p,q} \Longrightarrow E,$$

but of course one should be aware that there is more than the E_2 term involved.

Example 17.4: At this point I would like to list some cases where spectral sequences appear. All these statements are proved and stated in more detail, for instance, in Rotman.

a) This is, in some sense, the basic example. Consider a complex C (for instance of (graded) modules) with a regular filtration; in other words there are subcomplexes $\cdots F^{p+1}C \subseteq F^pC \subseteq \cdots \subseteq C$ such that the filtration is finite, when restricted to each C_n. Note that the filtration induces a filtration of $H(C)$, the homology of the complex. There is a spectral sequence (starting at page 1) with

$$E_1^{p,q} = H^{p+q}(F^pC/F^{p+1}C)$$

that converges to $H(C)$ with the induced filtration. In some sense, this spectral sequence measures the "difference" between $H(grC)$ and $grH(C)$, where given a filtered object, "gr" denotes the associated graded object.

b) A bicomplex gives rise to two spectral sequences that converge to the homology of the associated complex. Roughly speaking, the E_2 term of the first is obtained by taking the homology of the columns, and then the homology of the rows, while for the second spectral sequence one starts by taking the homology of the rows and then takes the homology of the columns.

c) *Grothendieck spectral sequence:* Let F and G be two functors on abelian categories (again, in our case, this will be the category of graded R-modules), such that the composition $F \circ G$ exists. Assume that both F and G are left exact (which will imply that $F \circ G$ is also left exact) and that all the categories have enough injectives, so that the derived functors $R^n(F \circ G)$, R^pF, R^qG all exist. Assume, furthermore, that G *takes injectives into F acyclic objects*, i.e, $R^pF(GQ) = 0$, for $p > 0$ and Q injective. Then there exists a spectral sequence for every object A of the category where G is defined:

$$R^pF(R^qG(A)) \implies R^{p+q}(F \circ G)(A).$$

A few remarks should be made at this point. Given a spectral sequence that converges to some filtered E, the only information that is provided concerns the composition factors

104

of E. This is, of course, weaker than knowing E, but in some cases it can be sufficient. Also the morphisms $d_r^{p,q}$ are fairly obscure! Often, in practice, the only way where one can manage to work ones way through the spectral sequence (by which I mean to try to compute the E_∞ term) is if there is enough vanishing in the E_2 term (note that, given (p,q), if $E_r^{p,q}$ is zero for some r, then all the $E_{r'}^{p,q}$ will also be zero for all $r' > r$).

The hypothesis in Proposition 17.1 are precisely what will be needed in order to have enough vanishing in the homogeneous component of a certain degree of the E_2 term of the spectral sequence that we will be using; we will not have to worry about how the $d_r^{p,q}$ look like and struggle through the higher pages!

Lectures 18 - Yves Pitteloud

In this lecture I will give a proof of Proposition 17.1, using a spectral sequence argument, and then show how to derive Green's Vanishing Theorem. We keep the notation introduced in the preceeding lecture.

Given a graded R-module M, we consider the Koszul cohomology modules $H^p(\underline{x}, M)$. These modules are defined to be the homology modules of the complex of graded modules $K^\bullet(\underline{x}, M) := Hom_R(K_\bullet(\underline{x}, R), M)$, where $K_\bullet(\underline{x}, R)$ is the Koszul complex associated to the variables $(x_0, \ldots, x_n)$. We have a first elementary result that will be quite helpful in the sequel.

Lemma 18.1: *Let M be a graded R-module, with $M_i = 0$. There are then equalities*

$$H^p(\underline{x}, M)_{i-p} = 0 \quad \text{for all} \quad p.$$

Proof: The complex $K^\bullet(\underline{x}, M)$ has the following shape:

$$0 \to M \to \oplus M(1) \to \cdots \to \oplus_{\binom{n+1}{p}} M(p) \to \cdots \to M(n+1) \to 0,$$

The assertion follows at once from degree considerations. $\square$

Knowing these Koszul cohomology modules is equivalent to knowing the Betti numbers of M, as shown in the following lemma (where $H(\underline{x}, M)$ denotes the usual Koszul homology).

Lemma 18.2: *There are isomorphisms of graded modules, for each p*

$$H^p(\underline{x}, N) \cong H_{n+1-p}(\underline{x}, M)(n+1),$$

in other words the graded modules $Ext_R^p(k, M)$ and $Tor_{n+1-p}^R(k, M)(n+1)$ are isomorphic, when R is the polynomial ring.

Proof: The second assertion follows immediately from the first assertion and the fact that the Koszul complex is a graded free resolution of the R-module k. The first assertion follows from the symmetry of the Koszul complex: the complexes $K^\bullet(\underline{x}, M)$ and $K_{n+1-\bullet}(\underline{x}, M)(n+$

1) are canonically isomorphic, the element $\sum_{|I|=p} x_I \otimes m_I$ of $K_p(\underline{x}, M)_i$ corresponding to the following element of $K^{n+1-p}(\underline{x}, M)_{i-n-1}$:

$$x_J \mapsto sign(I, J) m_I,$$

where $I \cup J = \{0, \ldots, n\}$ and $sign(I, J)$ denotes the sign of the corresponding permutation (I, J) of $\{0, \ldots, n\}$. $\square$

The following proposition will be essential for the proof of Proposition 17.1.

Proposition 18.3: *There is a spectral sequence $(E_r^{p,q}, d_r^{p,q})$, of graded R-modules with E_2 term $H^p(\underline{x}, H_\mathfrak{m}^q(M))$ that converges to $H^{p+q}(\underline{x}, M)$*

$$E_2^{p,q} = H^p(\underline{x}, H_\mathfrak{m}^q(M)) \Longrightarrow H^{p+q}(\underline{x}, M).$$

Proof: There are various ways to derive this spectral sequence. We will interpret it as a *Grothendieck Spectral Sequence.* We denote, as usual, by $\Gamma_\mathfrak{m}(M)$ the module $H_\mathfrak{m}^0(M)$. As $\Gamma_\mathfrak{m}(M)$ consists of those elements of M killed by some power of $\mathfrak{m}$, the modules $Hom_R(k, \Gamma_\mathfrak{m}(M))$ and $Hom_R(k, M)$ are canonically isomorphic. In other words, we have an equality of functors on the category of graded R-modules

$$Hom_R(k, \ ) \circ \Gamma_\mathfrak{m}(\ ) = Hom_R(k, \ ).$$

Next, we want to show that $Ext_R^p(k, \Gamma_\mathfrak{m}(M)) = 0$ for $p > 0$, when M is an injective graded R-module. Proposition 18.2 will then follow from general theorems about compositions of derived functors (c.f. *Grothendieck spectral Sequences*).

As mentionned above, the module $Ext_R^p(k, \Gamma_\mathfrak{m}(M))$ is isomorphic to the Koszul cohomology module $H^p(\underline{x}, \Gamma_\mathfrak{m}(M))$. By naturality of the Koszul complex, this latter is isomorphic to $H^p(\Gamma_\mathfrak{m}(K^*(\underline{x}, M)))$. But now, if M is injective then $K^*(\underline{x}, M))$ is an injective resolution of $Hom_R(k, M)$, and so $H^p(\Gamma_\mathfrak{m}(K^*(\underline{x}, M))$ is just $H_\mathfrak{m}^p(Hom(k, M))$. The conclusion follows now from the fact that $Hom(k, M)$ is a R-module of Krull dimension 0. $\square$

Note that Proposition 18.3 (but not the proof given above) remains valid if we replace the polynomial ring R by any graded quotient R/I, and the variables x_i by a parameter system of R/I.

107

Very roughly speaking, the spectral sequence of proposition 18.3 describes the "interaction" between the local cohomology modules and the Betti numbers. For instance, one could use it to give another proof of the Auslander-Buchsbaum Codimension - Multiplicity theorem (for a graded module over the polynomial ring). In our case, this spectral sequence will be the right tool to derive Proposition 17.1.

Proof of Proposition 17.1: We will use the spectral sequence above with M as in Proposition 17.1. Note that each $E_r^{p,q}$ is a graded R-module and that all the differentials $d_r^{p,q}$ are homogeneous maps of degree 0.

We will denote by $[E_r^{p,q}]_i$ the homogeneous part of degree i of $E_r^{p,q}$ (What an orgy of indices! in fact, throughout the proof, the reader is highly advised to draw a picture of what's happening in order to get a better understanding!). The vanishing hypothesis in Proposition 17.1 will be just what is needed to have enough vanishing on the homogeneous part of the E_2 term, in certain degrees.

Let s be an integer; we will look at the homogeneous part of degree $j - s$ of the E_2 term:

$$[E_2^{p,q}]_{j-s} = H^p(\underline{x}, H_{\mathfrak{m}}^q(M))_{j-s}.$$

We know that the modules $H_{\mathfrak{m}}^q(M)_{j-q+1}$ are zero for $q = 0, \ldots, m$. Applying Lemma 18.1 yields the following equalities

$$H^p(\underline{x}, H_{\mathfrak{m}}^q(M))_{j-s} = 0, \quad \text{for } p + q = s + 1 \quad \text{and } q \leq m.$$

In other words $[E_2^{p,q}]_{j-s}$ is zero for those values of p, q. This implies that the $d_r^{s-m-1,m+1}$ are zero for all $r \geq 2$ (recall that the $d_r^{p,q}$ have bidegree $(r, 1 - r)$). On the other hand, as the Krull dimension of M is precisely $m + 1$, $E_2^{p,q}$ is zero, in all degrees, for $q > m + 1$. These two facts imply that there are isomorphisms

$$[E_2^{s-m-1,m+1}]_{j-s} \cong [E_3^{s-m-1,m+1}]_{j-s} \cong [E_4^{s-m-1,m+1}]_{j-s} \cong \cdots \cong [E_\infty^{s-m-1,m+1}]_{j-s}.$$

We also have that the modules $H_{\mathfrak{m}}^q(M)_{j-q}$ are zero for $q = 0, \ldots, m$. We again apply Lemma 18.1 and obtain the following equalities

$$H^p(\underline{x}, H_{\mathfrak{m}}^q(M))_{j-s} = 0, \quad \text{for } p + q = s \quad \text{and } q \leq m.$$

In other words, $[E_2^{pq}]_{j-s}$ is zero for those values of p, q. As $E_2^{p,q} = 0$ when $p > m + 1$, the only non zero component on the line $p + q = s$ of the E_∞ term in degree $j - s$ is $[E_\infty^{s-m-1,m+1}]_{j-s}$. This in turn implies the following isomorphism

$$[E_\infty^{s-m-1,m+1}]_{j-s} \cong H^s(\underline{x}, M)_{j-s}.$$

Putting together all these observations, we obtain an isomorphism

$$H^s(\underline{x}, M)_{j-s} \cong H^{s-m-1}(\underline{x}, H_{\mathfrak{m}}^{m+1}(M))_{j-s}.$$

To conclude the proof of Proposition 17.1, it remains for us to identify the two vector spaces appearing in the isomorphism above.

Applying Lemma 18.2, we deduce that the lefthand side $H^s(\underline{x}, M)_{j-s}$ is isomorphic to $Tor_{n+1-s}(M, k)_{j-s+n+1}$ So setting $i = n + 1 - s$, this latter is precisely the lefthand side in the isomorphism of Proposition 17.1

Next, we have to identify the righthand side in the isomorphism above. Recall that the module ω_M that appears in Proposition 17.1 is isomorphic to the module $(H_{\mathfrak{m}}^{m+1}(M))^\vee$, where, as usual, $(\ )^\vee$ denotes the graded k-dual. If we suppose that the $H_{\mathfrak{m}}^{n+1}(m)_i$ are finite dimensional k-vector spaces for all i, we also have the isomorphism $H_{\mathfrak{m}}^{m+1}(M) \cong \omega_M^\vee$. By Lemma 18.4, below, we then have the following isomorphisms:

$$H^{s-m-1}(\underline{x}, H_{\mathfrak{m}}^{m+1}(M))_{j-s} \cong Ext_R^{s-m-1}(k, \omega_M^\vee)_{j-s} \cong Tor_{s-m-1}(k, \omega_M)_{s-j}.$$

Setting, as above, $i = n + 1 - s$, we obtain $Tor_{n-m-i}^R(k, \omega_M)_{n+1-i-j}$. This is precisely the righthand side in the isomorphism of Proposition 17.1. To complete the proof of Proposition 17.1, it remains for us to prove the following lemma, which we have been using above!

Lemma 18.4: *Let M and N be graded R-modules. There is then an isomorphism of R-modules*

$$Ext_R^i(M, N^\vee) \cong (Tor_i^R(M, N))^\vee.$$

Proof: There is an isomorphism of graded modules

$$(M \otimes_R N)^\vee \cong Hom_R(M, N^\vee)$$

109

which can be deduced, more or less, as in the non graded case (a detailed proof can be found in Stueckrad/Vogel, *Buchsbaum Rings and Applications*). Now, let $F^\bullet$ be a graded free resolution of M. As the functor $(\ )^\vee$ is exact the homology of the following complex,

$$(F^\bullet \otimes_R N)^\vee \qquad\qquad (*)$$

is precisely $(Tor_\bullet^R(M,N))^\vee$. On the other hand, by the isomorphism at the beginning of the proof, the complex $(*)$ is isomorphic to the complex $Hom_R(F^\bullet, N^\vee$, whose homology is precisely $Ext_R^\bullet(M, N^\vee)$. This concludes the proof of the lemma, as well as the proof of Proposition 17.1. $\square$

Next I would like to show how we can derive Green's Duality Theorem from our Proposition 17.1.

The setting is as follows. We consider:

> X a locally Cohen-Macaulay and equidimensional projective variety, of dimension, say m;
>
> $\mathcal{L}$ an ample invertible sheaf on X with a base point free linear system $W \subset H^0(X, \mathcal{L})$ of dimension, say $n + 1$;
>
> $\mathcal{F}$ a locally free sheaf on X.

We will denote by R the symmetric algebra $Sym(W)$; R is, of course, isomorphic to a polynomial ring in $n + 1$ variables. The following objects are considered in Green's paper:

$$\oplus_{q \in \mathbb{Z}} H^i(X, \mathcal{F} \otimes \mathcal{L}^{\otimes q}).$$

They are graded modules over the ring $\oplus_{q \in \mathbb{Z}} H^0(X, \mathcal{L}^{\otimes q})$, and so, by restriction of scalars, they are graded R-modules. Green proves the following theorem (but in the case of a compact complex manifold and of an arbitrary invertible sheaf) that corresponds to our Proposition 17.1.

Theorem 18.5: *Let X, $\mathcal{F}$, $\mathcal{L}$, W, R be as above. Consider the following R-modules*

$$M = \oplus_{q \in \mathbb{Z}} H^0(X, \mathcal{F} \otimes \mathcal{L}^{\otimes q}) \quad and \quad N = \oplus_{q \in \mathbb{Z}} H^0(X, \mathcal{F}^* \otimes \mathcal{K}_\mathcal{X} \otimes \mathcal{L}^{\otimes q}),$$

110

where $\mathcal{K}_X$ denotes the dualizing sheaf and "*" denotes the $\mathcal{O}_X$ dual. Suppose moreover that the following equalities are satisfied, for $q = 1, \ldots, m - 1$:

$$H^q(X, \mathcal{F} \otimes \mathcal{L}^{\otimes(j-q)}) = 0 \quad and \quad H^q(X, \mathcal{F} \otimes \mathcal{L}^{\otimes(j-q-1)}) = 0.$$

There are then isomorphisms for each i,

$$Tor_i^R(M, k)_{i+j} \cong Tor_{n-m-i}^R(N, k)_{n+1-i-j}.$$

The assertion of this theorem is very similar to the assertion of Proposition 17.1. Let's see now how Theorem 18.5 can indeed be deduced from Proposition 17.1.

The key is the following fact, which follows from EGA III.2.1 (and is well known in the case of a very ample divisor). We denote by $\mathfrak{m}$ the irrelevant ideal in R. We then have the following isomorphisms of R-modules

$$H_{\mathfrak{m}}^0(M) = H_{\mathfrak{m}}^1(M) = 0 \quad and \quad H_{\mathfrak{m}}^{i+1}(M) \cong \oplus_{q\in\mathbb{Z}} H^i(X, \mathcal{F} \otimes \mathcal{L}^{\otimes q}) \text{ for } i \geq 1.$$

Note that the hypothesis that W is base point free and that $\mathcal{L}$ is ample is essential.

The hypothesis, in Theorem 18.5, thanks to the isomorphisms above, implies the following equalities, for $q = 0, \ldots, m$:

$$H_{\mathfrak{m}}^q(M)_{j-q} = 0 \quad and \quad H_{\mathfrak{m}}^q(M)_{j-q+1} = 0.$$

As M is a Krull module of dimension $\leq m + 1$ (if we denote by I the ideal of the image of X by the morphism determined by W, then M is a R/I-module) the hypothesis of Proposition 17.1 is satisfied. We have now the following isomorphisms, using Serre Duality and the observations above:

$$N \cong \oplus_{q\in\mathbb{Z}} Hom_k(H^n(X, \mathcal{F} \otimes \mathcal{L}^{*\otimes q}), k) = (\oplus_{q\in\mathbb{Z}} H^n(X, \mathcal{F} \otimes \mathcal{L}^{\otimes q}))^\vee \cong H_{\mathfrak{m}}^{n+1}(M)^\vee.$$

Now if M has Krull dimension $m + 1$, then the module N is isomorphic to the module ω_M of Proposition 17.1 and Theorem 18.5 follows in that case. If the Krull dimension of M is $\leq m$, then the module N has to be zero, and so Theorem 18.5 follows also from Proposition 17.1 in that case. $\square$

111

Let's consider, now, the case of a reduced and irreducible curve $\mathcal{C}$. Let $\mathcal{L}$ be an invertible sheaf on $\mathcal{C}$. Without limiting our generality, we can assume that $\mathcal{L}$ is of the form $\mathcal{O}(\sum n_i P_i)$ where the P_i are smooth points of $\mathcal{C}$. The degree of $\mathcal{L}$ is $\sum n_i$. Note that $\mathcal{L}$ is ample if and only if $deg\mathcal{L} > 0$ (this is well known in the case of a smooth curve, and follows from exercise III 5.7 d) of Hartshorne in the general case).

Recall that an ample invertible sheaf $\mathcal{L}$ on $\mathcal{C}$ is said to be *normally generated* if the canonical maps

$$SymH^0(\mathcal{C}, \mathcal{L}) \to \oplus H^0(\mathcal{C}, \mathcal{L}^{\otimes n})$$

are surjective. Note that this implies that $\mathcal{L}$ is very ample (compare Munford, *Varieties defined by quadric equations*,...). Note also that the fact that $\mathcal{L}$ is normally generated is equivalent to the fact $\mathcal{L}$ embeds $\mathcal{C}$ as an arithmetically Cohen-Macaulay curve (to see this consider the Hartshorne-Rao module).

Remark 18.6: If we denote by R the ring $SymH^0(H^0(\mathcal{C}, \mathcal{L}))$ and by S the ring $\oplus H^0(\mathcal{C}, \mathcal{L}^{\otimes n})$, we have then the following equivalence:

$$\mathcal{L} \text{ normally generated iff } Tor_0^R(S, k)_j = 0 \text{ for all } j > 0.$$

The equivalence above follows from the fact that $\mathcal{L}$ is normally generated iff 1 is a minimal generator of the R-module S.

Mumford proved, in *Varieties defined by Quadratic Equations*, CIME, Varenna, 1969, Cremonese, Roma, (1970), that in the case of a smooth curve, an invertible sheaf $\mathcal{L}$ is normally generated as soon as $deg\mathcal{L} \geq 2g+1$ (where g denotes the genus). He also proved then that, if $degL \geq 3g+1$, then the kernel of the surjection of R on S is generated by quadrics. Saint-Donat (smooth case) and Fujita (general case) showed that this is the case as soon as $deg\mathcal{L} \geq 2g+2$. Theorem 18.7 below is a generalisation of these results to higher syzygies. It was proved by Green in *Koszul Cohomology and the geometry of projective varieties* in the case of a smooth curve.

We need first some notation: we say that $\mathcal{L}$ satisfies property (N_p) if $Tor_0^R(S, k) \cong k$ and $Tor_i^R(S, k) \cong k(-i-2)^{\alpha_i}, \alpha_i \in \mathbb{Z}$, for $1 \leq i \leq p$ (compare also Lecture 14 where N_p is denoted $N_{2,p}$). Let $\psi_{\mathcal{L}}(\mathcal{C})$ be the embedding of $\mathcal{C}$ into $\mathbb{P}(H^0(X, \mathcal{L})^*)$. Then $\mathcal{L}$ satisfies (N_0) iff $\psi_{\mathcal{L}}(\mathcal{C})$ is projectively normal (see above). $\mathcal{L}$ satisfies (N_1) iff (N_0) holds and the homogeneous ideal I of $\psi_{\mathcal{L}}(\mathcal{C})$ is generated by quadrics. $\mathcal{L}$ satisfies (N_2) iff $(N_0), (N_1)$ hold and the first syzygy module of I is generated by linear relations; and so on. We can now state Theorem 18.7.

Theorem 18.7: *Let C be an integral curve of arithmetic genus g over an algebraically closed field. Let $\mathcal{L}$ be an invertible sheaf on C of degree $\geq 2g+1+p$ for some $p \geq 1$. Then $\mathcal{L}$ satisfies property (N_p).*

Proof. Let N be the R-module $\oplus H^0(C, \mathcal{K} \otimes \mathcal{L}^{\otimes q})$, where $\mathcal{K}$ is the dualizing sheaf on C. Note that $\mathcal{L}$ is very ample and generated by global sections (see Fujita, Proposition 1.6). Hence, as in Theorem 18.5 we have $N \cong H^2_{\mathfrak{m}}(S)^\vee$. From this we deduce that N is a torsion free $R/\wp$-module, where $\wp$ denotes the ideal of $\psi_L(C)$ in R (to see this, dualize the exact sequence induced in local cohomology by any element x of $R/\wp$ and use the fact that $H^2_{\mathfrak{m}}(S/Sx) = 0$). Now, $rank[N]_0 = g < rank[R]_1 = d - g + 1$ where $d = \deg \mathcal{L}$ (by Riemann Roch). Hence $[N]_j = 0$ for all $j < 0$, thanks to the torsion freeness. Thus we obtain, by Theorem 18.5,

$$[Tor^R_{d-g-1-i}(S,k)]_{d-g+1-j} \cong [Tor^R_i(N,k)]_j = 0 \quad \text{for } j < i \text{ and for all } i.$$

Moreover, the *Vanishing Theorem* of Green/Eisenbud (compare Lecture 11, Theorem) gives

$$[Tor^R_{d-g-1-i}(S,k)]_{d-g+1-i} \cong [Tor^R_i(N,k)]_i = 0 \quad \text{for } i \geq g,$$

which establishes the claim. $\square$

CONTRIBUTED NOTES

A: On Projective Properties of Varieties with Smooth Normalization
E. Ballico, N. Chiarli, S. Greco

B: Bielliptic Curves: Special Linear Series and Plane Models
A. Del Centina, A. Gimigliano

C: Gaps in the Rao Module of an Algebraic Space Curve and the Property "Numerically Subcanonical"
E. D. Davis

D: On the Lifting Problem for Complete Intersection Homogenous Ideals in Polynomial Rings
T. Harima

E: On Graded Betti Numbers and Geometrical Properties of Projective Varieties
U. Nagel, Y. Pitteloud

F: Powers of Ideals and Growth of the Deficiency Module
C. S. Peterson

A: On Projective Properties of Varieties with Smooth Normalization

E. Ballico
Department of Mathematics
University of Trento
38050 Povo (TN)
Italy

N. Chiarli and S. Greco
Department of Mathematics
Politecnico di Torino
Corso Duca degli Abruzzi 24
10129 Torino
Italy

On projective properties of varieties with smooth normalization

E. Ballico - N. Chiarli - S. Greco

We think it is very interesting to study (say, on a smooth projective variety X) base point free linear systems which induce finite birational morphisms. This is strongly related to the theory of the conductors, since of course X will be the normalization of its image, Y, under the corresponding morphism. In turn this is related to the classical theory of the canonical divisors and to adjunction theory. We are even more interested in the case in which the opposite picture is the starting datum. We have an ambient space P (here by far the more interesting case is when $P = P^n$ is a projective space) and we have an integral subvariety Y of P whose normalization, X, is smooth. Here we will be concerned about the extension to this situation of very interesting results obtained under the assumption of the smoothness of Y. In this case the "amount of non normality" (i.e. the structure of the singular locus of Y) should enter into the picture. In the cases we will consider here it will enter essentially only numerically (e.g. for isolated singularities only the colength of the conductor will be important). In §1 and §2 we will consider two (very related) cases; we will assume always characteristic 0.

In §1 we will extend to our situation the main result of [EP] and obtain the following result.

Theorem 0.1. *Fix an integer c. Then there are only finitely many integral families of integral surfaces, S', in P^4 with only isolated singularities, with normalization, S, smooth, with conductor of S' in S of colength c and such that S is not of general type.*

As in [EP] we will prove indeed a more refined result (see Proposition 1.1)

In §2 we will exstend to our situation the main result of [BOSS] and obtain the following result.

Theorem 0.2. *Fix two integers c(1) and c(2). Then there are only finitely many families of integral 3-dimensional subvarieties, X', of P^5 with singular locus,*

Sing(X'), of dimension ≤1, with normalization, X, smooth and not of general type, whose normalization map f: X→X'→P⁵ has differential of rank 3 except at finitely many points and such that the quotient of O_X by the conductor ideal of $O_{X'}$ has c(1)t+c(2) as Hilbert polynomial.

In the statement of 0.2 the pair (c(1),c(2)) is just a bound on the " amount of non normality of X' "; any finite set of data which bound the difference of the Hilbert polynomials $\chi(O_{X'}(t))$ and $\chi(O_X(H^{\otimes t}))$ (with H:= f*($O_{X'}$)) will do and we will refer to c as such a data.

To prove Theorems 0.1 and 0.2 we will just show how to adapt to our setting the proofs for the smooth case of the corresponding results in [EP] and [BOSS]. Hence we will be telegraphic and to read any part of these sections it is necessary to read simultaneously the corresponding part in [EP] or [BOSS].

The authors are partially supported be MURST and GNSAGA of CNR (Italy).

§1. In this section we will show how to carry over the statements and the proofs in [EP] to the case of a singular surface in **P⁴** with only isolated singularities and with normalization smooth; note that any sufficiently general projection into **P⁴** of a smooth surface in a projective space **P^N** is of this type (but of course if N>4 the image will have too many singularities to apply this procedure). We will get in this very cheap way Theorem 0.1 and a more refined statement (Proposition 1.1), which is again just a translation in our setting of [EP], Prop. 1.

This section will be needed also for the proof (given in §2) of Theorem 0.2. In particular, since the proofs will give a bound on the degree of the surface or 3-fold in **P^k**, k = 4 or 5, we will need two standard results (Lemma 1.2 and step (h) in the proof of Theorem 0.2 in §2), which will give the boundness claimed in Theorems 0.1 and 0.2, knowing that the degree, d, of S' or X' is a priori bounded.

We fix the following notations. Let S be a smooth surface with a birational finite morphism f: S→**P⁴** whose image, S', has only finitely many singular points; hence f: S→S' is the normalization map. Set d:= deg(S'), H:= f*($O_{S'}(1)$), O= O_S, K:=K_S, g the sectional genus of the pair (S,H) (i.e. 2g-2 = H.(H+K)), $\chi = \chi(O_S)$ = 1-q+p_g, and c:= length(f*(O_S)/$O_{S'}$) (the weighted number of double points of

S'); in the setting of Theorem 0.2 and its proof in the next section we will have c:=
c(1). By the double point formula ([F]) we have

$$d^2 - 5d - 5(2g-2) - 2K^2 + 12\chi = c \qquad (1)$$

Now look at [EP]. Here are the modifications needed to obtain Theorem
0.1.

(a) Statemement (B) in [EP], p.4, (i.e. a quotation of a classical paper of L.
Roth) holds true for any integral surface, hence for S'.

(b) The main point is to obtain the following result which corresponds to
[EP], Prop. 1.

Proposition 1.1. *(i) If $6c<d^2 -90d -6(2K^2-12\chi)$ and $d\geq90$, then S' is
contained in a hypersurface of degree at most 5.*

*(ii) Fix the integer c; there is an integer d(c) such that if $d\geq d(c)$, then S' is
contained in a hypersurface of degree 5.*

(c) In the statement of Lemma 2 use $\chi(O_{S'})$ instead of $\chi(O)$; in its proof
use the fact that $\chi(O_{S'}(t)) = \chi(O_S(t))+c$.

(d) In the proof of Lemma 3, let V^+ be the normalization of V and let S^+ be
the strict transform of S' in V^+; S^+ is a partial normalization of S'; hence the
"weighted number", c^+, of nodes of S^+ is at most c. Lemma A of [EP] does not
depend on S. Lemmas 4 and 5 of [EP] apply to S' as to S in the smooth case
because they are concerned only with a general (smooth) hyperplane section of S'.
Lemma 6 of [EP] follows from this with a correction term in the extimates which
depends only on c^+ and is bounded in term of c. Lemma B of [EP] does not
depend on S and S' (and also its proof because it uses only V^+ and the curve
section C).

The next result concludes the proof of Theorem 0.1.

Lemma 1.2. *With the notations used in this section if there is a constant $d_0(c)$
depending only on c such that if $d:=deg(S')\geq d_0(c)$ for every possible S',then S
and S' varies only in bounded families.*

Proof. There are only finitely many possible Hilbert polynomials for S and S'.
Hence the result follows from [Ko], Th. 2.1.2; however, since Sing(S') is finite
and the normalization of S is smooth, the proof needed is much simpler than in
[Ko] (and the result "classical"). ♦

§2. In this section we will show how to modify the proofs in [BOSS] in
our setting to obtain Theorem 0.2. Again, we we will just show in a telegraphic

way the small modifications needed. All the references (pages and number of formulas) are to [BOSS] unless otherwise specified. We fix the following notations. Let X be a smooth complex projective 3-fold with a birational finite morphism f: $X \to P^5$ whose image X': = f(X) has at most 1-dimensional singular locus; we assume that u has differential of rank 3 except at finitely many points; hence f: $X \to X'$ (abuse of notations) is the normalization map. The data (denoted with c:= (c(1),c(2)) are the numerical data needed to bound the badness of the non normality locus, B, of X'; just for convention we will take as data c: = (c(1),c(2)). Set H:= $f*(O_{X'}(1))$, K:= K_X, d:= deg(X'):= H^3. Let σ be the minimal integer such that X' is contained in a hypersurface of degree σ. S will denote a general element of |H| and set S':= f(S); hence (S,S') are exactly the actors of §1. We will denote with C both a curve which is the intersection of 2 general surfaces in |H| and its isomorphic image in the corresponding P^3 of P^5. We will denote with a(i,c), i = 1,..., (or just a(*,c)) constants depending only on c = (c(1),c(2)); a(i,c) for i = 1, 2, 3, could be computed in terms of the numerical data of the pair (X,H), but we do not do that because it seemed to us hopeless to find an explicit bound for the other constants.

Now look at [BOSS].

(a) Page 313: By the double point formula, the formula (1.2) for HK^2 has now another term which is exactly -c(1)/2 (as in our eq. (1) in our §1). Now the formula (1.4) for K^3 has now one more additive term : +a(1,c). Instead of the formula for c_2 now we have:

$$H \cdot c_2 = (15-d^2)H^3 + 6H^2K + HK^2 + a(2,c)$$

for the following reasons (indeed a(2,c) depends only on c(1)). Now the normal sheaf N_f (which will be denoted also by N) to f is not a locally free sheaf on X, but it is locally free outside the points at which the differential of f has rank 3 (outside the cusps); we assumed the existence of only finitely many cusps; hence the restriction of N_f to a general surface section, S, of H is locally free and its c_2 (which by abuse we denote with $H \cdot c_2$) is defined; instead of the tangent/normal bundle short exact sequence of the smooth case now we have the corresponding exact sequence for Nf on X and we define a(3,c) as the length of the cokernel of the map $f*(TP^5) \to N_f$ (which is supported by the cusps) (hence depends only on c(2)).

A-4

(b): Page 314. Theorems 1.2, 1.3, 1.4 and 1.5 are OK in our situation (note that for 1.5 we consider the smooth X, not X'). We do not have formula (1.5) (i.e. the vanishing of $q(X):= h^1(O_X)$), hence we cannot use later formula (1.6) (i.e. $q(S) = 0$).

(c): Page 315. Instead of Proposition 2.1, see step (h) at the end of this section. About Proposition 2, we will not try to use Chern classes (except, as before $H.c_2$) for the non locally free sheaf $N:= N_f$, but use directly Segre classes. Since the cuspidal locus is finite, we still have $H \cdot s_2(N(-1)) \geq 0$, but we have only $s_3(N(-1)) \geq a(4,c)$. This is sufficient to modify Proposition 2.2 (and its proof at page 316) and obtain in parts 1. and 2. respectively the inequalities

$$12\chi(O_S) \geq d^2 - 7d - 18(g-1) + a(5,c)$$
$$24\chi(O_S) \geq d^2 - 3d + (d-15)(g-1) + 12\chi(O_X) + a(6,c).$$

(d): Page 316. With the modifications just given for the proof of Proposition 2.2, now Proposition 2.3 holds in the following form:

Proposition 2.1. *There is an integer a(7,c) such that if $s_2(N_f(-1)) \cdot H \leq a(7,c)$ and if $d \geq a(8,c)$, then X' is contained in a hypersurface of degree 6.*

(e): [BOSS], §3. A key step in [BOSS] is Proposition 3.1, whose proof needs pages 317-323. A key part of our note is the following discussion (and 'justification' in our setting) of its proof. At the end of this discussion we will obtain a proof of the following statements (which corresponds respectively to Proposition 3.1 and Corollary 3.1 of [BOSS]):

Lemma A. *There is a constant $d_0 := d_0(\sigma,c)$ (depending only on σ and c) and there is a polynomial $P_{\sigma,c}$ of degree 8 in $(d)^{1/2}$ and with positive leading term ($P_{\sigma,c}$ depending only on σ and c), such that if $d \geq d_0$ we have $P_{\sigma,c}((d)^{1/2})) \leq -\chi(O_X)$.*

Lemma B. *Fix σ and c; there are only finite many algebraic families of possible (X,X') with the invariants σ, c and not of general type.*

The essential point in the proof of [BOSS], Prop. 3.1, was the proof of Lemmas 3.1 and 3.2. Here again the main point would be the justification of the corresponding results (with an adaptation of their statements).

(f1) The first part of the analysis of the proof of Proposition 3.1 is the checking (which will be done just below in this substep (f1)) that everything works well for us in the proof of [EP], Lemma 1(or equivalently, the justification of eq. (3.1), (3.2) and (3.4) of [BOSS]). Set $N_S := N_f|S$ (which is a vector bundle by the finiteness assumption about the cuspidal locus); set m:= $c_2(NS(-\sigma))$. Now we do not have the formula " $c_2(N_S) = d^2$ " but there is just a correcting term - $c(1)/2$ (see step (a)). The inequality " $0\leq m$ " is OK since it is just (B) in [EP], p. 2 (hence it uses only C as remarked here in §1). The considerations about the jacobian ideal work well because f|S is unramified. The formula for $\dim(O_Z)$ works, and to apply the formula to obtain the inequality by the fact that $\dim(O_Z)\geq 0$ (and conclude the justification of the lemma) just note that (for instance by standard adjunction theory) the line bundle $3H|S+K_S$ is very ample.

(f2) To justify [BOSS], Lemma 3.3, it is sufficient to justify (up to constants depending only on s and c) [EP], Lemma 5 and Lemma D. Lemma D is OK since it is a general lemma on singular surfaces in $\mathbf{P}^3$. Lemma 5 concerns only C, which is smooth also in our situation (but with a correction term depending only on c for the relation between g and d). However, for [EP], Lemma 5, it is used [EP], Lemma 4. To extend it to our situation it seems to us necessary to make some modification to its statement and to the definition of the integer t_1 introduced in the statement of [BOSS], Lemma 3.2. Now we claim the existence of a computable integer a(9,c) (depending only on c) such that if t_1 is defined as the minimal integer t with $t\sigma-d\geq\sigma$ and $(t\sigma-d)^2-\mu-(t\sigma-d)\sigma(\sigma-4)>a(9,c)$, then Lemma 3.2, part 2, holds with $A = A(\sigma,c)$ constant depending only on σ and c, and Lemma 3.2, part 1, holds with the inequalities

$$d/\sigma<t_1\leq d/\sigma + (d)^{1/2} + \sigma + a(9,c)$$

We claim that with this statement everything will work. To prove this claim, first note that in the Observation of pages 321-322 the only difference is that now r = $r(\sigma,c)$ depends only on σ and c; hence the same holds for the constant $B:= B(\sigma,c)$. We consider only the case " n = 5 " needed for Theorem 0.2 in the general statements on $\mathbf{P}^n$ in [BOSS], lemma 3.3 and 3.4. In Lemma 3.3 we have $A_1 = A_1(c)$ depending only on c. By our modification of the statement of part 1 of Lemma 3.2 of [BOSS] now in the proof of the inequality (3.4) in Lemma 3.3 we use as δ_1 an integer with $\delta_1<\sigma(d)^{1/2}+\sigma^2+a(10,c)$. In the eq. (3.5) of Lemma 3.3 the coefficient of the leading term $d^{5/2}$ is now a constant b(σ,c) depending only on σ and c, not just the constant $\sigma/2$ as in [BOSS}. In Lemma 3.4 we have $B_0 = B_0(c)$ and $B_i = B_i(c)$ (depending only on c); the claim is OK; the constant D = $D(\sigma)>0$ at the beginning of page 324 is now $D(\sigma,c)$, i.e. it depends only on σ and c. Lemma B of [EP] is OK and everything works well (with constants depending on c) until the claim at page 326. Here the big trouble is the quotation of [L] which requires S' smooth. This problem is solved in the next step (f3).

(f3) Note that for our aims about [L] we need only the following far weaker statement:

There are integers a(11,c) and a(12,c) (depending only on c) such that for all integers $t \geq (d-3+a(11,c))$ the restriction map $r_S(t)$:

$$(f/S)^*(H^0(P^4, O_P(t))) \rightarrow H^0(S, H^{\otimes t})$$

has $dim(Coker(r_S(t)) \leq a(12,c)$.

We claim that the proofs in [L] give this statement with a(11,c) = 0 and a(12,c) = c(1). First note that the statement of [L], lemma 1.2, cannot holds in our situation if $c(1) \neq 0$; the best could be $dim(Coker(w_2)) = c(1)$ and this is exactly what follows from the proof of the smooth case in [L]; we only remark explicitly that to obtain it without modifying the proof it is not necessary to assume anything about the goodness of the singularities of S'; we need only to have the finite integer c(1) as a datum. The sheaf E appearing in [L] is again defined using $f^*(O_X)$ (with X the smooth surface as in [L]), not $f^*(O_{X'})$ (in which now, following the notations of [L] f is the composition of the morphism $X \rightarrow P^4$ with a general projection into P^3); in this way, since X is locally Cohen - Macaulay, E is again locally free. With this convention, everything in [L] works verbatim and gives our claim.

(f4) To conclude the proof of the part corresponding to part 1 of Lemma 3.2 (hence to conclude the proof of Lemma A) just note that [EP], Lemma 4, is OK in our situation.

(f5) To obtain Lemma B having Lemma A (which in [BOSS] is just the proof that Corollary 3.1 follows from Proposition 3.1) the only trouble (taking for granted the next step (h) which is just "general knowledge") is that now we do not have, a priori, q(S) = 0 to obtain a bound on $p_g(X)$. However, by [EP] and our §1 we may assume that S is of general type. Hence we have $q(X) = q(S) \leq p_g(S)/2$. This is sufficient to carry over the proofs in [BOSS], pages 327 and 328, and obtain Lemma B from Lemma A (modulo step (h)).

(g) Proposition 4.1 works verbatim with the addition of a term +a(*,c) on the right hand side of the inequality (4.1). Instead of [BOSS], Proposition at page 329, we use again the key inequality $q(X) \leq p_g(S)/2$ to conclude the fact that d must be bounded and (modulo the next step (h)) to conclude proof of Theorem 0.2.

(h) By step (g) we may fix one degree, d. Call $P_{X,H}(t)$, $P_{S,H}(t)$, $P_{X',H}(t)$ the Hilbert polynomial of X, X' and S with respect to the line bundle induced by P^5. First note that the possible Hilbert polynomials $p_{S,H}(t)$ are finite (hence, as in lemma 1.2, we get the boundness for all S since c(1) is fixed). Since $p_{X,H}(t) - p_{X,H}(t-1) = p_{S,H}(t)$, we get only finitely many choices for the coefficients of $p_{X,H}(t)$ except the constant one. It is a general fact (see essentially [Kl] or [KM] or [Ko], statement and proof of Th. 2.1.3) that this is sufficient to obtain the boundness for the set of all possible smooth X. In particular, we have only finitely many possible $p_{X,H}(t)$. Since $p_{X,H}(t) = p_{X',H}(t) + c(1)t + c(2)$, we have only finitely many $p_{X',H}(t)$. Now from the bounded set of all subschemes of P^5 with that Hilbert polynomial we delete the ones which are too good (the smooth ones) and then the ones which are too bad (non integral, with normalization non smooth, singular in codimension 1 or with a curve of cusps). We obtain a constructible (hence bounded) subset of the previous bounded set, as wanted.

The proof of Theorem 0.2 is over.

References

[BOSS]   R. Braun, G. Ottaviani, M. Schneider, F. O. Schreyer, Boundedness for non general-type 3-folds in P^n, in: Complex Analysis and Geometry, pp. 311-338, Plenum, 1992.

[EP]   G. Ellingsrud, C. Peskine, Sur les surfaces lisses de P^4, Invent. math. **95** (1989), 1-11.

[F]   W. Fulton, Intersection theory, Ergebnisse der Math. vol. **2**, Springer-Verlag, 1985.

[Kl]   S. Kleiman, Les Theoreme de Finitude pour le Foncteur de Picard, in: Theorie des intersections et Theorem de Riemann Roch (SGA VI), Exp. XIII, pp. 616-666, Lect. Notes in Math. **225**, Springer-Verlag, 1971.

[Ko]   J. Kollar, Toward moduli of singular varieties, Compositio Math. **56** (1985), 369-398.

[KM]   J. Kollar, T. Matsusaka, Riemann - Roch type inequalities, Amer. J. Math. **105** (1983), 229-252.

[L]   R. Lazarsfeld, A sharp Castelnuovo bound for smooth surfaces, Duke Math. J. **55** (1987), 423-427.

E. Ballico

Dept. of Mathematics, University of Trento, 38050 Povo (TN), Italy

e-mail: (bitnet) ballico@itncisca   or   ballico@itnvax.cineca.it

fax: italy + 461881624

N. Chiarli

Dept. of Mathematics, Politecnico di Torino,

Corso Duca degli Abruzzi 24,10129 Torino, Italy

e-mail: chiarli@itopoli.bitnet

fax: italy + 11-5647599

S. Greco

Dept. of Mathematics, Politecnico di Torino,

Corso Duca degli Abruzzi 24,10129 Torino, Italy

e-mail: sgreco@itopoli.bitnet

fax: italy + 11-5647599

B: Bielliptic Curves: Special Linear Series and Plane Models

A. Del Centina
Dipartimento di Matematica
Università di Ferrara
Via Machinavelli 35
I - 44100 Ferrara
Italy

A. Gimigliano
Dipartimento di Matematica
Università di Bologna
Piazza di Porta S. Donato 5
I - 40127 Bologna
Italy

BIELLIPTIC CURVES: SPECIAL LINEAR SERIES AND PLANE MODELS

A.Del Centina , A.Gimigliano **

Introduction

Let C be a *bielliptic* (also *elliptic-hyperelliptic* in the literature) curve, i.e. a curve which admits a $2:1$ morphism π onto an elliptic curve. This paper is devoted to :

a) giving a description of all the special linear series g_n^r that can exist on C , and;

b) finding plane models of minimal degree for such a C.

Question a) is not new in the literature. It has been considered e.g. in [F] and in [H1]. More precisely, in [F] it is proved that for $n \leq g(C) - 2$ and n odd, every g_n^r is composed with the algebraic family γ_2^1 of the fibers of π, while in [H1] this result is extended to the case when n is even (these results are stated in terms of gap order for the existence of meromorphic function on Riemann surfaces).

The existence of g_{g-1}^1's not composed with γ_2^1 can be found in [H1],[H2], in [M] and in [W]. In this paper we approach question a) with quite straightforward methods based on the peculiar geometry of the canonical model of C.

The paper is organized as follows:

In the first section (after the preliminaries) we determine for which values r, n there exist linear series g_n^r on C and which of them are composed with the γ_2^1 or have fixed points.

The second section is dedicated to the study of plane models of minimal degree for the curve C. In particular, when $g = g(C) \geq 10$, we are able to characterize the curves which are bielliptic in some families of plane curves, by imposing certain conditions on the 0-dimensional scheme of their singular points.

0. Notation and preliminary results.

In this paper we will always work on a projective, irreducible, smooth curve C with genus $g \geq 3$, defined over an algebraically closed field of characteristic 0.

We denote by $K = K_C$ a canonical divisor, by ω the sheaf $\mathcal{O}_C(K)$ on C and with $< A >$ the linear subspace of the canonical space of C generated by a divisor A dominated by K.

In the next two sections we make frequent use of the following well known fact (geometric version of Riemann-Roch Theorem):

** As members of the G.N.S.A.G.A. of the C.N.R. (Work partially supported by M.P.I. funds). A.M.S. Subject Classification : 14H30.

Lemma 0.1 : *Let C be a non-hyperelliptic curve of genus g and let $\varphi : C \to \mathbb{P}^{g-1}$ be its canonical map.*

If $P_1, \ldots, P_n$ are points on C such that $|P_1 + \ldots + P_n| = g_n^r$, then the points $\varphi(P_1), \ldots, \varphi(P_n)$ span a linear subspace of $\mathbb{P}^{g-1}$ of dimension $\dim < \varphi(P_1), \ldots, \varphi(P_n) > = n - r - 1$.

For curves C possessing two non-constant morphisms $\nu_i : C \to X_i$, where X_i is a smooth curve of genus g_i and $\deg \nu_i = d_i$, such that ν_1, ν_2 do not jointly factor over another morphism on a third curve, we have the following inequality, known as the *Castelnuovo-Severi Inequality* (see **[Ca]**, or **[K]** for a more modern exposition):

0.2
$$g(C) \leq d_1 g + d_2 g' + (d_1 - 1)(d_2 - 1).$$

We recall that a linear series g_n^r on C is said to be *composed* if there exist a smooth curve X, a non-constant morphism $\nu : C \to X$ with $1 < d = \deg(\nu) < r$ and a linear series g_p^s on X such that $\nu^*(g_p^s)$ is the moving part of the g_n^r; in this case we denote the algebraic family of the fibers of ν by γ_d^1 and we say that the g_n^r is composed with γ_d^1. In particular, two linear series g_n^r are said to be *independent* if they are not composed with the same γ_d^1.

A curve C is called *bielliptic* if there exists a degree two morphism $\pi : C \to E$ over an elliptic curve E ; in this case we call the triple (C, π, E) a *bielliptic structure* on C.

We denote by i the automorphism of C associated to π (so that the quotient of C by the action of i is E) and by γ_2^1 the family of divisors of degree 2 whose points are coupled under i (i.e. the fibers of π).

Let us suppose C to be bielliptic. From 0.2 one immediately gets the following facts:

0.3   *If $g \geq 4$, then C cannot be hyperelliptic and if $g \geq 5$ then C cannot be trigonal.*

0.4   *If $g \geq 6$, , then the bielliptic structure on C is unique.*

0.5   *If $g \geq 6$, , then there are no g_4^1's that are independent from the γ_2^1.*

The covering $\pi : C \to E$ is determined by its branch divisor B on E (whose degree is $2g - 2$) and a half $\mathcal{A}$ of $|B|$, such that

$$\pi^* \mathcal{A} = \mathcal{O}_C(\pi^{-1}(B)).$$

Let us recall some well known facts about the canonical model $\tilde{C}$ of C. $\tilde{C}$ lies on the surface $S = \bigcup_{e \in E} < \pi^{-1}(e) > \subseteq \mathbb{P}^{g-1}$, ruled on E. We view $| \omega_E |^*$ and $| \omega_E(\mathcal{A}) |^*$ in $| \omega_C |^* \cong \mathbb{P}^{g-1}$ as the two invariant spaces of the projectivity of $| \omega_C |^*$ which induces the involution on C, and we have that all the lines of S intersect $| \omega_E |^*$ which is a point (since $\omega_E = \mathcal{O}_E$). Hence S is a cone; moreover the lines also intersect the curve $E \subseteq | \omega_C(\mathcal{A}) |^* \cong \mathbb{P}^{g-2}$(again a slight abuse in notation) which is given by the embedding of E by the series $\mathcal{A}$, hence S is an elliptic normal cone in $\mathbb{P}^{g-1}$. For more details we refer to [**DC**]. In the cases $g = 4, 5$, we can have more γ_2^1's on $\mathcal{C}$, so we suppose that we have fixed one of them when we consider $\mathcal{S}$ and we speak of "the" γ_2^1 on $\mathcal{C}$.

1. Special complete g_n^r on $\mathcal{C}$.

Let $g_n^r = |D|$, $r > 0$, be a complete special linear series on $\mathcal{C}$, without fixed points.

LEMMA 1.1 : *Suppose we have a $g_n^r = |D|$, without fixed points. Then there exists a divisor $D' \in |K - D|$ containing a divisor of the γ_2^1 if and only if $|D|$ is composed with the γ_2^1 .*

Proof: Let $K, \tilde{\mathcal{C}}$ and $\mathcal{S}$ be as in §0.

It is trivial to check that if $|D|$ is composed with the γ_2^1 then $|K - D|$ is composed with it also (the hyperplane sections in $|K|$ which contain divisors of $|D|$ pass through the vertex of the cone).

Now suppose $D' \in |K - D|$ contains a divisor of the γ_2^1 ; then the hyperplanes through the linear span $< D' > \subseteq \mathbb{P}^{g-1}$ cut out $|D|$ on $\mathcal{C}$.

Since $< D' >$ contains the vertex V of the elliptic cone $\mathcal{S}$, the intersection with $\mathcal{S}$ of every hyperplane H passing through $< D' >$ will split into $g - 1$ lines, so $D + D'$ is given by $g - 1$ divisors of γ_2^1. Then either:

> *a)* every line in $H \cap \mathcal{S}$ contains two or no points of D : hence $|D|$ is composed with the γ_2^1 and we are done, or
> *b)* some of those lines contain only one point P of D , and we are finished also, because P would be a fixed point for $|D|$ since all the hyperplanes through D' would contain the point P' which is associated to P in the γ_2^1.

Now we can enunciate the main result in this section:

Theorem 1.2 : *There exists on $\mathcal{C}$ a complete, special g_n^r , without fixed points and not composed with the γ_2^1, if and only if r and n satisfy the following conditions :*
1.2.1) $\qquad\qquad g - 1 \leq n \leq 2g - 2$;
1.2.2) $\qquad\qquad r = n - g + 1 \qquad if \ n > g - 1$;
1.2.3) $\qquad\qquad r = 1 \ if \ n = g - 1$.

Proof : Consider a generic divisor $D \in g_n^r$. Suppose that $n > g - 1$ and consider, in the canonical embedding of $\mathcal{C}$, a hyperplane H which contains D. Let $\Gamma = H \cap \mathcal{S}$; then if Γ is a smooth elliptic curve of degree $g - 1$, we have $< D >=< \Gamma >$, by Bezout.

If Γ were composed of $g - 1$ lines (H contains the vertex V of $\mathcal{S}$), note that we would have again $< D >=< \Gamma >$ since $V \in < D >$ (we have at least one of the lines containing two points of D) and any of the $g - 1$ lines must intersect D otherwise the residue D' of D

B-3

with respect to the intersection $H \cap \tilde{C}$ would contain a divisor of the γ_2^1 , in contradiction with Lemma 1.1.

Hence $g - 2 = \dim < D >= n - r - 1$ (by Lemma 0.1), and so $r = n - g + 1$.

If $n \leq g - 1$, note that D cannot contain a divisor of the γ_2^1 , otherwise D' would contradict Lemma 1.1 again.

In this case there exist a hyperplane H containing D and cutting a smooth elliptic curve Γ on S (this follows from Riemann-Roch Theorem and $r > 0$, which implies that the hyperplanes through D form at least a pencil). The fact that D is contained in the elliptic normal curve Γ implies that $\dim < D > \geq n - 2$, in fact otherwise we could choose a set, B , of $g - n$ other points on Γ such that the linear space $\Pi =< B, D >$ would have $\dim \Pi < g - 2$. Hence we would have $\Gamma \subseteq \Pi$, by Bezout, a contradiction. So $n - r - 1 = \dim < D > \geq n - 2$, and $r = 1$. But in the case that $|D| = g_n^1$, we can apply the Castelnuovo-Severi inequality to get that $n \geq g - 1$. Hence $n = g - 1$ and one of the implications of the theorem is proved.

Now suppose that $r, n \in \mathbb{N}$ are such that 1.2.1 and 1.2.2 hold. We can choose a generic set A of $2g - 2 - n$ points on $\tilde{C}$ such that no two of them are on the same line of S. The hyperplanes H through $< A >$ cut on S a family of curves whose generic member, say Γ, is an elliptic normal curve. So this family of curves cuts on $\tilde{C}$, outside of A , a linear series of degree n and dimension r', with

$$r' \leq g - 1 - 2g + 2 + n = n - g + 1.$$

Since by Riemann's inequality, $r' \geq n - g + 1$, we actually have

$$r' = n - g + 1 = r.$$

Such a series is without fixed points. In fact, any such point would be fixed also for the series that our hyperplanes H cut on Γ and this is impossible since no complete linear series of degree greater than one on an elliptic curve can have fixed points.

Now let r, n be as in 1.2.3 and let us show how to construct a g_{g-1}^1 on $\tilde{C}$ (without fixed points and not composed with the γ_2^1).

We can choose a set of $g - 3$ points on $\tilde{C}$: $P_1, \ldots, P_{g-3}$, in such a way that the projection of $\tilde{C}$ from the space $< P_1, \ldots, P_{g-3} >$ into $\mathbb{P}^2$ is a curve C' of degree $g + 1$, birational to $\tilde{C}$ and whose only singularities are an ordinary $(g - 3)$-fold point, O, and $2g - 6$ double points $O_1, \ldots, O_{2g-6}$ (this fact will be proved in Theorem 2.3).

The lines of $\mathbb{P}^2$ passing through O cut on C' a g_4^1 which is composed with γ_2^1, while the lines through any of the O_i will cut a g_{g-1}^1 which is not composed with the elliptic involution and has no fixed points.

Our next step is to describe the g_n^r's on C which are composed with the γ_2^1.

Remark 1.3 : *For every pair (n, r) of positive integers, with n even, there exists on C a special, complete g_n^r without fixed points composed with the γ_2^1 if and only if (n, r) satisfies the condition :*

1.3.1) $$4 \leq n \leq 2g - 4 \qquad \text{and} \qquad r = (n/2) - 1 .$$

Proof: Suppose that $g_n^r = |D|$ is composed with the γ_2^1. Then n has to be even and so $r = (n/2) - 1$, by the Riemann-Roch theorem on the elliptic curve.

Note also that, for $n = 2g - 2$, $|K|$ is the only special linear series, and it is not composed with the γ_2^1. Now suppose that (n, r) satisfies 1.3.1 and consider, on E, a divisor Z of degree $n/2$.

Let $|\pi^{-1}(Z)|$ be our g_n^r ; then $r = \dim |\pi^{-1}(Z)| \geq (n/2) - 1$ but, by Clifford's Theorem, $r \leq n/2$ and C cannot be hyperelliptic (by 0.3), so $r = (n/2) - 1$.

Corollary 1.4 : *The only special complete g_n^r's which do have fixed points and are not composed with the γ_2^1 must have $(r, n) = (1, g)$, and are of type: $g_g^1 = g_{g-1}^1 + P$.*

Proof: Suppose the g_n^r has $m > 0$ fixed points. By removing them we get a special, complete g_{n-m}^r without fixed points and, by Theorem 1.2 , the triple (n, r, m) must satisfy the following conditions:

1.4.1) $$g - 1 \leq n - m \leq 2g - 2,$$
1.4.2) $$r = n - m - g + 1, \text{ if } n - m > g - 1,$$
1.4.3) $$r = 1, \text{ if } n - m = g - 1 .$$

Let i, i' be the indices of specialty of the g_n^r, g_{n-m}^r, respectively. By the Riemann-Roch Theorem we have : $r = n - m - g + i = n - g + i'$, hence $i = i' + m$.

If $n - m > g - 1$ then, by 1.4.2 , the index of specialty of the g_n^r is $1 - m$. So we must have $1 - m > 0$, and we get the contradiction $m \leq 0$.

If $n - m = g - 1$, then 1.4.3 implies that $r = 1$ and $i = 2 = i' + m$. so $i' = m = 1$ and $n = g$.

Corollary 1.5 : *There exists on C a special complete g_n^r composed with the γ_2^1 and having $m > 0$ fixed points if and only if the triple $(n, r, m) \in \mathbb{N}^3$ satisfies the conditions :*
1.5.1) $$n = 2r + m + 2,$$
1.5.2) $$r \leq g - m - 3.$$

Proof: Let g_n^r be a special complete linear series on C composed with the γ_2^1 and having $m > 0$ fixed points. The moving part of this g_n^r is a g_{n-m}^r so 1.5.1 follows immediately from Theorem 1.3.

If i is the index of specialty of the g_{n-m}^r, then that of the g_n^r is $i - m$. So 1.5.2 follows from Riemann-Roch and Theorem 1.3.

Now suppose that the triple (n, r, m) verifies 1.5.1 and 1.5.2 (recall $r > 0, m > 0$).

Every set of $r+1$ lines of S (since $r \leq g-3$) is contained in a hyperplane which cuts S in $g-r-2$ other lines intersecting $\tilde{C}$ in the union of $g-r-2$ divisors of the γ_2^1. Let A be the associated set of points. By 1.5.1 and 1.5.2, we have $2g-4-2r-m > g-2-r > 0$.

Then consider a subset $A' \subseteq A$ of $2g-4-2r-m$ points of A such that on each of the $g-2-r$ lines determined by A there is at least one of them.

Clearly dim $<A'> = g-2-r$ so the hyperplanes through $<A'>$ cut on $\tilde{C}$ a special complete linear series g_n^r which has m fixed points (those of the set $A \backslash A'$) and is composed with the γ_2^1 by Lemma 1.1 (there is at least a line of S in $<A>$).

The above results give us a way to describe the subvarieties $W_n^r(C)$ of $\mathrm{Pic}^n(C)$ parameterizing the complete linear series of degree n and dimension at least r :

$$W_n^r(C) = \{| D |: \deg D = n, h^0(C, \mathcal{O}_C(D)) \geq r+1\}.$$

We refer to [**A.C.G.H**] for the study of the cases with $g \leq 5$, so we will consider $g \geq 6$.

For $n = g + k \geq g$, passing to the residual series with respect to $|K|$ provides an isomorphism $W_{g+k}^r(C) \cong W_{g-k-2}^{r-k-1}(C)$, so we can restrict ourselves to studying the case $n \leq g-1$.

The dimension of $W_n^r(C)$ is at least equal to the Brill-Noether number $\rho = g - (r+1)(g-n+r)$, and it is known that $W_n^r(C)$ is connected when $\rho \geq 1$.

When $r > 0, 4 \leq n \leq g-2$, or $r \geq 2$ and $n = g-1$, from Theorem 1.2 and Corollary 1.5 we get that such g_n^r's must be composed with the γ_2^1 and have $m = n - 2r - 2 \geq 0$ fixed points, so (we will always write $W_n(C)$ for $W_n^0(C)$) :

$$W_n^r(C) = \pi^*(W_{r+1}^r(E)) + W_m(C)$$

and thus, in this case (see also [**A.C.G.H**], pg. 198) :

$$\dim W_n^r(C) = m + 1 = (\text{by } 1.5.1) \ n - 2r - 1$$

Note that these schemes are all irreducible (topologically they are quotients of $E \times C^{(m)}$).

When $n = g-1$, $W_{g-1}^1(C)$ is equidimensional (see [**K-L**]) and reduced (see [**Te**]). By [**W**] we have :

$$W_{g-1}^1(C) = \Sigma \cup \Sigma'$$

where $\Sigma = W_4^1(C) + W_{g-5}(C)$ is the component which parameterizes the g_{g-1}^1's with $g-5$ fixed point while Σ' parameterizes (outside its intersection with Σ) the g_{g-1}^1's without fixed points.

We have $\Sigma \cong \pi^*(W_2^1(E)) + W_{g-5}$, so $\dim \Sigma = \dim \Sigma' = g-4$ (hence we always have $\dim W_n^r(C) = n - 2r - 1$).

2. Plane models of minimal degree.

We can apply Theorem 1.2 in order to get the minimal order of a plane model of $\mathcal{C}$.

Corollary 2.1 : *A bielliptic curve $\mathcal{C}$ of genus $g \geq 3$ cannot be birational to a plane curve of order less than $g + 1$. In particular, the only smooth bielliptic plane curves are those with $g = 3$.*

Proof: In fact, a plane model of $\mathcal{C}$ must be given by a g_n^2 on the curve: if the g_n^2 is complete, either it is regular, and then $n = g + 2$, or it is special and $n = g + 1$ by Theorem 1.2.

If the g_n^2 is not complete, it is part of a complete g_n^r, $r \geq 2$, and if this is a regular g_n^r, then $n = r + g \geq g + 2$, hence the plane model of $\mathcal{C}$, say $\mathcal{C}'$, has degree $\geq g + 2$. When the g_n^r is special, Theorem 1.2 applies to get that $n \geq g + 2$ again.

Remark 2.2 : With the same kind of proof as above, one has that if a bielliptic curve $\mathcal{C}$ of genus g is birational to some curve of degree d in $\mathbb{P}^n$, then $d \geq n + g - 1$.

Let us recall the following fact that will be useful in the proof of the next theorem, in which we give a construction for plane models of minimal degree of a bielliptic curve $\mathcal{C}$.

Fact : Let $E_n \subseteq \mathbb{P}^{n-1}$ be an elliptic normal curve. Then for a generic choice of $n - 2$ points $P_1, \ldots, P_{n-2}$ on E_n (i.e. in an open set of $E_n^{(n-2)}$), the following is true :

$$(*) \qquad \text{For any choice of } i, j = 1, ..., n - 2, \ i \neq j, \text{ the following}$$
divisor (on E) spans $\mathbb{P}^{n-1}$:

$$D = P_1, + \ldots + 2P_i + \ldots + 2P_j + \ldots + P_{n-2}$$

In fact, for any choice of two distinct points $P_i, P_j \in E_n$, the divisor $2P_i + 2P_j$ generates a 3-space, and the hyperplanes containing it cut a g_{n-4}^{n-5} on E_n outside $2P_i + 2P_j$. Hence, a generic set of $n - 4$ points on E_n is not contained in the g_{n-4}^{n-5} and the corresponding divisor D generates $\mathbb{P}^{n-1}$, i.e. it is not contained in a hyperplane section.

Theorem 2.3 : *Any bielliptic curve $\mathcal{C}$ of genus $g \geq 4$ can be birationally transformed into a plane curve $\mathcal{C}'$ of degree $g + 1$ having a $(g - 3)$-fold point O and $2g - 6$ distinct double points $O_1, \ldots, O_{2g-6}$ as its only singularities.*

Proof: Consider a set of $g - 3$ points, say
$P_1, \ldots, P_{g-3}$, "general enough" on $\tilde{\mathcal{C}}$, the canonical model of $\mathcal{C}$. We require that the P_i's impose independent conditions on hyperplanes, none of them is a ramification point for the γ_2^1, no two of them are on the same line of S and their projections on a smooth hyperplane section Γ of S are generic with respect to property $(*)$.

The series $| K - (P_1 + \ldots + P_{g-3}) |$ on $\tilde{\mathcal{C}}$ is a (special, complete) g_{g+1}^2 without fixed points and is not composed with the γ_2^1 ; we want to check that it is not composed with any other γ_ν^1.

Suppose that the g_{g+1}^2 is composed with some γ_ν^1 and let $P_1', \ldots, P_\nu'$ be the set of points on $\tilde{\mathcal{C}}$ belonging to any divisor passing through P_1'. Then $S = < P_1, \ldots, P_{g-3}, P_1', \ldots, P_\nu' >$

has dimension $g - 3$ and the hyperplanes through S cut out on $\tilde{C}$ a special, complete, $g^1_{g+1-\nu}$, not composed with the γ^1_2 (we can easily see that $P_1, \ldots, P_{g-3}, P'_1$ can be chosen so that in the whole set $\{P_1, \ldots, P_{g-3}, P'_1, \ldots, P'_\nu\}$ there are no divisors belonging to γ^1_2). By Theorem 1.2 it follows that $\nu = 2$.

The map into $\mathbb{P}^2$ associated to the g^2_{g+1} can be seen as the projection of $\tilde{C}$ from the space $< P_1, \ldots, P_{g-3} >$; let $C' \subseteq \mathbb{P}^2$ be the image of $\tilde{C}$ under this projection.

Note that the points $i(P_1), \ldots, i(P_{g-3})$ are all projected onto the same point $O \in C'$ and, if the g^2_{g+1} is composed with an involution of degree 2, we can choose them "generic enough" so that they do not contain any divisor of such involution , so that C' would be a plane curve of degree $(g+1)/2$ (hence g is odd) having at O a point of multiplicity at least $(g - 3)$. This is impossible if $g \geq 6$, while for $g = 5$, C' would be rational (a cubic with a node) and the map $C \to C'$ is $2 : 1$, then C would be hyperelliptic in contradiction to 0.3.

Hence $\tilde{C} \to C'$ is birational and $\deg C' = g + 1$. By Bezout, it follows immediately that C' cannot have singular points of multiplicity ≥ 5 , since C' has multiplicity $g - 3$ at O.

Let us observe that the

$$g^1_4 = \mid K - (P_1 + \ldots + P_{g-3} + i(P_1) + \ldots + i(P_{g-3})) \mid$$

is cut out on C' by the pencil of lines passing through O.

Note that the multiplicity of O cannot be greater, otherwise the lines through it would cut a g^1_3 or a g^1_2 on C'.

We have also that O is an ordinary multiple point for C', in fact if C' had a multiple tangent L at O, L would cut a divisor of type $2O + Q_1 + Q_2 \in g^1_4$. This means that there are two points P_i, P_j among $P_1, \ldots, P_{g-3}$, such that the two tangents to $\tilde{C}$ at $i(P_i), i(P_j)$ lie in the same hyperplane containing $P_1, \ldots, P_{g-3}$ and the vertex of the cone. This would imply that the projections of $P_1, \ldots, P_{g-3}$ on a smooth hyperplane section of S would not be generic with respect to property (*), contrary to our choice of $P_1, \ldots, P_{g-3}$.

Now suppose that C' has a 4-fold point Q, i.e. suppose that there exist Q_1, Q_2, Q_3, Q_4 on $\tilde{C}$ with $Q_1 + Q_2 + Q_3 + Q_4 \in g^1_4$ and such that $\dim < Q_1, Q_2, Q_3, Q_4, P_1, \ldots, P_{g-3} > = g - 3$. Under this hypothesis the linear series

$$\mid K - (P_1 + \ldots + P_{g-3} + Q_1 + Q_2 + Q_3 + Q_4) \mid$$

would have positive dimension, which is impossible.

On the other hand we can easily see that if C' had a singular point of multiplicity at least 3 it would be, actually, of multiplicity 4 (it cannot be more, by Bezout) since the g^1_4 is the pullback of a g^1_2 on the elliptic curve. Hence the only other singularities on C' are double points and, since C' has genus g and degree $g + 1$, their number δ is given by the formula :

$$g = \binom{g}{2} - \binom{g-3}{2} - \delta$$

from which $\delta = 2g - 6$.

If some of the O_i's are infinitely near, we can operate with quadratic transformations based on O and two of the O_i's in order to obtain a curve with distinct nodes.

A result like our Theorem 2.3 has been proved by C.Ciliberto and E.Sernesi in $[\mathbf{C} - \mathbf{S}]$, which we received when the first version of this paper was finished.

Remark 2.4 : From the construction in the proof of the previous theorem it is not hard to see that the special complete g_n^r's on a bielliptic curve C are very ample if and only if $n \geq 2g - 3$ (see also $[\mathbf{A.C.G.H}]$, pg. 221, es. B.4). In particular, if $g(C) \geq 6$, then C cannot be embedded in $\mathbb{P}^3$ with degree $< g + 3$.

In all that follows a plane curve of the same degree, genus and type of singularities as in Theorem 2.3 will be called a curve *of type C'* .

Now let us denote by Z the adjoint divisor of C', i.e. the 0-dimensional subscheme of $\mathbb{P}^2$, which is given by the homogeneous ideal $I^{g-4} \cap I_1 \cap I_2 \cap \ldots \cap I_{2g-6}$, where each I_i is the ideal of the point O_i and I is the ideal of O. Let Z' and Z'' be the subschemes of Z defined by the ideals :
$$I^{g-5} \cap I_1 \cap I_2 \cap \ldots \cap I_{2g-6} , \quad I^{g-6} \cap I_1 \cap I_2 \cap \ldots \cap I_{2g-6}.$$

Proposition 2.5 : *Let C be a bielliptic curve of genus $g \geq 6$, and let C' be a plane model of minimal degree of C , constructed as in our Theorem 2.3. Then C' possesses four bitangent lines (and $2g - 2$ tangent lines) passing through O . Moreover*

    i) Z' imposes independent conditions to the plane curves of degree $g - 3$.

    ii) Z'' does not impose independent conditions to the plane curves of degree $g - 4$.

Proof: Denote by $| D |$ the complete linear g_4^1 cut out on C' by the lines through O. Since $| D |$ is composed with the γ_2^1, $| D |$ is the lift of a g_2^1 on E , which has exactly four divisors of type $2P$, $P \in E$. Hence the four lines through O which cut on C the divisors $\pi^{-1}(2P)$ are bitangent to C'.

The remaining $2g - 2$ tangents corresponds to the ramification points of π (see $[\mathbf{DC}]$).

The last part of the corollary follows immediately by observing that the residual linear series to $| D |$ and to $| 2D |$ with respect to the
canonical series are complete and of dimensions $g - 4$ and $g - 6$, respectively.

Remark 2.6 : From the data in the plane it is possible to recover the elliptic curve E. In fact let H be the hyperplane in the canonical space of C containing the $2g - 2$ ramification points of π. In the projection from $P_1, \ldots, P_{g-3}$, the elliptic normal curve $\Gamma = S \cap H$ is projected into a plane curve Γ' of degree $g - 1$ possessing a $(g - 3)$-fold point in O. It is easy to check that the four bitangent lines to C' are tangents for Γ'. So, viewing $\mathbb{P}^1$ as the space parameterizing the pencil of lines through O, its double covering branched at those four points which represent the four bitangent lines is E.

Among the curves of type C' with genus ≥ 10, the conditions $i)$ and $ii)$ above do characterize the bielliptic ones. Namely we have

Proposition 2.7: *Let B be a plane curve of type C', with genus $g \geq 10$. Let Z' and Z'' be as defined above. If Z' and Z'' satisfy conditions $i)$ and $ii)$ of Prop.2.5, then B is bielliptic.*

In order to prove the proposition we need the following two results:

Remark 2.8. Let C be a 4-gonal curve of genus ≥ 7, then any g^1_4 on C is complete, without fixed points and such that (by Clifford's Lemma) :

$$3 \leq h^0(\mathcal{O}_C(2D)) \leq 4, \text{ where } D \in g^1_4.$$

According to the two possibilities $h^0(\mathcal{O}_C(2D)) = 3, 4$, we will say that a g^1_4 is of *type I* or *II* , respectively. This definition is due to M.Coppens (see [**Co**] also for a result similar to the following) :

Lemma 2.9 : *Let C be a 4-gonal curve of genus $g \geq 10$.*
Then either C has a unique g^1_4, which must be of type I, or C is bielliptic.

Proof: Let g, g' be two g^1_4's on C. If they were independent we would have that $g(C) \leq 9$, by 0.2, contrary to our hypothesis.

Then g and g' are dependent i.e. they are both composed with the same involution on C (necessarily an involution of degree 2).

In this case let $\psi : C \to \mathbb{P}^1 \times \mathbb{P}^1$ be the map associated to (g, g'); viewing $\mathbb{P}^1 \times \mathbb{P}^1$ as a quadric in $\mathbb{P}^3$ we have $\deg \psi(C) = 4$, so its genus can only be 0 or 1. The first case cannot occur otherwise C would be hyperelliptic so $g(\psi(C)) = 1$, i.e. C is bielliptic.

Now suppose that there is a unique g^1_4 on C. If the g^1_4 is of type II, denote by g^3_8 the linear series $|2D|$, for $D \in g^1_4$.

Since the g^1_4 is without fixed points, the same is true for our g^3_8, hence it defines a morphism whose image is a curve of degree 8 or 4 in $\mathbb{P}^3$ (necessarily non-degenerate); in the latter case C is bielliptic. In the first case it is well known that all such curves must have genus ≤ 9, against our hypothesis, so the g^1_4 must be of type I.

Proof of 2.7: From $i)$ it follows that the g^1_4 cut out by the lines through O is complete and without fixed points, so B cannot be hyperelliptic. Note that B cannot be trigonal either, by 0.2.

If D is a divisor of the above g^1_4, from $ii)$ it follows that $h^0(\mathcal{O}_B(2D)) = 4$ and therefore, by Lemma 2.9, we have that B is bielliptic.

For curves of type C' with $4 \leq g \leq 9$ one can find stronger conditions on Z' and Z'' which imply the biellipticity, but for the moment we have not been able to put them in a "nice enough" form, so we are not going to treat this case.

REFERENCES

[**A.C.G.H**]: E. Arbarello, M. Cornalba, J. P. Griffiths, J. Harris: *Geometry of Algebraic Curves* , vol. I, Grun. der Math. Wiss. 267 Springer Verlag, 1985

[**Ca**] : G.Castelnuovo. *Sulle serie algebriche di punti appartenenti ad una curva algebrica.* Rend. d. R. Acc. Lincei (5) **15**, (1906), 337-359.

[**C – S**]: C.Ciliberto, E.Sernesi: *Singularities of the theta divisor and congruences of planes.* Preprint.

[**Co**]: M.Coppens. *A study of 4-gonal curves of genus $g \geq 7$.* Preprint, R.U. Utrecht, **221**.

[**DC**] : A.Del Centina. *Remarks on curves admitting an Involution of genus ≥ 1 and some applications.* Boll. U.M.I. (6) $4 - B$, (1985), $671 - 683$.

[**E – C**]: F.Enriques, O.Chisini. *Lezioni sulla teoria geometrica delle equazioni e delle funzioni algebriche.* Voll. III, Zanichelli, Bologna (1915-18).

[**F**]: H.Farkas. *Remarks on automorphisms of compact Riemann Surfaces.* Ann. Math. Studies **79** (1974), 121-144.

[**F – L**]: W.Fulton, R.Lazarsfeld. *On the connectedness of degeneracy loci and special divisors.* Acta Math. **146** (1981), 271-283.

[**H1**]: R.Horiuchi. *On the existence of meromorphic functions with certain lower order on non-hyperelliptic Riemann Surfaces.* J.Math. Kyoto Univ. **21-2** (1981), 397-416.

[**H2**]: R.Horiuchi. *Meromorphic functions on 2-hyperelliptic Riemann Surfaces.* Japan J. Math. **7** (1981), 301-306.

[**K**] : E. Kani. *On Castelnuovo's equivalence defect.* J.Reine Ang. Math. **352**, (1984), 24-69.

[**K – L**] : G. Kempf, D.Laksov. *The determinantal formula of Schubert Calculus.* Acta Math. **132**, (1974), 153-162.

[**M**] : G.Martens. *Funktionen von vorgegebenen Ordnung auf komplexen Kurven.* J.Reine Ang. Math. **320** (1980), 68-85.

[**Te**]: M.Teixidor. *For which Jacobi varieties is* Singθ *reducible ?* J. Reine Angew. Math. **354** (1984), 141-149.

[**W**]: G.E.Welters: *The surface $C - C$ on Jacobi varieties and second order theta functions.* Acta Math. 157 (1986), 1-22.

Andrea Del Centina, Dipartimento di Matematica, Università di Ferrara, Via Machiavelli 35, $I - 44100$, Ferrara, Italy.

Alessandro Gimigliano, Dipartimento di Matematica, Università di Bologna, Piazza di Porta S.Donato 5, $I - 40127$, Bologna, Italy.

C: Gaps in the Rao Module of an Algebraic Space Curve

and the Property "Numerically Subcanonical"

E. D. Davis
Department of Mathematics
State University of New York - Albany
Albany, New York 12222-0001
U.S.A.

GAPS IN THE RAO MODULE OF AN ALGEBRAIC SPACE CURVE AND THE PROPERTY "NUMERICALLY SUBCANONICAL"

Edward D. Davis*

ABSTRACT: It is well known that the Rao module of an integral (even smooth) projective algebraic curve in 3-space may have gaps in its support; but it seems not to be known if that can be so for subcanonical curves. An earlier work suggested that the existence of a gap would imply the failure of a certain numerical condition necessarily satisfied by subcanonical curves; and this note shows that a gap does force that failure—*for nonsubcanonical curves*—and that furthermore, there do not exist "numerically small" examples of subcanonical curves with gaps. Any such example must be the zerolocus of a section of a vector bundle with a rather large "spectrum", many members of that spectrum occurring with multiplicity at least 2. Indeed, there exists no integral example with index of speciality less than 25 or of degree less than 260; and there exists no example (allowing reducible and/or nonreduced) of degree less than 76.

KEYWORDS: (subcanonical) curves and vector bundles in 3-space, support of the Rao module, spectrum of a vector bundle, Castelnuovo theory, Hilbert function, plane section.

1991 MATHEMATICS SUBJECT CLASSIFICATION: 14H50, 14F05.

ACKNOWLEDGEMENTS: For many stimulating conversations on the subject of this article, special thanks to L. Chiantini, A. Lascu, M. Roggero and P. Valabrega.

AUTHOR'S ADDRESSES:
    MATH DEPT SUNYA, ALBANY NY 12222 (USA)
    EDAVIS@MATH.ALBANY.EDU

* Supported in part by the Consiglio Nazionale delle Ricerche as Professore Visitatore at the Politecnico di Torino.

INTRODUCTION AND SOME STANDING NOTATION

This paper is the sequel to [D2], *grosso modo*, the phantom §4 to which the concluding remarks of §3 of that paper allude. To explain what that is all about we must first set a bit of notation and recall the concepts "gap" and "numerically subcanonical".

P denotes $\mathbf{P}^3$ (over an algebraically closed field), and *curve* means "1–equidimensional *CM* closed subscheme of **P**". X is always a curve. Any unexplained notation is that of [AG]. We put: $e = e(X) = \max\{j|h^1\mathcal{O}_X(j) \neq 0\}$ (index of speciality of X); $d = d_X = \deg X$; $g = g_X = p_a(X)$ (arithmetic genus of X). "X is f-$\mathcal{SC}$" means $\omega_X = \mathcal{O}_X(f)$, in which case $h^1\mathcal{O}_X(i) = h^0\mathcal{O}_X(f-i)$ $(\forall i)$ and (hence) $2g-2 = fd$. $\mathcal{SC}$ (subcanonical) means f-$\mathcal{SC}$ for some f. Recall: reduced and $\mathcal{SC}$ implies e-$\mathcal{SC}$.

Definitions. γ is a *gap* in the function f from **Z** to **N** if there exist $i < \gamma < j$ with $f(\gamma) = 0 \neq f(i)f(j)$. In case $f(\cdot) = h^1\mathcal{F}(\cdot)$ for some coherent sheaf $\mathcal{F}$ on **P**, we say "γ is an $\mathcal{F}$-gap" (a "gap in the Rao module" of $\mathcal{F}$); and when $\mathcal{F} = \mathcal{I}_X$, we say "$\gamma$ is an X-gap". NSC is the acronym of [D1] for "numerically subcanonical". $NSC(j)$ holds for X means: $h^1\mathcal{O}_X(i) = h^0\mathcal{O}_X(e-i)$ $(\forall i \geq j)$. NSC denotes $NSC(j)$ $(\forall j)$, in which case $2g-2 = ed$.

The rest of this introduction concerns integral curves. Then [Ro, (2.2)]: $\mathcal{SC}$ iff NSC; $NSC(j)$ iff $h^1\mathcal{O}_X(j) = h^0\mathcal{O}_X(e-j)$. And for γ an X-gap: $e+1 \geq \gamma \geq 5$ ([B], [D2]); if $NSC(\gamma-1)$ holds, then $e \geq \gamma \geq 6$, and $NSC(4)$ fails if $\gamma = 6$, in which case $e = \gamma$ [D2, (3.1b)]. By Rao [Ra], curve–gaps abound. However, there is apparently no known example of a subcanonical curve (equivalently, a rank 2 vector bundle on **P**) with a gap. For the purposes of exposition, consider this assertion, hereafter denoted $\mathcal{A}(n)$.

$$\gamma \leq n \text{ an } X\text{-gap} \implies NSC(e+4-\gamma) \text{ fails (i.e., } h^1\mathcal{O}_X(e+4-\gamma) \neq h^0\mathcal{O}_X(\gamma-4)).$$

$\mathcal{A}(n)$ implies "no gaps for subcanonical X with $e \leq n$"; and $\mathcal{A}(n)$ $(\forall n)$ implies "no gaps for rank 2 vector bundles on **P**". So [D2, §3] proves $\mathcal{A}(6)$, but also explains how certain technical impediments block extending its methods (in general) beyond $n = 6$. However, it further remarks that at least those impediments disappear in characteristic 0, because of Harris' Uniform Position Lemma and Laudal's Lemma.

This paper blends those methods with certain vector bundle techniques to test the validity of $\mathcal{A}(n)$ in characteristic 0. §1 recalls certain facts of "Castelnuovo Theory" and does that (unfortunately extensive) elaboration of [D2, §3] called for there, and in doing so proves: $\mathcal{A}(n)$ $(\forall n)$ for *nonsubcanonical* X. So the question returns to: *Can subcanonical curves have a gaps?* Perhaps. But in §2 we see that there can be no "numerically small" examples: $\mathcal{A}(24)$ holds, and $d \geq 260$ if X has a gap. Moreover, if there were such an X with $d = 260$, then the unique gap would be $e = 25$, and X would necessarily be the zerolocus of a section of $\mathcal{F}(15)$, $\mathcal{F}$ a (normalized) stable rank 2 bundle on **P** with Chern classes $c_1 = -1$ and $c_2 = 50$. The familiar examples of bundles with those Chern classes of course do not have gaps. If we look for examples (of subcanonical X with a gap) defined by stable bundles with $c_1 = 0$, then the first possibility is an $\mathcal{F}$ with $c_2 = 53$, X defined by a section of $\mathcal{F}(15)$, with $e = 26$ the unique gap. With nonstable bundles the numbers for those "first chances" are: in the semistable case, $c_2 = 94$, X defined by a section of $\mathcal{F}(26)$, with $e = 48$ the unique gap; in the nonsemistable case, $c_2 = 97-c_1$, X defined by a section of $\mathcal{F}(28)$, with $e = 52+c_1$ the unique gap. §2 develops those numbers, showing that they uniquely determine the "spectrum" of that (possibly nonexistent) bundle $\mathcal{F}$.

Which would be the better answer to our motivating question? "No Gaps" would be an intellectually satisfying (albeit probably useless) theorem; but "Gaps Exist" would augment (intertestingly?) the catalog of known bundles on **P**. §3 begins to decipher, for what seem to be the most promising cases, the geometric information (both curvewise and bundlewise) encoded in the numerical data developed by §2—with the hope of delivering suggestive (and possibly usable) material into the hands of the bundle specialists.

§1. Some points of Castelnuovo theory recalled and applied.

We subsume all notation and definitions of our introductory section, and let $\bar{\mathbf{P}}$ denote *the* general plane in $\mathbf{P}$, $R \equiv H^0_* \mathcal{O}_{\mathbf{P}}$ and $\bar{R} \equiv H^0_* \mathcal{O}_{\bar{\mathbf{P}}}$ the homogeneous coordinate algebras. For our curve X: $\bar{X} \equiv X \cap \bar{\mathbf{P}}$; $I = I_X \equiv H^0_* \mathcal{I}_X$, its homogeneous ideal in R; $M = M_X \equiv H^1_* \mathcal{I}_X$, its Rao Module; H is its Hilbert Function ($H(\jmath) = H(X; \jmath) \equiv h^0 \mathcal{O}_{\mathbf{P}}(\jmath) - h^0 \mathcal{I}_X(\jmath)$). $\mathcal{I}_{\bar{X}}$, $\bar{I}$, $\bar{M}$ and $\bar{H}$ denote the corresponding entities for $\bar{X}$, viewed as a subscheme of $\bar{\mathbf{P}}$. For S any projective scheme: $\alpha(S) \equiv \min\{\jmath | (I_S)_\jmath \neq 0\}$; if $\mathrm{codim} S \geq 2$, $\beta(S) \equiv \min\{\jmath | \gcd(I_S)_\jmath = 1\}$. CI means "2-codimensional complete intersection" (in any projective space), $CI(m,n)$ denoting such defined by hypersurfaces of degrees $m \leq n$. This from [D1] and/or [D2].

$\quad s = s(X) \equiv \sigma(\bar{X}) \equiv \min\{\jmath | h^1 \mathcal{I}_{\bar{X}}(\jmath-1) = 0\} = \max\{\jmath | h^1 \mathcal{I}_{\bar{X}}(\jmath-2) \neq 0\}$.

$\quad a = a(X) \equiv \alpha(\bar{X})$; $\alpha = \alpha(X)$. (Clearly: $\alpha \geq a$.)

$\quad b = b(X) \equiv \beta(\bar{X})$; $\beta = \beta(X)$. (Clearly: $\beta \geq b$; for integral X with $\alpha \neq a$, $\alpha \geq b$.)

Aside ([CV], [RV]) for integral SC X: either $CI(\alpha, \beta)$ (iff $M = 0$) or $\mathrm{supp} M \supset [\alpha-2, \beta-2]$.

As in [D2, §3], we first recall (here in (1.1)-(1.3) below) certain basic numerical data concerning the growth of $\bar{H}$, the relationships among I, $\bar{I}$, M and $\bar{M}$, and the those between the Rao modules and plane sections of linked curves. (See [D2] for references.)

Notation. Hereafter: $\rho_\jmath = \rho_\jmath(X) \equiv h^1 \mathcal{I}_X(\jmath)$; when $\rho \neq 0$, $\mu_0 = \mu_0(X)$ and $\mu_1 = \mu_1(X)$ denote the min and max, respectively, of its support; $\delta_\jmath = \delta_\jmath(X) \equiv \Delta \bar{H}(X; \jmath)$. ($\Delta$ denotes the difference operator on maps from $\mathbf{Z}$ to $\mathbf{Z}$: $\Delta f(\jmath) = f(\jmath) - f(\jmath-1)$.) $\Gamma(m, n) = \Gamma(m, n; \cdot)$ denotes the first difference of the Hilbert function of a $CI(m,n)$ in $\bar{\mathbf{P}}$—more precisely:

$$\Gamma(m, n; \jmath) = \max\{\Theta(\jmath), 0\}, \text{ where } \Theta(\jmath) = \min\{\jmath+1, m, m+n-1-\jmath\}.$$

Define: $\mu = \mu(X) \equiv \max\{\jmath < s | \delta_\jmath = \Gamma(a, b; \jmath)\}$. *The arguments below lean heavily on the behavior of $\Delta \bar{H}$, and are best understood by thinking in terms of the graph of that function and its relationship to the graphs of the several $\Gamma(m, n)$ encountered in those arguments.*

(1.1) RECALL: on the growth of $\bar{H}$ (valid for any 1-dimensional subscheme of $\mathbf{P}$).

$\quad$ (a) $a \leq b \leq s \leq a+b-1$; $0 \leq \delta_\jmath \leq \Gamma(a, b; \jmath) \, (\forall \jmath)$; $\delta_\jmath \neq 0 \Longleftrightarrow 0 \leq \jmath \leq s-1$.

$\quad$ (b) $\delta_\jmath = \Gamma(a, b; \jmath) \, (\forall \jmath \leq \mu)$; $a-1 \leq \mu$; $\Delta \delta_\jmath \leq \Delta \Gamma(a, b; \jmath) \, (\forall \jmath \leq s)$.

$\quad$ (c) $\Sigma\{\delta_\imath | \imath \leq \jmath\} = \bar{H}(\jmath) \leq d \, (\forall \jmath)$; $\bar{H}(\jmath) = d \Longleftrightarrow \jmath \geq s-1$.

(1.2) RECALL: the "Castelnuovo sequence". The restriction from $\mathbf{P}$ to $\bar{\mathbf{P}}$ induces this exact sequence (of cohomology modules) in the category of graded R-modules.

$$0 \to I(-1) \to I \to \bar{I} \to M(-1) \to M \to \bar{M} \to H^1_* \mathcal{O}_X(-1) \to H^1_* \mathcal{O}_X$$

The sequel denotes the Hilbert functions of $\mathrm{coker}(M(-1) \to M)$, $\ker(M(-1) \to M)$ and $\mathrm{coker}(I \to \bar{I})$ by C, K and $\bar{C}$, respectively, and uses these consequences of that sequence (which, with those consequences, is valid for any 1-dimensional subscheme of $\mathbf{P}$).

$\quad$ (a) $K(\jmath) = 0 \, (\forall \jmath \leq a-1)$; $C(\jmath) = 0 \, (\forall \jmath \geq s-1)$.

$\quad$ (b) $\bar{C} = K = h^0 \mathcal{I}_{\bar{X}}(\cdot) - \Delta h^0 \mathcal{I}_X(\cdot) = \Delta H - \bar{H}$.

$\quad$ (c) $e = \max\{\jmath | \mathrm{coker}(M_{\jmath+1} \to \bar{M}_{\jmath+1}) \neq 0\} \leq s-3$.

(1.3) RECALL: on Liaison. Consider a curve Y linked to X by a $CI(m, n)$, using this notation: $\delta'_\jmath \equiv \Delta \bar{H}(Y; m+n-2-\jmath)$; $\rho'_\jmath \equiv h^1 \mathcal{I}_Y(m+n-2-\jmath)$. Then:

$\quad$ (a) $\delta_\jmath + \delta'_\jmath = \Gamma(m, n; \jmath) \, (\forall \jmath)$. Hence: $s(Y) = m+n-2-\mu$ if $m = a$, $m+n-1-a$ if $m > a$.

$\quad$ (b) $\rho'_\jmath = \rho_{\jmath-2} \, (\forall \jmath)$. Hence: $\mu_0(Y) = m+n-4-\mu_1$; $\mu_1(Y) = m+n-4-\mu_0$.

(1.4) LEMMAS: on the vanishing and nonvanishing of C and K. Recall that $\mu_0 > 0$ when X is integral, because $\rho_\jmath = h^0 \mathcal{O}_X(\jmath) - H(\jmath) \, (\forall \jmath)$. In addition to (1.2a), these facts obtain.

$\quad$ (a) Suppose: $\jmath > b$ and $\Delta \delta_\jmath \geq -1$. Then: $K(\jmath-1) = 0 \Longrightarrow K(\jmath) = 0$.

$\quad$ (b) For $\mu_0 \leq \jmath < a$: $C(\jmath) \neq 0 \, (\jmath \neq a-1)$; $C(a-1) \neq 0$ if $\delta_a = a$.

$\quad$ (c) For integral X with $\alpha = a$: $K(\jmath) = 0 \, (\forall \jmath \leq b-1)$.

$\quad$ (d) For integral X with $\alpha = a$ and $\mu_0 \leq \jmath < b$: $C(\jmath) \neq 0 \, (\jmath \neq b-1)$; $C(b-1) \neq 0$ if $b \leq \mu$.

(1.5) LEMMAS: for γ an X-gap.

    (a) $a \leq \gamma \leq \min\{s-3, e+1\}$ in any case; $\gamma \geq b-1$ if X is integral.

    (b) For $\gamma \geq b-1$: $\beta \leq \gamma+1$; $s \leq a+b-2$; $\delta_J > s-J$ $(b-1 \leq J \leq \gamma+1)$; $\gamma \leq \mu \implies \alpha \neq a$.

    (c) For $\gamma \geq b-1$ and $s = a+b-2$: $\gamma+1 \leq \mu$ (so by (b), $\alpha \neq a$); $\beta > b$.

    (d) For $\gamma = b-1$: $s \leq a+b-3$; $a < b$; $\mu < b$; $\alpha = \beta = b$ if X is integral.

Proofs. [D2, (3.6)] (or its proof) contains (1.4a, b); and [D2, (3.7)] contains all of (1.5) but the last two assertions of (b) and the last assertion of (d). By (1.1), $b \leq s \leq a+b-1$ and for all $b-1 \leq J \leq s$: $\delta_J \geq s-J$, equality iff $\Delta\delta_\imath = -1$ $(J < \imath \leq s)$. So (1.4a) gives the third assertion of (1.5b). Assume $\gamma \leq \mu$, whence by (1.1), $\delta_\imath = \Gamma(a, b; \imath) (\forall \imath \leq \gamma)$. Suppose further: $\gamma \geq b-1$ is an X-gap and $\alpha = a$. Take Y as in (1.3), with $(m, n) = (a, \gamma+1)$. Then by (1.3): $s(Y) \leq a-1$ and $a-3$ is a Y-gap. Impossible, by (1.5a) applied to Y. That proves the fourth assertion of (1.5b). In any case, if X is integral and $\alpha = a$, then I_a contains irreducible forms, whence $b-1 \leq \mu$. That remark implies, by (1.5b), the last assertion of (1.5d), and by (1.2b), proves (1.4c). To prove (1.4d) take Y as in (1.3), with $m = a$ and $n \gg 0$. (1.4d) then follows from (1.3) by applying (1.4a) to Y.

    Aside: the sequel makes no further use of (1.3).

(1.6) RECALL: on [D1, §1], the functions F and G and the formulas (†) and (‡).

    Notation: $\tilde{J} \equiv e+1-J$; $\Phi(J) \equiv \Sigma\{\delta_\imath | \imath > J\}$.

    Definitions: $F(J) \equiv h^1 \mathcal{O}_X(J) - h^0 \mathcal{O}_X(e-J)$; $G(J) \equiv \bar{H}(J) + \bar{H}(\tilde{J}) - d$.

    Observations: $G(J) = G(\tilde{J}) = \bar{H}(\tilde{J}) - \Phi(J) = \bar{H}(J) - \Phi(\tilde{J})$; $G(J) = 0 (\forall J \geq s-1)$.

First these formal consequences of the definitions (the first two are (†) and (‡) of [D1]).

    (a) $\Delta F(J) = C(J) + C(\tilde{J}) + G(J)$.

    (b) $\Delta G(J) = \delta_J - \delta_{\tilde{J}+1}$; so by (1.1), $\Delta G(J) = J - \tilde{J} - 1$ if $a-1 \geq J > \tilde{J} \geq -1$.

    (c) $NSC(J-1) \iff \Delta F(\imath) = 0 (\forall \imath \geq J) \iff C(\imath) + C(\tilde{\imath}) = -G(\imath) (\forall \imath \geq J)$.

    (d) $NSC \iff NSC(J) (\exists J \leq \frac{e}{2})$.

Then these two excerpts from [D1, (1.3)], really addenda to (1.1) and (1.2c) above.

    (e) For $J \geq b-1$: $\Delta G(J) \geq 0$, equality iff $G(J-1) = 0$.

    (f) For $b-1 \leq J \leq s-1$: $\Delta G(J) = 0 \iff e = s-3$ and $\Delta\delta_\imath = -1 (J < \imath \leq s)$.

(1.7) LEMMAS: for $\gamma \geq b-1$ an X-gap.

    (a) In case $\mu_0 > 0$ and $NSC(\gamma-1)$ holds: $\gamma \leq e$.

    (b) In case $NSC(\gamma-1)$ holds: $\gamma > a$; $C(\tilde{\gamma}) = -G(\gamma) > -G(\gamma+1) > 0$.

    (c) In case $a = b = \gamma-1$ and $s = 2a-2$: $NSC(\tilde{\gamma}+3)$ fails.

Proof. It suffices to prove (c) because [D2, (3.10)–(3.11)] contain (a) and (b). Since $e \leq s-3$, by (1.2c), $\tilde{\gamma} \leq a-5$; whence it suffices to deduce an absurdity from $NSC(a-2)$. Put: $A = \Sigma\{-G(\imath) | a-1 \leq \imath \leq a+1\}$; $B = \Sigma\{C(\imath) + C(\tilde{\imath}) | a-1 \leq \imath \leq a+1\}$. Then by (1.6c, f) and (b): $A = B$; $A \geq 9$. The absurdity will come from showing $B \leq 8$. Now since in any case, $C(\imath) = \rho_\imath - \rho_{\imath-1} + K(\imath)$, by (1.2a, b):
$$B = \rho_{\tilde{\gamma}+2} - \rho_{\tilde{\gamma}-1} - \rho_{a-2} + K(a) + K(a+1) \leq h^0 \mathcal{I}_{\bar{X}}(a) + h^0 \mathcal{I}_{\bar{X}}(a+1).$$
But by (1.1) and the definition of "Hilbert Function":
$$h^0 \mathcal{I}_{\bar{X}}(a) + h^0 \mathcal{I}_{\bar{X}}(a+1) = 2(a+1-\delta_a) + (a+2-\delta_{a+1}).$$
Consequently, since by (1.5c), $\delta_J = \Gamma(a, a; J) (\forall J \leq a+2)$, $B \leq 8$. QED.

    Remarks. Suppose γ is an X-gap. Recall (cf. introductory section above) that we aim to prove (at least in certain cases) the failure of $NSC(\tilde{\gamma}+3)$ when X is integral. Then there is no loss in assuming: $\mu_0 > 0$; $NSC(\tilde{\gamma}+3)$ holds; and, by (1.5a), $\gamma \geq b-1$. Under the last two of those hypotheses, a simple calculation taking into account (1.5a, b, d) and (1.2c) shows: $\gamma-1 \geq \tilde{\gamma}+3$, whence the implications of $NSC(\gamma-1)$ developed in (1.7) hold. The reader may now safely assume "integral and characteristic 0"; we do so in stages in order to indicate where its several implications come into play.

STANDING HYPOTHESES ON X: $\gamma \geq b-1$ is an X-gap; $NSC(\tilde{\gamma}+3)$ holds; $\mu_0 > 0$.

Notation. Apart from the material recalled in (1.1)–(1.7) above and to be recalled in §2 below, the sequel is based on the ideas in the proof of (1.7c). To facilitate the further implementation of those ideas we define for our curve X these integers:

$$\xi \equiv \gamma-(b-1); \quad \eta \equiv b-a; \quad \zeta \equiv a+b-4-e; \quad z \equiv a+b-1-s; \quad \lambda_j \equiv -G(j); \quad \lambda \equiv \lambda_{b-1}.$$

(1.8) OBSERVATIONS. As already noted, $NSC(\gamma-1)$ necessarily holds. Moreover:
   (a) By (1.2c) and (1.5): $\zeta \geq z \geq 1$; $\xi+\zeta \geq 2$; $\zeta+\alpha-a \geq 2$; $\xi+\alpha-a \geq 1$ for integral X.
   (b) By (1.7a,b): $e \geq \gamma > a$; $\tilde{\gamma} = a-2-(\zeta+\xi) \geq \mu_0 \geq 1$; $\gamma \geq 2\xi+2+\zeta+\eta$; $\lambda_\gamma > \lambda_{\gamma+1} > 0$.
   (c) For $b-1 \leq j \leq e+3$. By (b) and (1.1): $\delta_j - \delta_{\tilde{j}+1} = \delta_j - (e+3-j) = \delta_j - (\Gamma(a,b;j)-\zeta)$. $\lambda_j \geq \gamma-j+2$ $(j \leq \gamma+2)$, $\lambda = \lambda_j + \Sigma\{\delta_i - \Gamma(a,b;i)+\zeta | b \leq i \leq j\} \geq \xi+2$, and $\Delta^2\lambda_j \geq 0$: by (1.6b,e), because $-\Delta\lambda_i = \delta_i - \delta_{\tilde{i}+1}$ $(\forall i)$ and $\lambda_{\gamma+1} \neq 0$. And so, again by (1.6b,e): $\lambda_i \geq 0 \geq \Delta\lambda_i$ $(\forall i \geq \gamma+2)$; $\Delta\lambda_i < 0$ $(b-1 \leq i \leq \gamma+2)$; $\Delta^2\lambda_i \geq 0$ $(\forall i \geq b)$.
   (d) Because $\lambda = \Phi(b-1) - \bar{H}(\tilde{\gamma}+\xi)$: $d = \bar{H}(b-1) + \binom{a-\zeta}{2} + \lambda$.
   (e) By (b), $NSC(a-\zeta-\xi+1)$ holds; by (1.6c), $\lambda_i = C(i) + C(\tilde{i})$ $(\forall i > j)$ if $NSC(j)$ holds.

REVISED HYPOTHESES ON X: integral; γ an X-gap; $NSC(\tilde{\gamma}+3)$ holds; $b-1 \leq \mu$.

Remarks. The new hypotheses of course include the old ones. Obviously any X with $a = b$ satisfies the last hypothesis, as does any X with $\bar{I}_a$ containing an irreducible form, in particular any integral X with $\alpha = a$ or with $\bar{X}$ in "uniform position" (in the sense of Harris [Hs]). Recall that $\bar{X}$ is in uniform position for all integral "reflexive" X [Rn], and so for all integral X in characteristic 0 [Hs]. By "integral": $h^0\mathcal{I}_X(j) \geq h^0\mathcal{O}_{\mathbf{P}}(j-\alpha)$, equality iff $j < \beta$; $\alpha \geq b$ if $\alpha \neq a$. In any case: $b-1 \leq \mu$ iff $h^0\mathcal{I}_{\bar{X}}(j) = h^0\mathcal{O}_{\bar{\mathbf{P}}}(j-a) + \Sigma\{a-\delta_i | b \leq i \leq j\}$ $(\forall j)$.

OBSERVATION (characteristic 0): $\alpha \neq a \implies z > \eta$.

Proof. In any case, by (1.1), $d = \bar{H}(b-1) + \Phi(b-1)$. But since $b-1 \leq \mu$, by (1.1), $\bar{H}(b-1) = ab - \binom{a}{2} = a^2+a\eta - \binom{a}{2}$; and by (1.5b) and (1.1), $\Phi(b-1) \geq \binom{a-z}{2}$. But "Laudal's Lemma" (Gruson–Peskine version [GP]) says: $d \leq a^2+1$. Hence: $\binom{a}{2} - \binom{a-z}{2} \geq a\eta$. So $z > \eta$, because $\binom{a}{2} - \binom{a-z}{2} = az - \binom{z+1}{2}$ and $z \geq 1$.
   Because $\zeta \geq z$ in any case, *that observation motivates this.*

ADDITIONAL STANDING HYPOTHESIS ON X: $\zeta > \eta$ when $\alpha \neq a$.

(1.9) PROPOSITION. X is subcanonical. Moreover: $\xi \geq 2$ if $\eta \leq 1$ (or if $\alpha = a$).

Proof. By (1.6d) and the hypothesis $NSC(\tilde{\gamma}+3)$: NSC (and so SC, on account of "integral") holds if $e \geq 2(\tilde{\gamma}+3)$. Hence this formal consequence of that fact and definitions: $2\xi+\zeta+\eta \geq 6 \implies SC$. So we need only eliminate the few possibilities for (ξ, η, ζ) not covered by that fact but permitted by (1.8a), which is subsumed below in checking those cases. We may assume $\eta \neq 0$: otherwise, by (1.7b,c), $\xi \geq \max\{2, 4-\zeta\}$. Suppose $a = \alpha$, in which case $\zeta \geq 2$ and $\xi \geq 1$, and we need only eliminate the case $\xi = 1$ (i.e., $\gamma = b$). In that event, applying (1.8c,e), and then (1.2a,b), (1.4d) and (1.1), and then (1.8c) again yields:

$$0 < \lambda_\gamma = C(\tilde{\gamma}) \leq \rho_{\tilde{b}} - \rho_{b-1} + K(b) \leq \tilde{b}+1-a+h^0\mathcal{I}_{\bar{X}}(b) - \Delta h^0\mathcal{I}_X(b) \leq \delta_{\tilde{b}+1} - \delta_b = \Delta\lambda_b < 0.$$

So we may assume $\alpha \neq a$. Then: $\zeta > \eta$; by (1.2b), $K(j) \leq h^0\mathcal{I}_{\bar{X}}(j)$, equality for $j < b$. If $\eta = 1$, then by (1.8b), $\xi \geq 1$ and we must eliminate the possibility $\xi = 1$ ($\gamma = b$ again). In that event, by (1.8b,e), (1.2a,b) and (1.4b):

$$\lambda_\gamma + \lambda_{\gamma-1} = C(a) + C(a-2-\zeta) + C(a-3-\zeta) \leq K(b) + K(a) - \rho_{a-1} + \rho_{a-2-\zeta} \leq 3+a-\delta_b-\zeta.$$

But by (1.8c): $\lambda_\gamma + \lambda_{\gamma-1} = 2\lambda - (\delta_\gamma - \delta_{\bar\gamma+1}) \geq 5 + a - \delta_b - \zeta$. That leaves only the possibility $(\xi, \eta, \zeta) = (0, 2, 3)$. In that event, by (1.8b, e), (1.4b) and (1.2b):
$$\lambda_\gamma + \lambda_{\gamma-1} \leq K(b-1) + K(b-2) - \rho_{b-3} + \rho_{a-4} \leq h^0\mathcal{O}_{\bar{\mathbf{P}}}(1) + h^0\mathcal{O}_{\bar{\mathbf{P}}}(0) - 3 = 1.$$
But by (1.8b, c): $\lambda_\gamma + \lambda_{\gamma-1} \geq 5$.

(1.10) COROLLARY: for nonsubcanonical integral curves Y. $\mathcal{A}(n)$ (see introductory section) is valid for all n in characteristic 0, and in arbitrary characteristic if $\alpha(Y) = a(Y)$.

(1.11) NOTATION-OBSERVATION. Define integers m, n, p, q and k as follows:
$$m \equiv \min\{\zeta, \eta\}; \quad n \equiv \max\{\imath | 2\imath \leq \zeta + \eta - 2m\}; \quad p \equiv |\zeta - \eta| - 2n;$$
$$\text{i.e., } n = [\tfrac{|\zeta - \eta|}{2}], \text{ and } p \text{ is the parity of } \zeta - \eta;$$
$$k \equiv \xi + m + n; \text{ for } m = \eta, \, q \equiv a - n; \text{ for } m \neq \eta, \, q \equiv a + n + p.$$
Then these formulas and estimates follow formally from definitions, (1.8b) and (1.9).

(a) $e + 4 = 2q - p$; $\gamma = q - 1 + k$; $q \geq k + 3 + p$, equality iff $\gamma = e$.
(b) $\tilde\gamma = (q - p) - (k + 2)$; $\tilde\gamma + p + k + 1 \leq a - 1$; $\tilde\gamma + p + k + 1 \leq b - 1$ if $m = \zeta$; $k - n = \xi + m \geq 2$.

Observe that since $b - 1 \leq \mu$, by (1.1), $\bar{H}(b-1) = ab - \binom{a}{2} = a^2 + a\eta - \binom{a}{2}$. Therefore (1.8d) and (a) apply to give these two formulas for d.

(c) $d = a(a + \eta - \zeta) + \binom{\zeta+1}{2} + \lambda$.
(d) $d = q(q - p) - n(n + p) + \binom{\zeta+1}{2} + \lambda$.

Finally, note that we have these cases to consider. (Recall that by (1.8a) and our final standing hypothesis: $\zeta \geq 2$ when $\alpha = a$; $\zeta > \eta$ when $\alpha \neq a$.)

Case 1: $\alpha \neq a$ (so $m = \eta < \zeta$ and $n + p > 0$).
Case 2: $\alpha = a$, $m = \eta < \zeta$ (so $n + p > 0$).
Case 3: $\alpha = a$, $m = \eta = \zeta$ (so $n + p = 0$).
Case 4: $\alpha = a$, $m = \zeta < \eta$ (so $n + p > 0$).

Bear in mind that each of Cases 1, 2 and 4 has two subcases, "odd" and "even", determined by the value of p, that is, by the parity of e (and $\zeta - \eta$).

(1.12) KEYLEMMA: estimates for d in terms of k, n, and q.

(a) $(\frac{2k+2+p}{2})d + h^0\mathcal{I}_X(\gamma) + \rho_{\bar\gamma-1} = \binom{q+k+2}{3} - \binom{q-k-p}{3} = (\frac{2k+2+p}{2})(q(q-p) + \frac{(k+p)(k+2)}{3})$.
(b) $d - q(q - p) \leq \frac{(k+p)(k+2)}{3} - \vartheta$, where ϑ is as follows.
  Case 1: $\vartheta = 0$.
  Cases 2 and 3: $\vartheta = \frac{(k+2-n)(k+1-n)(k-n)}{3(2k+2+p)}$.
  Case 4: $\vartheta = \frac{(k+2+p+n)(k+1+p+n)(k+p+n)}{3(2k+2+p)}$.
(c) Equality holds in (b) iff $\tilde\gamma = \mu_0$ and either $\alpha > \gamma$ or $\beta > \gamma > \alpha = a$.

Proof. $h^0\mathcal{O}_X(\jmath) - h^1\mathcal{O}_X(\jmath) = \jmath d + 1 - g$ for any curve; but $h^1\mathcal{O}_X(\jmath) = h^0\mathcal{O}_X(\bar\jmath - 1)$ and $ed = 2g - 2$, by "integral and subcanonical". That and the formulas of (1.11a, b) yield:
$$h^0\mathcal{O}_X(\gamma) - h^0\mathcal{O}_X(\bar\gamma - 1) = \gamma d + 1 - g = (\tfrac{2k+2+p}{2})d.$$
Now for any $\imath$: $h^0\mathcal{O}_X(\imath) = H(\imath) + \rho_\imath$; $H(\imath) = \binom{\imath+3}{3} - h^0\mathcal{I}_X(\imath)$. Substituting that information into the equation above and applying the formulas of (1.11a, b) yield the formulas of (a). Then (b) and (c) follow formally, because when $\alpha = a$: $h^0\mathcal{I}_X(\gamma) \geq h^0\mathcal{O}_{\mathbf{P}}(\gamma - a) = \binom{\xi+\eta+2}{3}$.

An immediate corollary of (1.11d) and (1.12b) is this upper bound on λ, which we apply to conclude this section expositorily with provisional estimates of ξ, d, e and γ, and again in §2 to improve those estimates.

(1.13) COROLLARY. With ϑ as in (1.12b): $\lambda \leq n(n + p) - \binom{\zeta+1}{2} + \frac{(k+p)(k+2)}{3} - \vartheta$.

Preview. Our upper and lower bounds on λ given by (1.13) and (1.8c) produce in each of our four cases a lower bound on ξ. Then the formula of (1.11c) and the inequalities of (1.8b) produce lower bounds on d, e and γ. The resulting data are these.

Case 1: $\xi \geq 3$; $d \geq 48$; $e \geq \gamma \geq 9$.
Case 2: $\xi \geq 4$; $d \geq 72$; $e \geq \gamma \geq 12$.
Case 3: $\xi \geq 5$; $d \geq 110$; $e \geq \gamma \geq 16$.
Case 4: $\xi \geq 5$; $d \geq 120$; $e \geq \gamma \geq 17$.

Consequently, no gaps for any integral subcanonical curve Y satisfying either of these two hypotheses: (1) characteristic 0 and $e(Y) \leq 8$; (2) $\alpha(Y) = a(Y)$ and $e(Y) \leq 11$. (2.8) below improves those hypotheses: for (1), $e(Y) \leq 24$; and for (2), $e(Y) \leq 26$. More precisely, (2.7) below shows: $\gamma \geq 26 - p$ in Case 1; $\gamma \geq 28 - p$ in Case 2; $\gamma \geq 48$ in Case 3; $\gamma \geq 52 - p$ in Case 4. Those data result from two new lower bounds on λ (compare (2.5) below with (1.8c) above) and the re-interpretation of (1.12b) as an upper bound on the second Chern class of a certain vector bundle $\mathcal{F}$ associated to X. One of those lower bounds sharpens that of (1.8c), the other bounds that Chern class, which, modulo a certain function of m, n and p is our λ. In fact, η and ζ (and hence m, n and p), as well as ξ and λ are numerical characters of $\mathcal{F}$, and are the same for every (necessarily integral and subcanonical) curve defined (in the sense of [H1]) by any sufficiently general section of any sufficiently high twist of $\mathcal{F}$. More about that at the end of §2.

§2. Application of vector bundle techniques.

The notation and standing hypotheses of the previous sections remain in force. (We have in effect hypothesized that X is an integral subcanonical curve in characteristic 0, with a gap γ, but we do not formally impose that until the end of this section. X is *necessarily* subcanonical, by (1.9) above; and except for one more property—see (2.3f) below—we have assumed all we need of "integral and characteristic 0".) This section continues the examination of the implications of those hypotheses by putting in play: (1) the relationship developed in [H1] between curves and rank 2 reflexive sheaves in $\mathbf{P}$; (2) the theory of the spectra of such sheaves initiated in [H1, §7] and further developed in [H2] and [S]. Because our curve X is subcanonical, the associated reflexive sheaf is locally free, a *vector bundle*. The use of (1) and (2) is strongly motivated by the success of their applications in [RV].

(2.1) RECALL: the "normalized vector bundle" $\mathcal{F}$ associated to X, according to [H1].

$\mathcal{F}$ is a rank 2 vector bundle on $\mathbf{P}$, with Chern classes $c_1 = c_1(\mathcal{F})$ and $c_2 = c_2(\mathcal{F})$ interpreted as integers, and such that $0 \leq -c_1 \leq 1$. Recall that in the notation of (1.11): $q = a - n$ if $m = \eta$; $q = a + n + p$ if $m \neq \eta$; $e + 4 = 2q - p$. Letting $\mathcal{O}$ denote $\mathcal{O}_\mathbf{P}$ and $\mathcal{I}$ denote $\mathcal{I}_X$, by [H1, (4.1)], there exists the exact sequence

(a)　　$0 \longrightarrow \mathcal{O} \longrightarrow \mathcal{F}(q) \longrightarrow \mathcal{I}(e+4) \longrightarrow 0$,

and so by restriction to our general plane $\bar{\mathbf{P}}$, the exact sequence

(b)　　$0 \longrightarrow \bar{\mathcal{O}} \longrightarrow \bar{\mathcal{F}}(q) \longrightarrow \bar{\mathcal{I}}(e+4) \longrightarrow 0$,

where $\bar{\mathcal{O}}$ denotes $\mathcal{O}_{\bar{\mathbf{P}}}$, $\bar{\mathcal{I}}$ denotes $\mathcal{I}_{\bar{X}}$, and $\bar{\mathcal{F}}$ denotes the restriction of $\mathcal{F}$ to $\bar{\mathbf{P}}$.

(c) By [H1, (4.1) & (2.2)]: $c_1 = -p$; $d = c_2(\mathcal{F}(q)) = c_2 + q(q-p)$.

(d) By [H1, (3.1)]: $\mathcal{F}$ is *stable* iff $h^0 \mathcal{F} = 0$.

As in [S], *define for nonstable* $\mathcal{F}$: $r \equiv \max\{\imath | h^0 \mathcal{F}(p-\imath) \neq 0\}$. (By [H1, (3.1)] then, $\mathcal{F}$ is *semistable* iff it is either nonstable with $r = 0$ or stable.) *Define for stable* $\mathcal{F}$: $r \equiv 0$.

(2.2) OBSERVATION–DEFINITION. (2.1a) and the fact that $e+4=2q-p$ give this.

(a) $\rho_j = h^1\mathcal{F}(j+p-q)$ $(\forall j)$. Hence: $\gamma_{\mathcal{F}} \equiv \gamma+p-q$ *is the* $\mathcal{F}$*-gap corresponding to* γ.
That formula, (1.2b) and (1.4c) then give this formula.

(b) $C(j) = \Delta h^1\mathcal{F}(j+p-q)$ for $j<a$, and for $j<b$ if $\alpha=a$.

Recall: $R=H^0_\bullet\mathcal{O}$; $I=H^0_\bullet\mathcal{I}$; $\bar{R}$ and $\bar{I}$ are the analogs for $\bar{\mathbf{P}}$ and $\bar{X}$. So (2.1a) induces the first of these two isomorphisms, and (2.1b) the second.

(c) $I(e+4) \cong \operatorname{coker}(R \to H^0_\bullet\mathcal{F}(q))$; $\bar{I}(e+4) \cong \operatorname{coker}(\bar{R} \to H^0_\bullet\bar{\mathcal{F}}(q))$.

To develop certain formulas derived from (c) consider an arbitrary finitely generated graded R-module $E \neq 0$. Then any homogeneous basis of E of minimal cardinality is just a set of representatives of a homogeneous basis of the vector space E/R_1E; whence the number of members of degree j in such a basis is just the dimension of the vector space E_j/R_1E_{j-1}. So if the members of such a basis are arranged in a sequence with their degrees nondecreasing, then the degree of the ith member of that sequence, *hereafter denoted* $\alpha_i(E)$, is independent of the choice of basis. (So: $\alpha_1(I)=\alpha$ and $\alpha_1(\bar{I})=a$; because X is integral, $\alpha_2(I)=\beta$; because $b-1\le\mu$, $\alpha_2(\bar{I})=b$.) Put: $\alpha_i \equiv \alpha_i(H^0_\bullet\mathcal{F})$; $a_i \equiv \alpha_i(H^0_\bullet\bar{\mathcal{F}})$. Given any nonzero graded submodule E' of E, the definitions imply: $\alpha_i(E/E')=\alpha_i(E)$ if $\alpha_i(E)<\alpha_1(E')$. Therefore, because $e+4=2q-p$, (c) yields:

(d) $\alpha_i-q=\alpha_i(I)+p-2q$ if $e+4>\alpha_i(I)$; $a_i-q = \alpha_i(\bar{I})+p-2q$ if $e+4>\alpha_i(\bar{I})$.

(2.3) LEMMAS: applications of (2.1) via (2.2).

(a) $\alpha_1=\alpha+p-q$; $\alpha_2=\beta+p-q$; $a_1=a+p-q$; $a_2=b+p-q$.

(b) Hence: $\eta=a_2-a_1$; $\zeta=a_1+a_2-p$; $\gamma_{\mathcal{F}}=a_2-1+\xi=k+p-1$.

(c) For $\alpha\neq a$ (so $\zeta>\eta$): $\alpha_1=\alpha-a+n+p$; $a_1=n+p\neq0$; $\mathcal{F}$ and $\bar{\mathcal{F}}$ are stable.

(d) For $\alpha=a$ and $m=\eta$: $\alpha_1=a_1=n+p$; $\mathcal{F}$ and $\bar{\mathcal{F}}$ are semistable, stable iff $n+p\neq0$.

(e) For $\alpha=a$ and $m\neq\eta$: $\alpha_1=a_1=-n$; $\mathcal{F}$ and $\bar{\mathcal{F}}$ are nonstable, with $r=n+p\neq0$.

(f) In characteristic 0: $\alpha\neq a \implies \eta\le1$.

Proof. Recall: $q=a-n$ if $m=\eta$, and $q=a+n+p$ if $m\neq\eta$. Given that and the fact that $\max\{a,b,\alpha\}\le\beta$, to justify (a) through (e), by (2.2a,d), it suffices to show $\beta<e+4$. But by (1.5b) and (1.8b): $\beta-e-4\le\gamma-e-3\le-3$. Then (f) follows from (b) and (c) because by [H2,(4.1)], $a_2-a_1\le1$ when $\alpha_1>a_1\ge0$.

(2.4) RECALL: the spectrum $\mathcal{S}$ of $\mathcal{F}$, according to [H1], [H2] and [S].

$\mathcal{S}$ is a function from $\mathbf{Z}$ to $\mathbf{N}$ such that: $\Sigma\{\mathcal{S}(i)\}=\kappa>0$, where $\kappa=c_2$ in the stable cases, and otherwise, $\kappa=c_2(\mathcal{F}(-r-c_1))=c_2+r^2+c_1r$. (Recall: $c_1=-p$.) $\mathcal{S}$ is *symmetric* and *connected*, in the senses described as follows. *Symmetry:* $\mathcal{S}(i)=\mathcal{S}(-i-p)$. *Connectedness:* $\mathcal{S}$ has no gaps in the stable cases; in the nonstable cases, $\mathcal{S}(r+1-p)\neq0$ and $\mathcal{S}$ has no gaps greater than $r+1-p$. Moreover:

(a) For $j\le r-1$: $\Delta h^1\mathcal{F}(j)=\Sigma\{\mathcal{S}(i)|i\ge-j-1\}$. (See [H1,(7.1)] and [S,(3.1)].)

(b) In the stable cases: $\mathcal{S}(j)=1$ with $j\ge1 \implies \mathcal{S}(j+1)\le1$. (See [H2,(5.1)].)

(c) In the nonstable cases: $\mathcal{S}(j)=1$ with $j\ge r+2-p \implies \mathcal{S}(j+1)\le1$. (See [S,(6.1)].)

Note that (2.1c) and the formula for κ recalled above in this item yield these points.

(d) In the stable cases: $d = \kappa+q(q-p)$.

(e) In the nonstable cases: $d = \kappa+q(q-p)-n(n+p)$.

Then (d), (e) and the formula of (1.11d), in view of (2.3c,d,e), yield the connection between λ and κ in each of the four "Cases" defined by (1.11).

(f) In Cases 1 and 2: $\kappa-\lambda = \binom{\zeta+1}{2}-n(n+p)$. (Note: $\zeta=2n+m+p$ in these cases.)

(g) In Cases 3 and 4: $\kappa-\lambda = \binom{\zeta+1}{2}$. (Note: $\zeta=m$ in these cases.)

(2.5) KEYLEMMAS: applications of (2.4) via (2.2b).

    (a) For $\jmath \leq \tilde{\gamma} + k + 1 + p$: $\Delta C(\jmath) = S(q - p - \jmath - 1)$.

    (b) $S(\jmath) \geq 2$ $(r + 2 - p \leq \jmath \leq k + 1)$; $S(k+2) = 0$ iff $\mu_0 = \tilde{\gamma}$; $S(1) \geq 2$ in the stable cases.

    (c) $\zeta \geq \delta_\jmath - \delta_{\tilde{\jmath}+1} \geq S(k) \geq 2$ $(b \leq \jmath \leq \gamma)$; $\gamma \leq \mu$ if $\zeta = S(k)$; $\zeta > S(k)$ if $\alpha = a$.

    (d) $\xi\zeta + \lambda_\gamma \geq \lambda \geq 2\xi + \lambda_\gamma \geq 2\xi + 2$; $\lambda_\gamma = 2$ iff $S(k+1) = 2$ and $S(k+2) = 0$.

    (e) In Cases 1 and 2: $\kappa \geq 4k + 5 + p$; $S(k+2) = 0$ and $S(\jmath) \leq 2$ $(\forall \jmath)$ if $\kappa \leq 4k + 6 + p$.

    (f) In Cases 3 and 4: $\kappa \geq 4(k-n) + 2$; $S(k+2) = 0$ and $S(\jmath) \leq 2$ $(\forall \jmath)$ if $\kappa \leq 4(k-n) + 3$.

Proof. The proof subsumes the formula (2.2b), the facts of (1.11b), and from (1.8b, e), that $C(\tilde{\gamma}) = \lambda_\gamma \geq 2$. So (2.4a) implies (a), which (applied for $\jmath \leq \tilde{\gamma}$ with the connectedness of S) implies: $S(k+1) > 0$; $\mu_0 = \tilde{\gamma}$ iff $S(k+2) = 0$. Suppose $S(k+1) = 1$. Then by (a) and (2.4b, c), $\Delta C(\imath) = 1$ $(\mu_0 \leq \imath \leq \tilde{\gamma})$; whence by (1.6c, e), $C(\jmath) = 0$ $(\forall \jmath \geq \gamma)$, and so the absurdity $\gamma > \mu_1$. That proves $S(k+1) \geq 2$, which implies the second assertion of (d) and, by (2.4b, c), also (b); and (b) implies (e) and (f), by the connectedness and symmetry of S. It remains to prove the first two assertions of (c), because they imply: by (1.15b), the third assertion of (c); by (1.8c), the first assertion of (d). Now (1.8c) gives this.

    (†) For $b \leq \jmath \leq \gamma$: $\delta_\jmath - \delta_{\tilde{\jmath}+1} \leq \Gamma(a, b; \jmath) - \delta_{\tilde{\jmath}+1} = \zeta$; $\delta_\gamma - \delta_{\tilde{\gamma}+1} \leq \delta_\jmath - \delta_{\tilde{\jmath}+1}$.

And (1.8c, e) with the formula of (a) (applied for $\jmath = \tilde{\gamma} + 1$) give this.

    (‡) $\delta_\gamma - \delta_{\tilde{\gamma}+1} = -\Delta\lambda_\gamma = \Delta C(\tilde{\gamma}+1) + C(\gamma-1) \geq S(k)$.

By (b), $S(k) \geq 2$. That fact, (†), (‡) and (1.1b) imply the first two assertions of (c). QED

(2.6) THEOREM: numerical possibilities for $(\xi, \eta, \zeta, \kappa)$. Recall: by (2.5c), $\zeta \geq 2$, equality possible only in Case 1, but constrained by (2.5d, e). By definition: p is the parity of $\zeta - \eta$; $m = \eta$ in Cases 1 and 2, $m = \zeta = \eta$ in Case 3, $m = \zeta$ in Case 4; $|\zeta - \eta| = 2n + p$; $k = \xi + m + n$.

    Case 1. $(k, \kappa) \geq (12 - p, 53 - 3p)$; $k = 12 - p$ iff $\kappa \leq 56 - 4p$.

        For $\eta \leq 1$ (as, by (2.3f), in characteristic 0): $\xi \geq 6$, and $k = 12 - p$ if $\xi = 6$; $56 - \eta \leq \kappa \leq 56$ if $(\xi, p) = (6, 0)$; κ is 50 or 52 if $(\xi, p) = (6, 1)$.

    Case 2. $(k, \kappa, \xi) \geq (13 - p, 58 - 4p, 7)$; $k = 13 - p$ iff $\kappa \leq 59 - 5p$ iff $(k, \xi, \eta) = (13 - p, 7, 0)$.

    Case 3. $(k, \kappa, \xi) \geq (23, 94, 12)$; $k = 23$ iff $\kappa \leq 95$, in which case $\xi \leq 18$.

    Case 4. $(k - n, \kappa, \xi) \geq (24, 98, 13)$; $k - n = 24$ iff $\kappa \leq 100$, in which case $n + p = 1$, $\xi \leq 19$.

(2.7) COROLLARY: numerical possibilities for d, e and γ.

    Case 1: $d \geq 278 - 18p$; $e \geq \gamma \geq 26 - p$.

    Case 2: $d \geq 314 - 20p$; $e \geq \gamma \geq 28 - p$.

    Case 3: $d \geq 770$; $e \geq \gamma \geq 48$.

    Case 4: $d \geq 881 - 27p$; $e \geq \gamma \geq 52 - p$.

In all seven subcases: e (and hence also γ) achieves its lower bound if d does.

(2.8) COROLLARY: for any integral subcanonical curve Y. No gaps under either of these hypotheses: (1) characteristic 0 and $e(Y) \leq 24$; (2) $\alpha(Y) = a(Y)$ and $e(Y) \leq 26$.

(2.9) COROLLARY: for any rank 2 vector bundle $\mathcal{E}$ on **P** with $0 \leq -c_1(\mathcal{E}) \leq 1$. The existence of an $\mathcal{E}$-gap, say t, implies these estimates.

    Stable case (characteristic 0): $\frac{(t+1)(t+3+c_1(\mathcal{E}))}{3} \geq c_2(\mathcal{E}) \geq 4t + 9 + 3c_1(\mathcal{E})$; $t \geq 11$.

    Nonstable semistable case: $\frac{(t+1)(t+3)}{6} \geq c_2(\mathcal{E}) \geq 4t + 6$; $t \geq 22$.

    Nonsemistable case: $\frac{(t+1)(t+3+c_1(\mathcal{E}))}{6} \geq \kappa(\mathcal{E}) \geq 4t + 6 - 4r(\mathcal{E})$; $t \geq 23 + r(\mathcal{E})$.

$(r(\mathcal{E})$ and $\kappa(\mathcal{E})$, see (2.1) and (2.4), are defined for $\mathcal{E}$ as r and κ are defined for $\mathcal{F}$. The upper bound on $\kappa(\mathcal{E})$ recorded in the nonsemistable case is a simplification of the stronger bound, a more complicated function of t, $c_1(\mathcal{E})$ and $r(\mathcal{E})$, actually given by the proof.)

Proof of (2.6), *Cases* 1 *and* 3. The formulas of (2.4f, g) instantly convert the upper bounds on λ of (1.13) into upper bounds on κ. Those bounds taken with lower bounds on κ of (2.5d, e) produce these data. In Case 1: $k \geq 12-p$, whence $\kappa \geq 53-3p$; $\kappa \leq 56-4p$ when $k = 12-p$. In Case 3: $k \geq 23$, whence $\kappa \geq 94$; $\kappa \leq 95$ when $k = 23$. Suppose for a moment we are in Case 1 with $\eta \leq 1$. Straightforward calculation using the upper and lower bounds on λ of (1.13) and (2.5d) and the fact that $k \geq 12-p$ shows that the bound of (1.13) cannot hold with $\xi \leq 5$ or with $\xi = 6$ and $k > 12-p$. The same argument proves $\xi \geq 12$ in Case 3. The Case 1 restriction on κ when $\eta \leq 1$ and $(\xi, p) = (6, 0)$ and the Case 4 restriction on ξ when $\kappa \leq 95$ follow from (2.4f, g) and (2.5d, f).

Proof of (2.6), *Case* 4. As in Cases 1 and 3, we use (1.13), (2.4g) and (2.5f) to discover the lower bound on k; but it is better to write the resulting polynomial inequality in terms of $u = k-n$ (which by (1.9) is necessarily positive). What comes out is this.

For $p = 0$: $\quad u^3 - 21u^2 - (24n+34)u - 12(n+1) \geq 0$.

For $p = 1$: $\quad u^3 - 21u^2 - (24n+46)u - 18(n+1) \geq 0$.

Given that $n \geq 1-p$, those cubic inequalities prove: $u \geq 24$; equality implies $n+p = 1$. By (1.12b), (2.4e) and (2.5e) then: $\kappa \geq 98$; $\kappa \leq 100$ iff $u = 24$. As in Case 3: using (1.13) and (2.5d) proves $\xi \geq 13$; using (2.4g) and (2.5a, b, d) proves $\xi \leq 19$ when $\kappa \leq 100$.

Proof of (2.6), *Case* 2. We sketch the case $p = 0$, leaving $p = 1$ to the reader. First use (1.13) and (2.5d), as above, to make these provisional estimates: $\xi \geq 5$; so $k-n \geq 5$. Next (cf. proof in Case 4) use (1.13), (2.4f) and (2.5e) to obtain the cubic inequality with coefficients depending on n satisfied by k. Letting k_n be the smallest integer greater than $n+4$ satisfying that inequality, we obtain: $k_n > 13$ $(1 \leq n \leq 5)$; $k_6 = 13$. Then use those data and (as before) (1.13) and (2.5d) to upgrade those provisional estimates: $\xi \geq 7$; so $k-n \geq 7$. Thus: $k \geq 13$; and the only possibility for $k = 13$ is with $(\xi, n) = (7, 6)$. Then using (1.13), (2.4f) and (2.5d) as in the previous cases produces the data claimed by (2.6) for that possibility.

Proofs of (2.7), (2.8), (2.9). By (1.11a): $q \geq k+3+p$; $\gamma \geq 2k+2+p$; in each estimate equality holds iff $\gamma = e$. Those facts and the formulas of (2.4d, e) join with (2.6) to produce the data of (2.7), which clearly imply (2.8). To prove (2.9): passing as above from X–data to $\mathcal{F}$–data and viceversa, i.e., via (2.3) and (2.4f, g), apply (1.13), (2.5e, f) and (2.6).

FINAL STANDING HYPOTHESES: characteristic 0; X is integral; γ is an X–gap.

As noted in §1, those hypotheses imply all previously imposed standing hypotheses. So we now have the context set by the introductory section for §3; and moreover, by (2.3f), $\eta \leq 1$ when $\alpha \neq a$. We conclude this section by preparing the ground for the next via a revisiting of the relationship between X and $\mathcal{F}$ established in items (2.1)–(2.3) above. Provisionally suspend the meaning of $(X, \mathcal{F}, \gamma, \xi, \eta, \zeta, p, q)$. Let $\mathcal{F}$ be a rank 2 vector bundle on $\mathbf{P}$, with $0 \leq -c_1(\mathcal{F}) = p \leq 1$. Then [H1] applies: for $q \gg 0$, there exists an integral $\mathcal{SC}$ curve X with $e+4 = 2q-p$, and (2.1a, b, c, d) obtain. Assume further the existence of an $\mathcal{F}$–gap $\gamma_{\mathcal{F}}$. Then by (2.2a), $\gamma \equiv \gamma_{\mathcal{F}}+q-p$ is an X–gap. In view of (2.2) and (2.3), put: $\xi \equiv \gamma_{\mathcal{F}}-a_1+1$; $\zeta \equiv a_1+a_2-p$; $\eta \equiv a_2-a_1$. So the situation and notation provisionally suspended have been restored. But because $q \gg 0$, whence $e > \mu_1$, there is more to say. By (1.6c, e, f), taking $\jmath = e+2$ shows that the equivalent conditions of (1.6f) obtain—*in which event it is convenient to have these definitions*:

$$\Gamma(\jmath) \equiv \max\{\Gamma(a, b; \jmath)-\zeta, 0\} \ (\forall \jmath \geq b); \quad \Gamma(\jmath) \equiv \Gamma(a, b; \jmath) \ (\forall \jmath < b);$$

$$\varphi_\jmath \equiv \delta_\jmath - \Gamma(\jmath) \ (\forall \jmath); \quad \bar{\mu} \equiv \max\{\jmath|\varphi_\jmath \neq 0\}.$$

Then (1.6c, e, f), (1.8c), (2.5c) and (1.1) yield all of the following item but its part (f), and yield that point in conjunction with (1.4a).

(2.10) PROPOSITION. Replacing X, in the sense of the foregoing discussion, by a curve associated to $\mathcal{F}$ by a $q \gg 0$, we may assume $e > \mu_1$, so $e = s-3$ and these points obtain.

(a) $\gamma+2 \leq \bar{\mu} \leq s-1$; $\Gamma(a,b;\jmath) \geq \delta_\jmath \geq \Gamma(\jmath) \ (\forall \jmath)$; $\varphi_\jmath \geq 0 \ (\forall \jmath)$; $\varphi_\jmath \neq 0$ iff $b \leq \jmath \leq \bar{\mu}$.

(b) $\varphi_\jmath \geq 2 \ (b \leq \jmath \leq \gamma)$; $\Delta\varphi_\jmath \leq 0 \ (\forall \jmath > b)$; for $\jmath \geq b-1$, $\lambda_\jmath = \Sigma\{\varphi_\imath | \imath > \jmath\}$.

(c) $\xi\zeta + \lambda_\gamma \geq \lambda = \Sigma\{\varphi_\jmath | b \leq \jmath \leq \gamma\} + \lambda_\gamma \geq 2\xi + \lambda_\gamma$; $\lambda = 2\xi + \lambda_\gamma$ iff $\varphi_\jmath = 2 \ (b \leq \jmath \leq \gamma)$.

(d) $\lambda_\gamma \geq \varphi_{\gamma+1} + \varphi_{\gamma+2} \geq 2$; $\lambda_\gamma = 2$ iff $\bar{\mu} = \gamma+2$ and $\varphi_{\gamma+1} = \varphi_{\gamma+2} = 1$.

(e) When $\lambda = 2\xi + \lambda_\gamma$: $C(\gamma-\jmath) = 0 \ (1 \leq \jmath \leq \xi)$; $S(k-\jmath) = 2 \ (0 \leq \jmath \leq \xi-1)$.

(f) When $\lambda_\gamma = 2$ (by (2.5d), iff $S(k+1) = 2$ and $S(k+2) = 0$) these data obtain:
$$\mu_0 = \tilde{\gamma}; \quad \mu_1 = \bar{\mu} = \gamma+2; \quad \varphi_{\bar{\mu}} = \varphi_{\bar{\mu}-1} = \rho_{\bar{\mu}} = \rho_{\bar{\mu}-1} = 1; \quad K(\bar{\mu}) = 0.$$

It is useful (see comment immediately preceding (1.1) above) to bear in mind the picture described by (a) and (b), supplemented in the relevant special cases by (c) and (d), of the graph of $\Delta\bar{H}$ enveloped between those of $\Gamma(a,b)$ and Γ.

(2.11) OBSERVATION: on the "replacement" giving (2.10).

(a) By (1.6c, e, f): (2.10) holds without replacement if $\lambda_g = 2$, the minimum possible.

(b) By characteristic 0: with replacement X may be assumed smooth.

Before §3, a detour through the following technical appendix concerning (1.12) and (2.4d, e). The reader may pass directly to §3, for this appendix is not used below—and may not even be a novel observation. It is included here because of its possible applicability in contexts beyond that of this paper.

APPENDIX: an upper bound on the second Chern class.

The proof of (1.12) really doesn't use "gap", it needs only: $e \geq \gamma > \mu_0$ and $\rho_\gamma = 0$. The point of this appendix is to sketch what that implies for semistable bundles (in characteristic 0). Provisionally suspend all assumptions on X, except that it is an integral curve (necessarily subcanonical) associated by the formalism of (2.1, 2, 3) to a given semistable bundle $\mathcal{F}$, and that for some $\gamma_\mathcal{F}$: $h^1\mathcal{F}(\gamma_\mathcal{F}) = 0 \neq h^1\mathcal{F}(\jmath) \ (\exists\jmath < \gamma_\mathcal{F})$. *Do not assume* $\gamma_\mathcal{F}$ *is an* $\mathcal{F}$-*gap*. Put $\gamma = \gamma_\mathcal{F} + q - p$, and assume as we may by taking $q \gg 0$, as above, that $\gamma \leq e = s-3$. Now by (1.2b), $\gamma \geq \max\{a, b-1\}$; i.e., that part of (1.5a) uses only $\gamma > \mu_0$, not "gap". So we have enough to do the proof of (1.12), which with (2.4d, e) then produces upper bounds for $c_2(\mathcal{F})$ (in Cases 1, 2 and 3). Noting that by (2.3a, b), the numbers k, n and p are definable in terms of $\mathcal{F}$, we then have this.

PROPOSITION: for any rank 2 semistable vector bundle $\mathcal{E}$ on **P** with $0 \leq -c_1(\mathcal{E}) \leq 1$. Suppose: $h^1\mathcal{E}(t-1) \neq h^1\mathcal{E}(t) = 0$. Then: $t + c_1(\mathcal{E}) > -1$ and the upper bounds on $c_2(\mathcal{E})$ of (2.9) hold. Putting $p = -c_1(\mathcal{E})$ and $k = t+1-p$, suppose further that $\mathcal{E}$ is stable and for the restriction $\bar{\mathcal{E}}$ of $\mathcal{E}$ to $\bar{\mathbf{P}}$: $n = \min\{\imath | h^0\mathcal{E}(\imath+p) \neq 0\} = \min\{\imath | h^0\bar{\mathcal{E}}(\imath+p) \neq 0\}$. Then: $k > n$ and $c_2(\mathcal{E}) \leq \frac{(k+p)(k+2)}{3} - \frac{(k-n)(k-n+1)(k-n+2)}{3(2k+2+p)}$.

Remarks. Applying the proposition for $t = \mu_1(\mathcal{E})+1$ then gives an upper bound on $c_2(\mathcal{E})$. That estimate is sharp: a nullcorrelation bundle is stable, with $c_1 = c_2-1 = 0$ and $\mu_1 = -1$. There is no compelling need to restrict this appendix to "semistable", i.e., to exclude Case 4: the re-interpretation of (1.12), i.e., without regard to "gap", as a bound on κ is valid in that case too. However, although $\kappa \geq c_2$, it is possible that $\kappa \gg c_2$.

§3. "First chances" for gaps in the stable cases.

All previously established standing notation and hypotheses remain in force. Recall: $\gamma_{\mathcal{F}}$ denotes the $\mathcal{F}$–gap corresponding via (2.2a) to γ. Then by (2.10), we can pass to a "new" X, changing neither $(\xi, \eta, \zeta, \lambda)$ nor the "Case" in the sense of (1.11): those data are determined by $\mathcal{F}$ and $\gamma_{\mathcal{F}}$. Therefore, in looking for "small examples", it is perhaps better to think of "small" in terms of κ (or λ) and ξ rather than d, e and γ; i.e., we should probably focus on the theorem (2.6) rather than its corollary (2.7). *With that viewpoint then, there is no loss in assuming that (2.10a, b, c, d) obtain, and that $s > \mu_1$.*

Notation. For any finitely generated standardly graded R–module E, $\nu_i(E)$ is the dimension of the vector space $E_i / R_1 E_{i-1}$, and so by (2.3), the number of members of degree i in any *standard basis* for E, i.e., a homogeneous basis of minimal cardinality. $E<j>$ (notation of [BDM]) denotes the submodule of E generated by $\cup \{E_i | i \leq j\}$.

Convention: $\nu_i \equiv \nu_i(I)$; $\bar{\nu}_i \equiv \nu_i(\bar{I})$.

(3.1) LEMMA. Suppose: $b \leq j \leq \bar{\mu}$; $\bar{\nu}_{j+1} = -\Delta \varphi_{j+1}$; $K(j) = 0$. Let Z be the zerolocus of I_j. (Z is clearly 1–dimensional, not necessarily a curve, and contains X, possibly with multiplicity greater than 1.) Put: $\bar{Z} = Z \cap \bar{\mathbf{P}}$; Y the scheme residual to X in Z. Then:

(a) $I_Z = I<j>$; $I_{\bar{Z}} = \bar{I}<j>$; $h^1 \mathcal{I}_Z(i) = 0 \, (\forall i \geq j-1)$; $\Delta H(\bar{Z}; i) = s(Z) - i \, (j < i \leq s(Z))$.
Suppose further that $\varphi_j = 1$. Then:

(b) X is not a multiple component of Z.

(c) $\dim Y = 1$ and $\deg Y = s - \bar{\mu}$. (NB: Y need not be a curve, but will be when Z is.)
Assume further that $j = \bar{\mu}$ and $\rho_j \leq 1$. Then $\mu_1 \leq j$, and moreover:

(d) For $\mu_1 < j$: $\nu_{j+1} = \bar{\nu}_{j+1} \leq 1$; $\nu_i = 0 \, (\forall i > j+1)$.

(e) For $\mu_1 = j$: $\nu_{j+2} = 2$; $\nu_{j+1} = 0 = \nu_i \, (\forall i > j+2)$; so the general member of the "pencil" $H^0 \mathcal{I}_{X/Z}(j+2)$ cuts out on Z an irreducible scheme of degree d, with residual in Z a 1–dimensional scheme of degree $\deg Y$, Y when Z is a curve.

Preview. (3.1) is our vehicle for geometrizing the numerical data of (2.6). In Cases 1 and 2 those data show that in the (numerically) first chances for a gap, λ_γ attains or is very close to its minimal value, 2. That so restricts $\bar{H}$ that (3.1) comes into play, with the result that X must be cut from Z by a clearly identifiable (small) linear system of hypersurfaces, with the residual scheme Y of much smaller degree—possibly even 1.

To prove (3.1) we translate into the notation at hand certain known facts (some very well known) concerning the numbers ν_i and $\bar{\nu}_i$ and the relationship between them induced by the "Castelnuovo Sequence" of (1.2) above. The presentation in (the primarily expository paper) [D3] of Campanella's upper bound on $\bar{\nu}_i$ [C] is particularly well–suited to our applications here.

(3.2) LEMMAS: on the generation of I and $\bar{I}$. *For the purposes of this item:* $j > b$.

(a) For $\eta \neq 0$: $\bar{\nu}_a = 1$; $\bar{\nu}_b = a - \delta_b$. For $\eta = 0$: $\bar{\nu}_b = a + 1 - \delta_b$. For $a \neq i < b$: $\bar{\nu}_i = 0$.

(b) $\bar{\nu}_j \leq -\Delta \varphi_j$, so $\bar{\nu}_j = 0 \, (\forall j > \bar{\mu}+1)$; $\bar{\nu}_{j+1} = -\Delta \varphi_{j+1}$ if $\Delta \varphi_j = 0$.

(c) In case $\bar{\nu}_j = -\Delta \varphi_j$: $\bar{I}<j-1>$ is saturated (of height 2), and for its zerolocus, say W, $\Delta^2 H(W; i) = -1 \, (j \leq i \leq j-1+\delta_{j-1})$.

(d) $\nu_i \leq \bar{\nu}_i$ if $K(i-1) = 0$; $\bar{\nu}_i \leq \nu_i$ if $K(i) = 0$.

(e) For $j > \bar{\mu}+1$: $\nu_j = 0$ if $j > \mu_1+1$.

Proof. See [D3, (3.2)&(3.4)] for (a) and (b), [BDM, (4.1b)] for (c). (Those are general results on arbitrary perfect homogeneous polynomial ideals of height 2.) By (1.2b), the canonical map $I_i / R_1 I_{i-1} \to \bar{I}_i / R_1 \bar{I}_{i-1}$ is injective if $K(i-1) = 0$, surjective if $K(i) = 0$. That proves (d), which with (b) implies (e).

Proof of (3.1). Clearly I and I_Z agree up to degree $\jmath$. So by (3.2c), $I_{\bar{Z}} = \bar{I}<\jmath>$ and $\Delta H(\bar{Z};\cdot)$ is as claimed in (3.1a). It is straightforward to deduce the rest of (3.1a) from that. Next notice that by (1.1): $\deg Z = d + \Sigma\{\Delta H(\bar{Z};\imath) - \delta_\imath | \imath > \jmath\}$; $0 < s - \bar{\mu} < d$. In case $\varphi_\jmath = 1$ then: by (3.2c), $\deg Z = d + s - \bar{\mu}$; whence (3.1b,c) hold. Now assume $\jmath = \bar{\mu}$ and $\rho_\jmath \leq \varphi_\jmath = 1$. Then $\lambda_\jmath = 0$; whence $C(\imath) = 0$ $(\forall \imath \geq \jmath)$. Hence: $\mu_1 < \jmath$ iff $\rho_\jmath = 0$; $\mu_1 = \jmath$ iff $K(\jmath+1) \neq 0$. Suppose $\rho_\jmath = 0$. Then by (3.2a,d,e): $\nu_\imath = 0$ $(\forall \imath > \jmath+1)$ and $\nu_{\jmath+1} = \bar{\nu}_{\jmath+1} \leq 1$. That establishes (d). Suppose $\rho_\jmath \neq 0$. Then by (1.4a), $K(\jmath+1) \neq 0$; whence $\mu_1 = \jmath$ and, by (3.2d), $\nu_\imath = 0$ $(\forall \imath > \jmath + 2)$. Moreover $\nu_{\jmath+1} = 0$: otherwise, because $\bar{C}(\jmath) = 0$ and, by (3.2b), $\bar{\nu}_{\jmath+1} \leq 1$, $\bar{C}(\jmath+1) = K(\jmath+1) = 0$. Finally observe that $\nu_{\jmath+2} = H(Z;\jmath+2) - H(\jmath+2)$. A simple calculation using (1.2b) then shows $\nu_{\jmath+2} = 2$.

(3.3) LEMMA: the case $\lambda_\gamma = 2$. Then: all but the last set of hypotheses of (3.1) hold for $\jmath = \bar{\mu}-1$; $\mu_0 = \tilde{\gamma}$ and $\mu_1 = \bar{\mu}$; $\rho_{\bar{\mu}-1} = \rho_{\bar{\mu}} = 1$ and $\nu_{\bar{\mu}} = 0$; all hypotheses of (3.1) hold for $\jmath = \bar{\mu}$.

Proof. (2.10f) gives everything but $\nu_{\bar{\mu}} = 0$, and (3.2d) gives that.

(3.4) LEMMA: the case $\lambda_\gamma = 3$, with $\varphi_{\gamma+1} = 2$. Then: $\bar{\mu} = \gamma+2$ and $\varphi_{\bar{\mu}} = 1$; $\tilde{\gamma} = \mu_0$ and $S(k+1) = 3$; $K(\bar{\mu}) \leq \rho_{\bar{\mu}-1} = 1$; $\mu_1 = \bar{\mu}-1$ if $K(\bar{\mu}) = 1$; $\mu_1 = \bar{\mu}$ if $K(\bar{\mu}) = 0$, in which case all three sets of hypotheses of (3.1) hold for $\jmath = \bar{\mu}$. If $\mu_1 = \bar{\mu}-1$, these points obtain.
  (a) The first set of hypotheses of (3.1) holds for $\jmath = \bar{\mu}-1$.
  (b) $\nu_{\bar{\mu}+1} = 3$; $\nu_{\bar{\mu}} = 0 = \nu_\imath$ $(\forall \imath > \bar{\mu}+1)$.
  (c) $\dim Y = 1$ and $\deg Y = 2(s-\bar{\mu}+1)$.

Proof. By (2.10b), $\bar{\mu} = \gamma+2$ and $\varphi_{\gamma+2} = 1$. Because $C(\tilde{\gamma}) = \lambda_\gamma = 3$, by (2.5a,b), either $S(k+1) = 3$ and $\tilde{\gamma} = \mu_0$ or $S(k+1) = 2$ and $S(k+2) = 1$. But in the latter event, $C(\gamma+1) = \rho_{\gamma+1} = 0$, which is absurd because in either case $C(\imath) = 0$ $(\forall \imath > \gamma+1)$. Besides showing $S(k+1) = 3$ and $\tilde{\gamma} = \mu_0$, that argument also gives: $\rho_{\gamma+1} = 1$; $\mu_1 = \gamma+1$ if $K(\gamma+2) = 1$; $\rho_{\gamma+2} = 1$ if $K(\gamma+2) = 0$. If $K(\gamma+2) = 0$, then $\bar{\nu}_{\gamma+3} = K(\gamma+3) = 1$: otherwise (1.2b) and (3.2b) give the absurdity $K(\imath) = 0$ $(\forall \imath \geq \gamma+2)$. So in case $K(\gamma+2) = 0$, the three sets of hypotheses of (3.1) hold for $\jmath = \gamma+2$. In case $K(\gamma+2) = 1$, a repeat of the argument just made shows that $\bar{\nu}_{\gamma+2} = 1$; whence (a) holds. We leave to the reader the proofs of (b) and (c), which are essentially the same as those of (3.1c,e).

(3.5) LEMMA: the case $\lambda_\gamma = 3$, with $\mu_0 = \tilde{\gamma}$ and $\varphi_{\gamma+1} = 1$. Then: $\bar{\mu} = \gamma+3$; the first two sets of hypotheses of (3.1) hold for $\jmath = \gamma+1$, $\gamma+2$, $\gamma+3$; $\mu_1 = \bar{\mu}+2$. Moreover:
  (a) $\rho_{\bar{\mu}-2} = \rho_{\bar{\mu}+1} = 2$; $\rho_{\bar{\mu}-1} = \rho_{\bar{\mu}} = 3$; $\rho_{\bar{\mu}+2} = 1$.
  (b) For $\imath \geq \bar{\mu}-1$: $\nu_\imath = 0$ $(\imath \neq \bar{\mu}+2, \bar{\mu}+3)$; $\nu_{\bar{\mu}+2} = 1$; $1 \leq \nu_{\bar{\mu}+3} \leq 4$.
  (c) For X' the scheme cut out on Z by $I_{\bar{\mu}+2}$: $\deg X \leq \deg X' \leq \deg X + 1$.

The proof of (3.5) is left to the interested reader, for it will not be used below. The same goes for the glossed over part of (3.4). Those points have been included mainly for expository reasons. In future we may well have to look at those cases (and others) here set aside, but the rest of this paper is restricted to experimentation with $\lambda_\gamma = 2$.

Observe: when $\mu_0 = \tilde{\gamma}$ (especially, see (2.10f) and (2.5b,e,f), when λ_γ or κ is "lower bound extremal") the difference between κ and its upper bound imposed by (1.12) and (2.4d,e) determines precisely $h^0 \mathcal{I}_X(\gamma)$; in any case, by (1.12c), $\mu_0 = \tilde{\gamma}$ when κ attains that upper bound. Now we really care more about $h^0 \mathcal{I}_X(\gamma+1)$, because in most of the cases we have in mind the scheme Z of (3.1) will be the zerolocus of $H^0 \mathcal{I}_X(\gamma+1)$. But in those cases we can use (1.2b) to calculate $h^0 \mathcal{I}_X(\gamma+1)$, if $h^0 \mathcal{I}_X(\gamma)$ is known. Finally we observe that for our "first chances" in Cases 1 and 2, one or both of those extremal conditions which permit the calculation of $h^0 \mathcal{I}_X(\gamma)$ will obtain.

Now these four instances of "first chances", to serve as "testcases" for the gap question. Others later (noted only briefly); here I prefer to concentrate primarily on these because of their compellingly simple properties, to be recorded in detail presently.

(TC1) TESTCASE: Case 1 with $(\xi, \eta, \zeta) = (6, 0, 11)$ and $(\kappa, \lambda) = (50, 14)$.

(TC2) TESTCASE: Case 1 with $(\xi, \eta, \zeta) = (6, 0, 12)$ and $(\kappa, \lambda) = (56, 14)$.

(TC3) TESTCASE: Case 2 with $(\xi, \eta, \zeta) = (7, 0, 11)$ and $(\kappa, \lambda) = (54, 18)$.

(TC4) TESTCASE: Case 2 with $(\xi, \eta, \zeta) = (7, 0, 12)$ and $(\kappa, \lambda) = (58, 16)$.

In each of those testcases the equivalent conditions $\lambda_\gamma = 2$ and $\mathcal{S}(k+1) = \mathcal{S}(k+2)+2 = 2$ of (2.5d) obtain: in (TC2) because of extemality with respect to the lower bound on λ of (2.5d); in (TC3) because of extremality with respect to the lower bound on κ of (2.5e); in (TC1) and (TC4) for both reasons. Hence: in all four testcases the the conclusions of (3.3) obtain; by (2.5e), $\mathcal{S}$ is uniquely determined in every testcase but (TC2); by (2.10b, d), $\bar{H}$ is uniquely determined in every testcase but (TC3); and in those exceptional testcases $\mathcal{S}$ and $\bar{H}$ are determined "almost uniquely" (details below). Finally, note that in each case one can use the deficiency of κ from its upper bound imposed by (1.12) and (2.4d) to calculate $h^0 \mathcal{I}_X(\gamma)$, and then use that to estimate α and β and, with (1.2b), to calculate $h^0 \mathcal{I}_X(\gamma+1)$. This notation facilitates the analysis.

Notation: $\varepsilon_j \equiv \Gamma(j)+2 \ (b \le j \le \gamma)$; $\varepsilon_j \equiv \Gamma(j)+1 \ (\gamma < j \le \gamma+2)$; otherwise $\varepsilon_j \equiv \Gamma(j)$.

Observation for $j \ge b$: $\delta_j \ge \varepsilon_j$; $j \le \imath \le \gamma \implies \delta_j - \varepsilon_j \ge \delta_\imath - \varepsilon_\imath$; $\Sigma\{\delta_\imath - \varepsilon_\imath | \imath \ge b\} = \lambda - 2\xi - 2$.

(3.6) NUMERICAL DATA: the functions $\bar{H}$, $h^0 \mathcal{I}_X(\cdot)$ and $h^0 \mathcal{F}(\cdot)$. In all four testcases, $a_1 = a_2 = 6$ and $\delta_j = \varepsilon_j \ (j \ne b, b+1)$; in all but (TC3) $\delta_j = \varepsilon_j \ (\forall j)$. In (TC3) and (TC4), $\alpha_1 = 6$. In (TC3), either $\delta_j - \varepsilon_j = 1 \ (j = b, b+1)$ or $\delta_b - \varepsilon_b = 2$ and $\delta_{b+1} = \varepsilon_{b+1}$. Moreover:

(TC1): $8 \le \alpha_1 \le \alpha_2 \le \gamma_\mathcal{F} = 11$; $\alpha_2 \ge 10$ if $\alpha_1 = 8$; $h^0 \mathcal{F}(11) = 25$; $h^0 \mathcal{F}(12) = 145$.

(TC2): $\alpha_1 = \alpha_2 = \gamma_\mathcal{F}+1 = 12$; $h^0 \mathcal{F}(12) = 127$.

(TC3): $11 \le \alpha_2 \le \gamma_\mathcal{F} = 12$; $h^0 \mathcal{F}(12) = h^0 \mathcal{O}_\mathbf{P}(6)+6$; $h^0 \mathcal{F}(13) = h^0 \mathcal{O}_\mathbf{P}(7)+113$.

(TC4): $10 \le \alpha_2 \le \gamma_\mathcal{F} = 12$; $h^0 \mathcal{F}(12) = h^0 \mathcal{O}_\mathbf{P}(6)+14$; $h^0 \mathcal{F}(13) = h^0 \mathcal{O}_\mathbf{P}(7)+131$.

In any case: $\gamma - \alpha = \gamma_\mathcal{F} - \alpha_1$; $\gamma - \beta = \gamma_\mathcal{F} - \alpha_2$; $h^0 \mathcal{I}_X(\gamma+4-\imath) = h^0 \mathcal{F}(\gamma_\mathcal{F}+4-\imath) \ (\forall \imath > 0)$.

Proof. The final statement is an immediate consequence of (2.1, 2, 3). The assertions concerning $\bar{H}$ follow immediately from these facts: in all cases but (TC3), $\lambda = 2\xi+2$; in (TC3), $\lambda = 2\xi+4$. Observe that (2.3a, b) and definitions yield these formulas:

$$2a_1 = \zeta - \eta + p; \quad 2a_2 = \zeta + \eta + p; \quad 2\gamma_\mathcal{F} = 2\xi + \zeta + \eta + p - 2.$$

Given those facts, it remains only to calculate $h^0 \mathcal{F}(\gamma_\mathcal{F})$ and $h^0 \mathcal{F}(\gamma_\mathcal{F}+1)$ and estimate α_2, in (TC1) and (TC2) also α_1. One does that by using (1.12) and (2.4d), and then (1.2b), as indicated in the discussion above.

(3.7) NUMERICAL DATA: the function $\mathcal{S}$ is determined by symmetry and these data.

(TC1): $\mathcal{S}(0) = 1$; $\mathcal{S}(j) = 2 \ (1 \le j \le 12)$; $\mathcal{S}(j) = 0 \ (\forall j > 12)$.

(TC2): $2 \le \mathcal{S}(j) \le 3 \ (1 \le j \le 6)$; $\mathcal{S}(j) = 2 \ (7 \le j \le 13)$; $\mathcal{S}(j) = 0 \ (\forall j > 13)$; $\mathcal{S}(0) = 4$ and $\mathcal{S}(j) = 2 \ (1 \le j \le 6)$, or $\mathcal{S}(0) = 2$ and $\exists! \ 1 \le j \le 6$ with $\mathcal{S}(j) = 3$.

(TC3): $\mathcal{S}(0) = 1$; $\mathcal{S}(j) = 2 \ (1 \le j \le 13)$; $\mathcal{S}(j) = 0 \ (\forall j > 13)$.

(TC4): $\mathcal{S}(j) = 2 \ (0 \le j \le 14)$; $\mathcal{S}(j) = 0 \ (\forall j > 14)$.

Proof. As already noted: $\mathcal{S}(k+1) = \mathcal{S}(k+2)+2 = 2$. By the connectedness of $\mathcal{S}$ then: $\mathcal{S}(j) = 0 \ (\forall j > k+1)$. (2.5b, e) yield the rest for all cases but (TC2), and with (2.10e) yield the rest for (TC2).

(3.8) NUMERICAL DATA: consequences of (3.6) and (3.7). $\bar{H}$ and S determine this.
  (a) $C(\jmath)$ $(\forall \jmath)$. Moreover, $C(\jmath) = 0$ $(b-1 \leq \jmath \leq \gamma)$, but for these exceptions.
     (TC3): $C(b-1) = 2$; $C(b) = \delta_{b+1} - \varepsilon_{b+1}$.
  (b) $H(\jmath)$ $(\forall \jmath)$, but for these exceptions.
     (TC1): $\alpha \leq \jmath < \gamma$. (Note: $\gamma - 3 \leq \alpha \leq \gamma$.)
     (TC3): $\beta \leq \jmath < \gamma$. (Note: $\gamma - 1 \leq \beta \leq \gamma$.)
     (TC4): $\beta \leq \jmath < \gamma$. (Note: $\gamma - 2 \leq \beta \leq \gamma$.)
  (c) $K(\jmath)$ $(\forall \jmath)$, but for these exceptions.
     (TC1): $\alpha \leq \jmath \leq \gamma$; none if $\alpha = \gamma$. (See note for (b).)
     (TC3): $\beta \leq \jmath \leq \gamma$; none if $\beta = \gamma$. (See note for (b).)
     (TC4): $\beta \leq \jmath \leq \gamma$; none if $\beta = \gamma$. (See note for (b).)
  (d) $\rho_\jmath$ $(\forall \jmath)$, but for the exceptions noted for $H(\jmath)$ in (b).
  (e) In (TC1) with α known, the exceptions of (b), (c) and (d) become these.
     (Recall that by (3.6): $\gamma - 3 \leq \alpha \leq \beta \leq \gamma$; $\beta \geq \gamma - 1$ if $\alpha = \gamma - 3$.)
     For $H(\jmath)$: $\beta \leq \jmath < \gamma$.
     For $K(\jmath)$: $\beta \leq \jmath \leq \gamma$; none if $\beta = \gamma$.
     For $\rho_\jmath$: $\beta \leq \jmath < \gamma$.
The proof below in fact shows how to express those data explicitly in terms of S and $\bar{H}$.

Proof. In the cases at hand S determines $C(\jmath)$ $(\forall \jmath \leq a - 1 - n - p)$ via the formula of (2.5a). (In those cases $\zeta = 2n + p$.) Furthermore, (1.8e) and the definition of $\lambda_\jmath$ give this.

$$\text{For all } \jmath \in \mathbf{Z}: \; C(\jmath) + C(\tilde{\jmath}) = \lambda_\jmath = d - \bar{H}(\jmath) - \bar{H}(\tilde{\jmath}).$$

That shows how to calculate $C(\jmath)$ $(\forall \jmath)$, and by (3.6), gives the values of $C(\jmath)$ claimed in (a). (Aside: note that (2.5a) and (1.8c) show how C is determined by S and $\bar{H}$ in any case, not just our testcases.) Now (2.10f) gives $K(\jmath)$ $(\forall \jmath > \gamma)$; whence (3.6) and (1.2b) give $H(\jmath)$ $(\forall \jmath \geq \gamma)$. Since (for any integral curve) $H(\jmath) = h^0 \mathcal{O}_P(\jmath - \alpha)$ $(\forall \jmath < \beta)$, that establishes (b), and by (1.2b) also (c). For any $\jmath$, $C(\jmath) = \Delta \rho_\jmath + K(\jmath)$; so (a) and (c) give (d). Again, (for any integral curve), $H(\jmath) = h^0 \mathcal{O}_P(\jmath - \alpha)$ $(\forall \jmath < \beta)$; so (e) is clear.

It seems that none of the possibilities permitted by (3.6)–(3.8) is inconsistent with the developments of §§1–2. That is, one thing those testcases successfully test is whether or not the methods of those sections can alone establish "no gaps" as a theorem—they cannot. The question becomes whether or not any of those testcases is a genuine obstruction to that "theorem". A "yes" would of course end the gap problem for subcanonical curves, and with it the apparently unsolved problem of whether or not the Rao module of such a curve can be decomposed. But whether "yes" or "no", successfully answering the question should be of interest for whatever new ideas are brought into play in doing so. What follows are are my naïve thoughts on those testcases, which I hope may be suggestive to the reader who may care to consider the question—especially the reader who knows more than I about vector bundles and general position arguments.

Now we enter the world of *Let's Pretend*. Since in each of our testcase $\lambda_\gamma = 2$, by (2.11), there is no need to replace q by a $q \gg 0$ to bring about the properties collected in (2.10). Therefore, in addition to having those properties, it is also possible that $\gamma = e = s - 3$. In that event: (a, b, e, d, g) becomes a quintuple of honest numbers, not just functions of q and $(\xi, \eta, \zeta, \kappa)$; taking the $\jmath$ of (3.1) to be $\gamma + 1$ (or $\gamma + 2$, the schemes Z and Y are the same for either choice because $\nu_{\gamma+2} = 0$), $\deg Y = 1$. Now the 1–dimensional scheme Z need not be a curve—but it could be. So let's pretend that it is, in which case then, Y is a line and Z is the (scheme-theoretic) union of X and Y. Put $D \equiv X \cap Y$, the "divisor of common points". Let's pretend also that D is reduced. Now recall that by (2.11b), X can be assumed smooth by taking $q \gg 0$. But that would destroy the condition $\gamma = s - 3$, and thereby all the good properties just listed. So let's pretend that we have it all: X is smooth (if the need arises); $\gamma = e = s - 3$; the Z defined by $H^0 \mathcal{I}_X(e+1)$ is a curve.

The next item assembles the relevant numerical data for our testcases under those hypotheses. We let $\ell(D)$ denote the length of D. Notice that D is a divisor on X (if X is smooth) and on the line Y, and is the fixed divisor of the linear system cut out on Y by that pencil, call it $\mathcal{P}$, of (3.1e). In (TC1) and (TC2), let $\mathcal{L}$ denote the linear system defined by $H^0\mathcal{I}_X(\gamma+1)$. In (TC3) and (TC4) let S denote the unique surface S of degree $\alpha = a$ containing X and let $\mathcal{L}$ denote the linear system on S defined by $H^0\mathcal{I}_{X/S}(\gamma+1)$. Let's pretend also that S is smooth. (Perhaps assuming smoothness for X and S is overkill; integrality probably suffices.)

(3.9) NUMERICAL DATA: subsuming the conventions of preceding paragraphs. In all four cases $\ell(D) = \gamma+4 = e+4$. (So the linear system cut by the pencil $\mathcal{P}$ on the line Y consists only of the fixed divisor D.) Moreover, these data obtain.

(TC1): $(a,b,e,d,g) = (20, 20, 25, 260, 3251)$; $\dim\mathcal{L} = 144$.
(TC2): $(a,b,e,d,g) = (21, 21, 26, 281, 3654)$; $\dim\mathcal{L} = 126$.
(TC3): $(a,b,e,d,g) = (21, 21, 27, 294, 3970)$; $\dim\mathcal{L} = 112$.
(TC4): $(a,b,e,d,g) = (22, 22, 28, 314, 4397)$; $\dim\mathcal{L} = 130$.

Proof. By definition: $e = a+b-4-\zeta$; $\gamma = b-1+\xi$. But in each case $\eta = 0$, i.e., $a = b$, and $\gamma = e$. That determines (a,b,e), and consequently $q = a-n$. By (2.4d), $d = \kappa+q(q-p)$; and in any case $2g-2 = ed$. That completes the determination of (a,b,e,d,g). Now the exact sequence $0 \to \mathcal{O}_Z \to \mathcal{O}_X \oplus \mathcal{O}_Y \to \mathcal{O}_D \to 0$ yields: $\ell(D) = g_Z - g_X - g_Y + 1$. Therefore, since $g_Y = 0$, to calculate $\ell(D)$, it is enough to determine $g_Z - g_X$. That can be done using these facts: $H(Z;\jmath) = (\jmath-\gamma-2)d_Z + H(Z;\gamma+2)$ $(\forall \jmath \geq \gamma+2)$, by (1.2b) and (3.1a); $d_Z = d+1$; $H(Z;\gamma+2) = H(\gamma+2)$ because by (3.3), $\nu_{\gamma+2} = 0$. Then (cleverly or straightforwardly) one obtains: $g_Z - g_X = \gamma+3$.

Given (3.9) and the discussion preceding it, an obvious thing to go for is the pair $(\mathcal{L}, \mathcal{P})$, in (TC3) and (TC4) the triple $(S, \mathcal{L}, \mathcal{P})$, after having fixed our line Y and the divisor D, consisting of $e+4$ general points on Y. Perhaps in (TC1) we should assume that $\alpha = e-3$, the minimum permitted by (3.6), and $\beta = e$, the maximum permitted, thereby eliminating the indeterminacy in H, in which case we should consider the triple $(S, \mathcal{L}, \mathcal{P})$, where S is here the unique surface of degree α containing X, and $\mathcal{L}$ is viewed as a linear system on S. Likewise it might be well in (TC3) and (TC4) to require that β be the maximum permitted by (3.6). (Perhaps in (TC1) it would be preferable to specify $\alpha = \beta = e$, the maximum possible.) It would seem that there are so many degrees of freedom relative to the number of conditions on H and $\bar{H}$, that there should be no difficulty in constructing pairs (Z, X) that are postulationally correct, with many degrees of freedom left over. The problem then becomes that of further restricting those remaining degrees of freedom so that X has the right Rao module. (In that event "subcanonical" will be forced by the numerical condition NSC, because of integrality.) I don't know how to do that job. But I think there are those who do know—or at least know enough to show nothing can come of that approach.

Concerning choices for S and $\bar{H}$. If with (TC2) the need arises to make a choice from among the seven possibilities for S allowed by (3.7), perhaps the best choice would be that with $S(0) = 4$. At least there do exist bundles with that kind of spectrum; as for the other "2-humped" type, I don't know (perhaps the bundle specialists do) if there exist bundles of that type. (On the other hand, there is the possibility that "gap" is a rare phenomenon that goes with certain weird spectra.) In any event my naïve expectation is that for that choice it would be most difficult to disprove the existence of a (TC2) curve and least difficult to prove existence. For similar motives, if with (TC3) a choice of $\bar{H}$ is required, from among the two allowed by (3.6), I would opt for the one with $\delta_b - \varepsilon_b = 2$. Note that with that choice the $\bar{X}$ is slightly less special than with the alternative choice:

$\bar{\nu}_b = 9$ with the first choice, with the alternative $\bar{\nu}_b = 10$; with either choice and $i > b$, $\bar{I} < i >$ has the properties described for $\bar{I} < j-1 >$ in (3.2c); for $i = b$, that is also true for the alternative choice, but not necessarily for the first choice. I don't think that will make a significant difference, but we should keep it in mind.

Two naïve comments on $\mathcal{F}$. If one prefers to concentrate more on constructing the bundle $\mathcal{F}$ or on disproving its existence, perhaps it would be well to go back to the analytic-geometric origins of "spectrum" [BE]. That development associates to the bundle $\mathcal{E}$ on $\mathbf{P}$ (rank 2, stable with $c_1 = 0$) and a line Λ in $\mathbf{P}$ a certain bundle $\mathcal{H}$ on Λ. Then $\mathcal{S}_\mathcal{E}(j)$ is exactly the multiplicity of $\mathcal{O}_\Lambda(j)$ in the decomposition of $\mathcal{H}$. (See [H1,§7] for discussion, and [BE] for the full story.) In our situation, we do have a distinguished line, and we do have the numbers $\mathcal{S}(j)$. Can some clever bundle maker manufacture the $\mathcal{F}$ out of those data? Presumably that would involve playing with the normal bundle of the (conjectural) curve X. Another bundle–theoretic approach might be to consider for each of our testcases the moduli space $M(-p, \kappa)$ of bundles (stable, rank 2 on $\mathbf{P}$) with $c_1 = -p$ and $c_2 = \kappa$, and its "stratification by spectrum". There at least exists such a stratification in the set–theoretic sense; but perhaps, as is sometimes the case with "stratification of Hilbert scheme by Hilbert function", one can attach geometric meaning to that stratification. Then, if "gap" is possible, but rare, one could expect to find $\mathcal{F}$ as a "degenerate member" of the stratum defined by the desired $\mathcal{S}$. The two approaches I've just suggested were made possible by the fact that my knowledge of this subject is almost nil—maybe less than nil. Perhaps someone who really does know something about it can determine whether or not those suggestions are complete nonsense.

Further testcases. If things do not go well with the first four—especially if without proving "no gaps" in general, one proves that there are no such curves—then it might be well to look at these two somewhat more complex testcases. (Perhaps it would be better first to look at the $\eta = 1$ variant of (TC2); but I susupect one can do nothing with that variant if nothing can be done with (TC2).)

(**TC5**) TESTCASE: Case 1 with $(\xi, \eta, \zeta) = (6, 0, 11)$ and $(\kappa, \lambda) = (52, 16)$.

(**TC6**) TESTCASE: Case 2 with $(\xi, \eta, \zeta) = (7, 0, 12)$ and $(\kappa, \lambda) = (59, 17)$.

Those two have the advantage that κ is upper bound extremal, and consequently: in both cases $\mathcal{S}(k+2) = 0$; for (TC5), $\alpha = \beta = \gamma+1$; for (TC6), $\beta = \gamma+1$. The disadvantages: $\lambda - 2\xi - 2 = 2$ in (TC5), 1 in (TC6); both cases have the possibility that λ_γ is either 2 or 3. I suspect that the $\lambda_\gamma = 2$ alternatives will show no more than than do (TC1)–(TC4); but the (more complicated) $\lambda_\gamma = 3$ alternatives (in which cases $\mathcal{S}$ and $\bar{H}$ are uniquely determined, but $\mathcal{S}$ is "2–humped") may give some new insight. For a first try I'd avoid the situation covered by (3.5), and look at that covered by (3.4). There the second of the two alternatives, $\mu_1 = \bar{\mu} - 1 = \gamma + 1$, is intriguing: given that X has a gap, it is as close to having no gap as can be; and one of the two components in the decomposition (resulting from the gap) of the Rao module looks like the Rao module of a nullcorrelation bundle. (Does that suggest anything?) By (3.4), with that alternative, Y can't be a line—but its degree could be as small as 4. (Could four skew lines be the "right" choice for Y?) And if nothing comes of that, then there remain the variants of (TC5) and (TC6) covered by (3.5). And if nothing comes of that, there remain to be investigated a few testcases with $\lambda_\gamma = 4$. And if nothing comes of that, the last gasp for this point of view would probably be $\lambda_\gamma = 2$ with $c_2 \gg 0$ (i.e., $k \gg 0$). And if nothing comes of that, it will be time to abandon this path and to re-double efforts to establish "no gaps" as a theorem.

REFERENCES

[AG]   R. HARTSHORNE, Algebraic Geometry (GTM 52), Springer–Verlag, 1977.

[BE]   W. BARTH and G. ELENCWAJG, *Concernant la cohomologie des fibrés algébriques sur* $P_n(C)$ (in: Variétés Analytiques Compactes) LNM **683** (1978) 1-24.

[BDM]   G. BECCARI, E. DAVIS and C. MASSAZA, *Extremality with respect to the estimates of Dubreil-Campanella: splitting theorems*, JPAA **70** (1991) 211-225.

[B]   A. BURAGGINA, *On the connectedness of the Hartshorne-Rao module of curves in* P^3, Arch. Math. **60** (1993) 96-102.

[C]   G. CAMPANELLA, *Standard bases of perfect homogeneous polynomial ideals of height 2*, J. Alg. **101** (1986) 47-60.

[CV]   L. CHIANTINI and P. VALABREGA, *On some properties of subcanonical curves and unstable bundles*, Comm. Alg. **15** (1987) 1877-1887.

[D1]   E. DAVIS, *Complements to a theorem of Gherardelli: the postulational viewpoint*, Ann. Univ. Ferrara **37** (1991) 205-219.

[D2]   E. DAVIS, *Some applications of Castelnuovo theory via residuation* (Conference on 0–dimensional Schemes, Ravello 1992), Verlag Walter De Gruyter, 1993.

[D3]   E. DAVIS, *Complements to a paper of P. Dubreil*, Ric. Mat. **37** (1988) 347-357.

[GP]   L. GRUSON and C. PESKINE, *Section plane d'une courbe gauche: postulation*, Progress in Math. **24** (Birkhäuser, 1982) 33-35.

[Hs]   J. HARRIS, *The genus of space curves*, Math. Ann. **249** (1980) 191-204.

[H1]   R. HARTSHORNE, *Stable reflexive sheaves*, Math. Ann. **254** (1980) 126-176.

[H2]   R. HARTSHORNE, *Stable reflexive sheaves II*, Inv. Math. **66** (1982) 165-190.

[Ra]   A. RAO, *Liaison among curves in* P^3, Inv. Math. **50** (1979) 205-217.

[Rn]   J. RATHMANN, *The uniform position principle in characteristic p*, Math. Ann. **276** (1987) 565-579.

[Ro]   M. ROGGERO, *On rank 2 reflexive sheaves and subcanonical curves in* P^3, Comm. Alg. **16** (1988) 1770-1790.

[RV]   M. ROGGERO and P. VALABREGA, *Some vanishing properties of the intermediate cohomology of a reflexive sheaf on* P^n, to appear in J. Alg.

[S]   T. SAUER, *Nonstable reflexive sheaves on* P^3, TAMS **281** (1984) 633-655.

Albany, October 1993

D: On the Lifting Problem for Complete Intersection

Homogenous Ideals in Polynomial Rings

T. Harima
Department of Management and Information Science
Faculty of Management and Information Science
Shikoku University
Furukawa Ohjin-cho Tokushima 771-11
Japan

On the lifting problem for complete intersection homogeneous ideals in polynomial rings

Tadahito HARIMA

0. Introduction

Let k be a field and J a homogeneous ideal of $S = k[X_1, \cdots, X_n]$. In [1, Definition 1.7], the following lifting problem is discussed:

Does there exist a homogeneous ideal I of $R = k[X_0, \cdots, X_n]$ such that
  (i) I is a radical ideal,
  (ii) X_0 is not a zero-divisor on R/I,
and (iii) $R/(I, X_0) \cong S/J$ as graded k-algebras ?

If such an ideal I exists, we say that I *lifts* J, or that J *can be lifted to* I.

Many results are known about this problem:
  (1) If J is generated by monomials and the cardinarity of k is large enough, then J can be lifted ([1], [2]).
  (2) If k has characteristic 0, then every homogeneous ideal of $k[X_1, X_2]$ can be lifted ([8]).
  (3) If k is any finite field, then for any $n \geq 2$ there exists a non-liftable homogeneous ideal of S generated by monomials ([8]).
  (4) If k is an algebraically closed field, then for any $n \geq 4$ there exists a non-liftable homogeneous ideal J of S with $\dim S/J = 1$ ([7]).

The main theorem of this paper is the following :

THEOREM. *Assume that k is an infinite field. Then every complete intersection homogeneous ideal of S can be lifted.*

Moreover as an application of the above theorem, we shall give a result on deformations of complete intersection closed subschemes of $\mathbf{P}_k^{n-1}$.

1. Preliminaries

Throughout this paper, let k be a field, $S = k[X_1, \cdots, X_n]$ and $R = k[X_0, \cdots, X_n]$. Let $J \subset S$ and $I \subset R$ be ideals, and let $f \in S$, $g \in R$ and $c \in k$. We put

$$f^* = X_0^{\deg f} f(X_1/X_0, \cdots, X_n/X_0) \text{ if } f \neq 0, \ 0^* = 0,$$
$$J^* = \{f^* \mid f \in J\}R,$$
$$g(c, X) = g(c, X_1, \cdots, X_n),$$
$$I(c, X) = \{g(c, X) \mid g \in I\},$$

and $\quad l(f) = $ the homogeneous component of f with the highest degree.

It is easy to show that $I(c, X)$ is an ideal of S, and the following lemma is well known.

LEMMA 1.1 ([9, Ch.VII, §5]). (1) *Let f and h be elements of S. Then $(fh)^* = f^* h^*$, and $X_0^{\deg f + \deg h} (f + h)^* = X_0^{\deg(f+h)}(X_0^{\deg h} f^* + X_0^{\deg f} h^*)$.*

(2) *Let g be an element of R. Then $g = X_0^s g(1, X)^*$, where X_0^s is the highest power of X_0 which divides g.*

(3) *If I is a radical ideal of S, then I^* is also a radical ideal of R.*

We recall the following conditions (R_i) and (S_i) in a Noetherian ring A, where i is a non-negative integer ([5, page 183]):

(R_i) A_p is regular for all $p \in \mathrm{Spec}(A)$ with $\mathrm{ht}(p) \leq i$.

(S_i) $\mathrm{depth}(A_p) \geq \min\{\mathrm{ht}(p), i\}$ for all $p \in \mathrm{Spec}(A)$.

It is well known that A is reduced if and only if A satisfies (R_0) and (S_1), and that A is Cohen-Macaulay if and only if A satisfies (S_i) for all i.

Now let $f_1, \cdots, f_m$ be elements of S, and we put $J = (f_1, \cdots, f_m)$ and $A = S/J$. For any prime ideal p of A, we denote by $M(J, p)$ the matrix $[\partial f_i / \partial X_j(x_1, \cdots, x_n)]_{i=1,\cdots,m, j=1,\cdots,n}$, where x_i is the image of X_i in A/p. Then the following proposition is well known.

PROPOSITION 1.2 ([4, Ch.VI, Theorem 1.15]). *Assume that k is perfect. Then for a prime ideal p of A, the following conditions are equivalent :*

(1) *A_p is regular.*

(2) *$\mathrm{rank}\, M(J, p) = n - \dim A$.*

Hence if $\{f_1, \cdots, f_m\}$ is a regular sequence, then the above conditions are also equivalent to the following condition :

(3) *There exists a maximal minor μ of the matrix $[\partial f_i / \partial X_j]_{i=1,\cdots,m, j=1,\cdots,n}$ such that $\mu \notin p$.*

2. Proof of the main theorem

First, we need some lemmas.

LEMMA 2.1. *Let $f_1, \cdots, f_m$ be elements of S, and put $J = (f_1, \cdots, f_m)$. Then the following conditions are equivalent :*

(1) *$J^* = (f_1^*, \cdots, f_m^*)$.*

(2) *X_0 is not a zero-divisor on $R/(f_1^*, \cdots, f_m^*)$.*

PROOF. $(1) \Rightarrow (2)$: Let g be a homogeneous element of R such that $X_0 g \in (f_1^*, \cdots, f_m^*) = J^*$. By Lemma 1.1, we have $g = X_0^s g(1, X)^*$, where X_0^s is the highest power of X_0 which divides g. Since $X_0 g \in (f_1^*, \cdots, f_m^*)$ and $f_i^*(1, X) = f_i$, we have $(X_0 g)(1, X) \in (f_1, \cdots, f_m) =$

J. Moreover since $(X_0 g)(1, X) = (X_0^{s+1} g(1, X)^*)(1, X) = g(1, X)$, we have $g(1, X) \in J$, and $g(1, X)^* \in J^*$. Hence $g = X_0^s g(1, X)^* \in J^* = (f_1^*, \cdots, f_m^*)$.

$(2) \Rightarrow (1)$: The inclusion $J^* \supset (f_1^*, \cdots, f_m^*)$ is trivial. So it is enough to show that $h^* \in (f_1^*, \cdots, f_m^*)$ for all $h \in J$. Put $h = h_1 f_1 + \cdots + h_m f_m$, where $h_i \in S$ $(1 \leq i \leq m)$. By Lemma 1.1, we obtain that $X_0^s h^* = X_0^t h_1^* f_1^* + \cdots + X_0^u h_m^* f_m^*$ for some non-negative integers $s, t, \cdots, u$, and therefore $X_0^s h^* \in (f_1^*, \cdots, f_m^*)$. Since X_0 is not a zero-divisor on $R/(f_1^*, \cdots, f_m^*)$, we have $h^* \in (f_1^*, \cdots, f_m^*)$.

LEMMA 2.2 ([6, Lemma 3.1]). *If $f_1, \cdots, f_m$ are elements of S such that $\{l(f_1), \cdots, l(f_m)\}$ is a regular sequence, then $\{f_1, \cdots, f_m\}$ is a regular sequence.*

The following lemma is the key to the proof of our Theorem.

LEMMA 2.3. *Let J be an ideal of S generated by a homogeneous regular sequence $\{f_1, \cdots, f_m\}$, and let $g_1, \cdots, g_m$ be homogeneous elements of R such that $g_i(0, X) = f_i$. Then the ideal $I = (g_1, \cdots, g_m)$ satisfies the following :*

(1) $R/(I, X_0) \cong S/J$ as graded k-algebras.

(2) X_0 is not a zero-divisor on R/I.

(3) Assume that k is perfect, and put $h_i = g_i(1, X)$ $(1 \leq i \leq m)$. If there exists a maximal minor μ of the matrix $[\partial h_i / \partial X_j]_{i=1,\cdots,m, j=1,\cdots,n}$ such that $\mathrm{ht}((\mu, h_1, \cdots, h_m)) \geq m + 1$, then I is a radical ideal (here put $\mathrm{ht}(S) = \infty$).

PROOF. (1) Let $\varphi : R \longrightarrow S/J$ be the natural ring homomorphism with $\ker(\varphi) = (X_0, J)$. Since $g_i(0, X) = f_i$, we have $(X_0, J) = (X_0, I)$, which yields an isomorphism : $R/(X_0, I) \cong S/J$ as graded k-algebras.

(2) Since $\{X_0, f_1, \cdots, f_m\}$ is a regular sequence and $g_i(0, X) = f_i$, $\{X_0, g_1, \cdots, g_m\}$ is a regular sequence. Hence $\{g_1, \cdots, g_m, X_0\}$ is a regular sequence, and in particular X_0 is not a zero-divisor on R/I.

(3) Since $g_i(0, X) = f_i$ and $g_i(1, X) = h_i$, we have $l(h_i) = f_i$. By Lemma 2.2, $\{h_1, \cdots, h_m\}$ is a regular sequence, and the ring $A = S/(h_1, \cdots, h_m)$ satisfies (S_1) condition. Moreover since $\mathrm{ht}((\mu, h_1, \cdots, h_m)) \geq m + 1$, we have $\mu \notin p$ for all $p \in \mathrm{Min}(A)$. Thus by Proposition 1.2, the ring A_p is regular for all $p \in \mathrm{Min}(A)$, and the ring A is reduced, and $(h_1, \cdots, h_m)$ is a radical ideal. By Lemma 1.1, $(h_1, \cdots, h_m)^*$ is a radical ideal. Therefore since $h_i^* = g_i$, $(h_1, \cdots, h_m)^* = (h_1^*, \cdots, h_m^*) = I$ is a radical ideal.

Assume that $m \leq n$. For elements $f_1, \cdots, f_m$ of S, we put

$$\mu(f_1, \cdots, f_m) = \det[\partial f_i / \partial X_j]_{1 \leq i,j \leq m}.$$

Then we have the following.

LEMMA 2.4. *For elements $f_1, \cdots, f_m$ of S, there exist elements $a_1, \cdots, a_m$ of k such that $\mu(f_1 + a_1 X_1, \cdots, f_m + a_m X_m) \neq 0$.*

PROOF. We prove our claim by induction on m. The case $m = 1$ is trivial. Suppose $m > 1$. Then by induction hypothesis, there exist elements $a_1, \cdots, a_{m-1}$ of k such that

$\mu(f_1 + a_1X_1, \cdots, f_{m-1} + a_{m-1}X_{m-1}) \neq 0$. If $\mu(f_1 + a_1X_1, \cdots, f_{m-1} + a_{m-1}X_{m-1}, f_m) \neq 0$, then we put $a_m = 0$, and if $\mu(f_1 + a_1X_1, \cdots, f_{m-1} + a_{m-1}X_{m-1}, f_m) = 0$, then let a_m be any non-zero element of k. Considering the mth-row cofactor expansion of $\mu(f_1 + a_1X_1, \cdots, f_m + a_mX_m)$, we obtain $\mu(f_1 + a_1X_1, \cdots, f_m + a_mX_m) = \mu(f_1 + a_1X_1, \cdots, f_{m-1} + a_{m-1}X_{m-1}, f_m) + (-1)^{m-1}a_m\mu(f_1 + a_1X_1, \cdots, f_{m-1} + a_{m-1}X_{m-1}) \neq 0$.

LEMMA 2.5. *Let A be a Noetherian ring containing an infinite field k, and let $f_1, \cdots, f_m$ be elements of A. Then there exist elements $b_1, \cdots, b_m$ of k such that $\mathrm{ht}((f_1 + b_1, \cdots, f_m + b_m)) \geq m$.*

PROOF. We prove our claim by induction on m. Suppose $m = 1$. Then since $\# k = \infty$, $\# \mathrm{Min}(A) < \infty$ and $\# \{c \in k \mid f + c \in p\} \leq 1$ for every $p \in \mathrm{Min}(A)$, there exists an element b of k such that $f + b \notin p$ for all $p \in \mathrm{Min}(A)$, i.e. $\mathrm{ht}((f + b)) \geq 1$. Suppose $m > 1$. Then by induction hypothesis, there exsist elements $b_1, \cdots, b_{m-1}$ of k such that $\mathrm{ht}((f_1 + b_1, \cdots, f_{m-1} + b_{m-1})) \geq m - 1$. We put $B = A/(f_1 + b_1, \cdots, f_{m-1} + b_{m-1})$, then since $\# k = \infty$, $\# \mathrm{Min}(B) < \infty$ and $\# \{c \in k \mid f_m + c \in p\} < \infty$ for every $p \in \mathrm{Min}(B)$, we can take an element b_m of k such that $f_m + b_m \notin p$ for all $p \in \mathrm{Min}(B)$. hence $\mathrm{ht}((f_1 + b_1, \cdots, f_m + b_m)) \geq m$.

PROOF OF THEOREM. Assume that J is generated by a homogeneous regular sequence $\{f_1, \cdots, f_m\}$. We may assume that $\deg f_i \geq 2$ for $1 \leq i \leq m$. By Lemma 2.4, there exist elements $a_1, \cdots, a_m$ of k such that $\mu \neq 0$, where $\mu = \mu(f_1 + a_1X_1, \cdots, f_m + a_mX_m)$. Let $\bar{k}$ be an algebraic clousure of k, $\bar{S} = \bar{k}[X_1, \cdots, X_n]$ and $\bar{R} = \bar{k}[X_0, \cdots, X_n]$. By applying Lemma 2.5 to $\bar{S}/\mu\bar{S}$, there exist elements $b_1, \cdots, b_m$ of k such that $\mathrm{ht}((\mu, h_1, \cdots, h_m)\bar{S}) \geq m + 1$, where $h_i = f_i + a_iX_i + b_i$ $(1 \leq i \leq m)$. We put $g_i = h_i^*$ and $I = (g_1, \cdots, g_m)R$. Then since $g_i(0, X) = f_i$, we have $R/(X_0, I) \cong S/J$ as graded k-algebras, and X_0 is not a zero-divisor on R/I. On the other hand, since $h_i = g_i(1, X)$, we obtain from Lemma 2.3 that the ideal $I\bar{R}$ is a radical ideal. Hence I is a radical ideal. This completes the proof.

EXAMPLE. Assume that k is an algebraically closed field, and put $S = k[X_1, X_2, X_3]$ and $J = (X_1^2 + X_2X_3, X_2^2 + X_1X_3, X_3^2 + X_1X_2)$. Then J is a complete intersection homogeneous ideal, and by the proof of Theorem a lifting of J is given by $(X_1^2 + X_2X_3, X_2^2 + X_1X_3, X_3^2 + X_1X_2 + aX_0^2)$, where a is any non-zero element of k.

3. An application

PROPOSITION. *Assume that k is an algebraically closed field. Then every complete intersection closed subscheme Z of $\mathbf{P}_k^{n-1}$ can be deformed over an open subscheme U of $\mathbf{A}_k^1$ into a reduced closed subscheme of $\mathbf{P}_k^{n-1}$, that is, there exists a closed subscheme W of $\mathbf{P}_k^{n-1} \times \mathbf{A}_k^1$ such that*
> (i) *the morphism $\pi : \pi^{-1}(U) \longrightarrow U$ induced by the projection $\pi : W \longrightarrow \mathbf{A}_k^1$ is flat,*
> (ii) *$\pi^{-1}(P) \cong Z$ for some point $p \in U$,*
and (iii) *the other fibres are reduced.*

PROOF. Let $J = (f_1, \cdots, f_m)$ be the complete intersection homogeneous ideal of S defining Z, where $m = \mathrm{ht}(J)$. Take a homogeneous element l of S with $\deg l = 1$ such that $\{f_1, \cdots, f_m, l\}$ is a regular sequence. Then by the proof of Theorem, there exists a finite subset T of k and homogeneous elements $g_1, \cdots, g_m$ of R such that for all $c \in k \backslash T$, the ideal $(g_1, \cdots, g_m, X_0 - cl)$ of R lifts $(f_1, \cdots, f_m, l)$. Let W be the closed subscheme of $\mathbf{P}_k^{n-1} \times \mathbf{A}_k^1$ defined by the ideal $(g_1(tl, X), \cdots, g_m(tl, X)) \subset k[t][X_1, \cdots, X_n]$, and let U be the open subscheme of $\mathbf{A}_k^1$ consisting of the prime ideal $(t - c)$, such that $c \in k \backslash T$, together with (t). For every closed point $p = (t - c)$ such that $c \notin T$, the fibre $\pi^{-1}(p) \subset \mathbf{P}_k^{n-1}$ has the homogeneous coordinate ring $S/(g_1(cl, X), \cdots, g_m(cl, X)) \cong R/(g_1, \cdots, g_m, X_0 - cl)$ which is reduced. Also it is easy to see that $\pi^{-1}((t)) \cong Z$. Thus the fibres of π have a constant Hilbert function over U. Hence by [3, Ch.III, §9, Theorem 2.2] the morphism $\pi : \pi^{-1}(U) \longrightarrow U$ is flat. This completes the proof.

References

[1] A. V. Geramita, D. Gregory and L. G. Roberts, Monomial ideals and points in projective space, J. Pure Appl. Algebra, 40 (1986), 33-62.

[2] R. Hartshorne, Connectedness of the Hilbert scheme, Inst. Hautes Etudes Sci. Publ. Math. 29 (1966), 261-304.

[3] R. Hartshorne, Algebraic Geometry, Springer, 1977.

[4] E. Kunz, Introduction to Commutative Algebra and Algebraic Geometry. Birkhäuser, 1985.

[5] H. Matsumura, Commutative Ring Theory, Cambridge University Press, Cambridge, 1986.

[6] L. G. Roberts and M. Roitman, On the Hilbert function of reduced and of integral algebra, J. Pure Appl. Algebra, 56 (1989), 85-104.

[7] L. G. Roberts, On the lifting problem over an algebraically closed field, C.R.Math. Rep. Acad. Sci. Canada, Vol.XI, No.1 (1989), 35-38.

[8] M. Roitman, On the lifting problem for homogeneous ideals in polynomial rings, J. Pure Appl. Algebra, 51 (1988), 205-215.

[9] O. Zariski and P. Samuel, Commutative Algebra Vol.II, Springer, 1975.

E: On Graded Betti Numbers and Geometrical Properties

of Projective Varieties

U. Nagel
FB Mathematik - Informatik/17
Universität-GH Paderborn
D - 33095 Paderborn
Germany

Y. Pitteloud
Department of Mathematics and Statistics
Queen's University
Kingston, Ontario K7L 3N6
Canada

On graded Betti numbers and geometrical properties of projective varieties

Uwe Nagel[1]

FB Mathematik - Informatik/17, Universität-GH Paderborn, D — 33 095 Paderborn, Germany; e-mail: uwen@uni-paderborn.de

Yves Pitteloud[2]

Department of Mathematics and Statistics, Queen's University, Kingston, Ontario, K7L3N6, Canada; e-mail: PITTELOU@QUCDN.QUEENSU.CA

Introduction

Given a projective variety in $\mathbb{P}^n$, one obtains a collection of invariants, the graded Betti numbers, by considering the minimal graded free resolution of the homogeneous coordinate ring of the variety. Recently a great deal of research has attempted to understand the interplay between the algebra and the geometry arising in such a situation.

This search was started in the pioneering paper [13], by M. Green. In this article new techniques were developed for the computation of Betti numbers, making strong use of the Koszul complex, and various connections with geometrical questions were explained. Most of the results of [13] are formulated in the setting of compact complex manifolds. The main object of the present paper is to examine how some of these results generalize to more general subschemes of $\mathbb{P}^n$.

The main computationals tools introduced in [13] are the following:

---

[1]Supported by Deutsche Forschungsgemeinschaft
[2]Supported by the Swiss National Research Fund

the Vanishing Theorem (cf. Theorem 3.a.1),

the Duality Theorem (cf. Theorem 2.c.6),

the $K_{p,1}$ Theorem (cf. Theorem 3.c.1).

An algebraic version of the vanishing theorem has been proved by D. Eisenbud and J. Koh in [7] (cf. theorem 1.7) and hence we will concentrate our attention in this paper on the Duality Theorem and on the $K_{p,1}$ Theorem.

We will adopt a slightly different approach from that in [13], where graded $Sym H^0(X, \mathcal{L})$-modules of the form $\oplus H^0(X, \mathcal{E} \otimes \mathcal{L}^{\otimes q})$ are studied, with $\mathcal{E}$, $\mathcal{L}$ locally free sheaves on a variety X, and $\mathcal{L}$ of rank one. Our projective varieties X will be already embedded in some $\mathbb{P}^n$ and we will consider arbitrary graded modules M over the polynomial ring $R = k[x_0, \ldots, x_n]$; of course, in the most interesting case M is the homogeneous coordinate ring of X, or its canonical module. Our techniques will be mainly algebraic, although inspired by the techniques introduced in [13].

Section 1 deals with the Duality theorem. Roughly speaking the problem considered is the following. Given a Cohen-Macaulay graded R-module M (where R is the polynomial ring in $n+1$ variables), of dimension, say $m+1$, one can dualize the minimal graded free resolution of M and obtains the minimal free resolution of $Ext_R^{n-m}(M, R)$. In other words, if we denote by ω_M the R-module $Ext_R^{n-m}(M, R)(-n-1)$ (the canonical module), we have an isomorphism for all i and j

$$Tor_i^R(M, k)_{i+j} \cong Tor_{n-m-i}^R(\omega_M, k)_{n+1-i-j}.$$

We show, using a spectral sequence argument, how the Cohen-Macaulay hypothesis on M can be weakened and replaced by a suitable cohomological hypothesis on M, if one is just willing to have the isomorphism above only for certain values of j (cf. theorem 1.2). We explain how Green's Duality Theorem fits in the pattern of our result. Then we extend to singular curves a result of Green (cf. [13] Theorem 4.a.1) on the syzygies of a curve embedded by a very ample line bundle to singular curves (cf. theorem 1.6) generalizing a serie of results by Mumford, Saint-Donat and Fujita (cf. [19], [22] and [11]) about projective normality, and generation by quadrics of embedded curves.

In section 2 we consider the graded Betti numbers of a finite scheme on a rational normal curve. In certain cases we are able to compute all of them. This is related to results in [9] and will be used later.

In section 3 we consider the problem of bounding the length of the 2-linear part of the minimal resolution of the coordinate ring of a projective variety. If the variety lies on many quadrics, the bound provided by the Vanishing Theorem of Green/Eisenbud-Koh is much too big. Green however showed, in the so called $K_{p,1}$ Theorem, that the codimension of the variety turns out to be a bound; moreover this bound is only reached in the case of a variety of minimal degree. We show how his results remain true under a much weaker hypothesis. We allow the schemes to be non-reduced and singular (cf. theorem 3.5). In particular we get a version of the $K_{p,1}$ theorem for ribbons, an interesting class of schemes introduced in [1].

Both the authors would like to warmly thank Tony Geramita for many interesting discussions during their stay at Queen's University. The first author would also like to thank Mark Green for valuable discussions.

The authors are grateful to the referee for his helpful comments.

1 Betti numbers and duality

Throughout the paper R will denote the polynomial ring $k[x_0, \ldots, x_n]$ over a field k. Given a graded R-module M, we denote by $[M]_j$ the homogeneous component of M of degree j; given an integer q, we write $M(q)$ for the qth shift of M (defined by the formula $[M(q)]_j = M_{q+j}$) and we write $M^\vee$ for the graded k-dual of M. By the dimension of a graded R-module M we will mean the Krull dimension of the ring $R/Ann(M)$.

The local cohomology modules of a graded R-module M, with respect to the irrelevant ideal $\mathfrak{m} = (x_0, \ldots, x_n)$, will be denoted by $H^q_{\mathfrak{m}}(M)$. Recall that they are graded R-modules. The Local Duality Theorem states that there is an isomorphism of graded R-modules (where Ext denotes the "graded Ext")

$$H^i_{\mathfrak{m}}(M)^\vee \cong Ext_R^{n+1-i}(M, R)(-n-1).$$

We write $K(\underline{x})$ for the Koszul complex of R associated to the variables $x_0, \ldots, x_n$. Given a graded R-module the Koszul homology modules $H_p(\underline{x}, M)$ are the homology modules of $K(\underline{x}) \otimes_R M$ and the Koszul cohomology modules $H^p(\underline{x}, M)$ are the homology modules of $Hom_R(K(\underline{x}), M)$ (where Hom denotes the "graded Hom"). The following properties of these Koszul modules are well known.

Remark 1.1 a) The Koszul complex $K(\underline{x})$ is a minimal graded free resolution of the R-module k. Consequently we have isomorphisms of graded modules

$$H_p(\underline{x}, M) \cong Tor_p^R(k, M) \quad \text{and} \quad H^p(\underline{x}, M) \cong Ext_R^p(k, M).$$

b) Let M be graded R-module; if $[M]_i = 0$ then

$$[H_p(\underline{x}, M)]_{i+p} = 0 \quad \text{and} \quad [H^p(\underline{x}, M)]_{i-p} = 0 \quad \text{for all } p.$$

This follows at once from degree considerations.

c) There are isomorphisms of graded modules

$$H^p(\underline{x}, M) \cong H_{n+1-p}(\underline{x}, M)(n+1), \quad \text{for every } p.$$

This follows from the symmetry of the Koszul complex.

d) There is a spectral sequence (hypercohomology) of graded R-modules

$$E_2^{p,q} = H^p(\underline{x}, H_{\underline{m}}^q(M)) \implies H^{p+q}(\underline{x}, M),$$

where the differentials $d_r : E_r^{p,q} \to E_r^{p+r,q-r+1}$ are homogeneous maps of degree zero.

The main result of this section is the following theorem, where given a graded R-module M of Krull dimension $m+1$, we denote by ω_M the graded R-module $Ext_R^{n-m}(M, R)(-n-1)$.

Theorem 1.2 *Let M be a R-module of Krull dimension $m+1$. Let j be an integer such that*

$$[H_{\underline{m}}^q(M)]_{j-q} = 0 \quad and \quad [H_{\underline{m}}^q(M)]_{j-q+1} = 0 \quad for \; q = 0, \ldots, m,$$

and such that all the vector spaces $[H_{\underline{m}}^{m+1}(M)]_i$ are of finite type. There is then an isomorphism of k-vector spaces

$$[Tor_i^R(M, k)]_{i+j} \cong [Tor_{n-m-i}^R(\omega_M, k)]_{n+1-i-j}, \quad for \; all \; i.$$

Remark 1.3 The hypothesis above includes, of course, the case where M is a Cohen-Macaulay module of finite type, and in this case the assertion is well known (cf., for example, [21], Lemma 2.1).

A special case of this theorem, Corollary 1.4, is a well known result about the Castelnuovo-Mumford regularity of a R-module M (cf. [6], Theorem 1.2). Recall that the Castelnuovo-Mumford regularity of a R-module M is defined to be the largest integer j such that there is a q with $H^q_{\mathfrak{m}}(M)_{j-q} \neq 0$.

Corollary 1.4 *Given a finitely generated graded R-module M, the following statements are equivalent:*

$\quad$ *a)* $[H^q_{\mathfrak{m}}(M)]_{j-q} = 0$ *for all q and all* $j > j_0$,
$\quad$ *b)* $[Tor^R_i(M, k)]_{i+j} = 0$ *for all i and all* $j > j_0$.

Proof of the Corollary: Suppose first that we have, for some integer j_0, $[Tor_i(M, k)]_{i+j} = 0$ for all $j > j_0$. This means that in the minimal graded free resolution of M

$$0 \to \oplus R(-e_{sj}) \to \cdots \to \oplus R(-e_{ij}) \to \cdots \to \oplus R(-e_{0j}) \to M \to 0$$

we have the inequality $e_{ij} \leq i + j_0$. Now applying $Hom_R(\ , R)$ to the resolution, we deduce that $[Ext^i_R(M, R)]_l$ is zero when $l < -i - j_0$ and the conclusion follows by local duality.

Suppose now that $[H^q_{\mathfrak{m}}(M)]_{j-q} = 0$ for all $j > j_0$; in particular the hypothesis of Theorem 1.2 is satisfied for those j, and hence we have the following isomorphism for all $j > j_0$:

$$[Tor_i(M, k)]_{i+j} \cong [Tor_{n-m-i}(\omega_M, k)]_{n+1-i-j}.$$

By local duality the module ω_M is isomorphic to $H^{m+1}_{\mathfrak{m}}(M)^{\vee}$ and so the hypothesis on the local cohomology implies that $[\omega_M]_l$ is zero for all $l < m + 1 - j_0$; this in turn implies that $[Tor_{n-m-i}(\omega_M, k)]_l$ is zero for all $l < n + 1 - i - j_0$ which concludes the proof of the Corollary.

For the proof of Theorem 1.2 we will use the spectral sequence of Remark 1.1 d): The vanishing hypothesis in Theorem 1.2 will be just what is needed to have enough vanishing on the homogeneous part of the E_2 term, in certain degrees.

Proof of Theorem 1.2: Let M and j be as in Theorem 1.2 and let s be an integer. We will look at the homogeneous part of degree $j - s$ of the E_2 term of the spectral sequence:

$$[E^{p,q}_2]_{j-s} = [H^p(\underline{x}, H^q_{\mathfrak{m}}(M))]_{j-s}.$$

E-5

As the modules $[H^q_{\mathfrak{m}}(M)]_{j-q+1}$ are zero for $q = 0, \ldots, m$, we obtain the following equalities by Remark 1.1 b):

$$[H^p(\underline{x}, H^q_{\mathfrak{m}}(M))]_{j-s} = 0, \quad \text{for } p + q = s + 1 \quad \text{and } q \leq m.$$

In other words $[E^{p,q}_2]_{j-s}$ is zero for those values of p, q. On the other hand, $E^{p,q}_2$ is zero, in all degrees, for $q > m + 1$, as the Krull dimension of M is $m + 1$. These two facts imply the following isomorphism:

$$[E^{s-m-1,m+1}_2]_{j-s} \cong [E^{s-m-1,m+1}_\infty]_{j-s}.$$

We also have that the modules $[H^q_{\mathfrak{m}}(M)]_{j-q}$ are zero for $q = 0, \ldots, m$, and this in turn implies the following equalities

$$[H^p(\underline{x}, H^q_{\mathfrak{m}}(M))]_{j-s} = 0, \quad \text{for } p + q = s \quad \text{and } q \leq m.$$

In other words, $[E^{pq}_2]_{j-s}$ is zero for those values of p, q. As $E^{p,q}_2 = 0$ when $p > m + 1$, the spectral sequence gives the isomorphism

$$[E^{s-m-1,m+1}_\infty]_{j-s} \cong [H^s(\underline{x}, M)]_{j-s}.$$

Putting together these observations, we obtain an isomorphism

$$[H^s(\underline{x}, M)]_{j-s} \cong [H^{s-m-1}(\underline{x}, H^{m+1}_{\mathfrak{m}}(M))]_{j-s}. \qquad (*)$$

To conclude the proof of Theorem 1.2, it remains to identify the two vector spaces appearing in the isomorphism above.

By Remark 1.1, $[H^s(\underline{x}, M)]_{j-s}$ is isomorphic to the vector space $[Tor_{n+1-s}(M, k)]_{j-s+n+1}$, so setting $i = n + 1 - s$, this latter is precisely the left handside in the isomorphism of Theorem 1.2.

Next, we have to identify the right handside of $(*)$. By local duality, the module $H^{m+1}_{\mathfrak{m}}(M)$ is isomorphic to the module $\omega^\vee_M$ (here we use the fact that the $[H^{n+1}_{\mathfrak{m}}(M)]_i$ are k-vector spaces of finite type). By Remark 1.1 a) and [23], Corollary 0.4.11, we have the following isomorphisms:

$$[H^{s-m-1}(\underline{x}, H^{m+1}_{\mathfrak{m}}(M))]_{j-s} \cong [Ext^{s-m-1}_R(k, \omega^\vee_M)]_{j-s} \cong [Tor_{s-m-1}(k, \omega_M)]_{s-j},$$

and setting, as above, $i = n + 1 - s$, this latter is isomorphic to the vector space $[Tor^R_{n-m-i}(k, \omega_M)]_{n+1-i-j}$. This concludes the proof of Theorem 1.2.

Remark 1.5 Given an m-dimensional locally Cohen-Macaulay equidimensional projective scheme over a field, an ample invertible sheaf $\mathcal{L}$ on X with a base point free linear system $W \subset H^0(X, \mathcal{L})$ of dimension $n+1$ and a locally free sheaf $\mathcal{E}$ on X, consider the $R \ (= Sym W)$-graded modules

$$M = \oplus_{q \in \mathbb{Z}} H^0(X, \mathcal{E} \otimes \mathcal{L}^{\otimes q}) \quad \text{and} \quad N = \oplus_{q \in \mathbb{Z}} H^0(X, \mathcal{E}^* \otimes \mathcal{K}_X \otimes \mathcal{L}^{\otimes q}),$$

where $\mathcal{K}_X$ denotes the dualizing sheaf and "$*$" denotes the $\mathcal{O}_X$ dual. Suppose moreover that the following equalities are satisfied, for $q = 1, \ldots, m-1$:

$$H^q(X, \mathcal{E} \otimes \mathcal{L}^{\otimes(j-q)}) = 0 \quad \text{and} \quad H^q(X, \mathcal{E} \otimes \mathcal{L}^{\otimes(j-q-1)}) = 0.$$

There are then isomorphisms

$$[Tor_i^R(M, k)]_{i+j} \cong [Tor_{n-m-i}^R(N, k)]_{n+1-i-j} \quad \text{for each } i.$$

This assertion, similar to the Theorem 2.c.6 of [13], can be derived from our Theorem 1.2 as follows. By [14], III 2.1, there are isomorphisms

$$H_{\mathfrak{m}}^{i+1}(M) \cong \oplus_{q \in \mathbb{Z}} H^i(X, \mathcal{E} \otimes \mathcal{L}^{\otimes q}) \text{ for } i \geq 1 \quad \text{and} \quad H_{\mathfrak{m}}^0(M) = H_{\mathfrak{m}}^1(M) = 0,$$

where $\mathfrak{m}$ denotes the irrelevant ideal in R. Hence, by Serre Duality, we have

$$N \cong \oplus_{q \in \mathbb{Z}} Hom_k(H^n(X, \mathcal{E} \otimes \mathcal{L}^{* \otimes q}), k) = (\oplus_{q \in \mathbb{Z}} H^n(X, \mathcal{E} \otimes \mathcal{L}^{\otimes q}))^\vee \cong H_{\mathfrak{m}}^{n+1}(M)^\vee.$$

The assertion is now a direct consequence of Theorem 1.2.

Now let $\mathcal{C}$ be an integral curve and let $\mathcal{L}$ be a very ample line bundle on $\mathcal{C}$. Let S be the ring $\oplus H^0(\mathcal{C}, \mathcal{L}^{\otimes n})$, considered as a graded module over the ring $R = Sym H^0(\mathcal{C}, \mathcal{L})$. We say that $\mathcal{L}$ satisfies property (N_p) if $Tor_0^R(S, k) \cong k$ and $Tor_i^R(S, k) \cong k(-i-2)^{\alpha_i}, \alpha_i \in \mathbb{Z}$, for $1 \leq i \leq p$ (cf. [4]). Let $\psi_{\mathcal{L}}(\mathcal{C})$ be the embedding of $\mathcal{C}$ into $\mathbb{P}(H^0(X, \mathcal{L}))$. Then $\mathcal{L}$ satisfies (N_0) iff $\psi_{\mathcal{L}}(\mathcal{C})$ is projectively normal. $\mathcal{L}$ satisfies (N_1) iff (N_0) holds and the homogeneous ideal I of $\psi_{\mathcal{L}}(\mathcal{C})$ is generated by quadrics. $\mathcal{L}$ satisfies (N_2) iff $(N_0), (N_1)$ hold and the first syzygy module of I is generated by linear relations; and so on.

The following result was proved by Green in the case of a smooth curve over $\mathbb{C}$ (cf. [13], Theorem 4.a.1). It could also be derived using Theorem 3 of [5] instead of our Duality Theorem. Note also that there is a generalization of Green's result by Ein and Lazarsfeld to higher dimensional smooth varieties over the complex numbers (cf. [4]).

Theorem 1.6 *Let C be an integral curve of arithmetic genus g over an algebraically closed field. Let $\mathcal{L}$ be an invertible sheaf on C of degree $\geq 2g + 1 + p$ for some $p \geq 1$. Then $\mathcal{L}$ satisfies property (N_p).*

Proof. Let N be the R-module $\oplus H^0(C, \mathcal{K} \otimes \mathcal{L}^{\otimes q})$, where $\mathcal{K}$ is the dualizing sheaf on C. Note that $\mathcal{L}$ is very ample and generated by global sections (see [11] Proposition 1.6). Hence, as in Remark 1.5 we have $N \cong H^2_{\mathfrak{m}}(S)^{\vee}$. From this we deduce that N is a torsion free $R/\wp$-module, where $\wp$ denotes the ideal of $\psi_L(C)$ in R (cf. [21], Lemma 2.6). Now, rank $[N]_0 = g <$ rank $[R]_1 = d - g + 1$ where $d = \deg \mathcal{L}$. Hence $[N]_j = 0$ for all $j < 0$. Thus we obtain, by Remark 1.5,

$$[Tor^R_{d-g-1-i}(S, k)]_{d-g+1-j} \cong [Tor^R_i(N, k)]_j = 0 \quad \text{for } j < i \text{ and for all } i.$$

Moreover, Theorem 1.7 below gives

$$[Tor^R_{d-g-1-i}(S, k)]_{d-g+1-i} \cong [Tor^R_i(N, k)]_i = 0 \quad \text{for } i \geq g,$$

proving the claim.

Theorem 1.7 (cf. [7], Theorem 1.1) *Let M be a graded module over the polynomial ring $R = k[x_0, \ldots, x_n]$ and suppose that M is torsion free over $R/\wp$ for some absolutely irreducible prime ideal $\wp$. Then $[Tor_i(M, k)]_{i+j} = 0$ for $i \geq$ rank $[M]_j$.*

Theorem 1.7, which we have been using in the proof of Theorem 1.6, is the generalization to the non smooth case of the vanishing theorem of Green (cf. [13] Theorem 3.a.1) due to Eisenbud and Koh.

2 Finite schemes on a rational normal curve

Recently, J. Harris and D. Eisenbud [9] have extended the notion of linearly general position from sets of points to arbitrary 0-dimensional subschemes. A finite subscheme $X \subset \mathbb{P}^n$ is said to be in linearly general position iff for every proper linear subspace L of $\mathbb{P}^n$ we have

$$\deg X \cap L \leq \dim L + 1.$$

Harris and Eisenbud could extend some results of Castelnuovo theory to schemes X in linearly general position. In particular, they have shown that X lies on a unique rational normal curve if deg $X = n + 3$ [9], Theorem 1 or deg $X \geq 2n + 3$ but X imposes only $2n + 1$ independent conditions on quadrics [10], Theorem 2.2. In this section we want to study the graded Betti numbers of finite schemes on a rational normal curve. Note that these schemes are always in linearly general positon. We need these results in the next section but they are also interesting in their own right.

For the remainder of the paper we will always assume that the ground field k is algebraically closed. The homogeneous ideal of a subscheme $S \subset \mathbb{P}^n$ will be denoted by I_S. It is always assumed to be a saturated ideal.

Lemma 2.1 *Let X be a finite scheme on a rational normal curve C of $\mathbb{P}^n$. Let p be an integer with $0 \leq p \leq n$. If deg $X \geq 2n + 1 - p$ then*

$$[Tor_i^R(k, I_X)]_{i+2} = [Tor_i^R(k, I_C)]_{i+2} \text{ for all } i \geq p.$$

Proof: The exact sequence

$$0 \longrightarrow I_C \longrightarrow I_X \longrightarrow I_X/I_C \longrightarrow 0$$

gives an exact sequence

$$[Tor_{i+1}^R(k, I_X/I_C)]_{i+2} \rightarrow [Tor_i^R(k, I_C)]_{i+2} \rightarrow [Tor_i^R(k, I_X)]_{i+2} \rightarrow$$

$$[Tor_i^R(k, I_X/I_C)]_{i+2}.$$

Since I_X does not contain a linear form we get $[Tor_{i+1}^R(k, I_X/I_C)]_{i+2} = 0$.

By [9], Theorem 3.2 we have for the Hilbert function of X, $h_X(2) \geq 2n + 1 - p$. Therefore we get rank $[I_X/I_C]_2 \leq 2n + 1 - p - (2n + 1) = p$. Since I_X/I_C is torsion free as an R/I_X-module, the Vanishing Theorem 1.7 gives $[Tor_i^R(k, I_X/I_C)]_{i+2} = 0$ for all $i \geq p$. The claim is now a consequence of the above exact sequence.

It is easy to compute the Betti numbers of a rational normal curve. Recall that a subscheme V of $\mathbb{P}^n$ is called variety of minimal degree if V is integral, nondegenerate and deg $V = $ codim $V + 1$. Note that this is the minimal possible degree of an integral nondegenerate subscheme of $\mathbb{P}^n$. For example, a curve of minimal degree is precisely a rational normal curve.

By a famous classification theorem of Bertini (cf. [8]), a variety of minimal degree is either a rational normal scroll or a cone over the Veronese surface in $\mathbb{P}^5$. In the first case the homogeneous ideal of the scroll is generated by the maximal minors of an 1-generic matrix of linear forms (see [8]). The resolution of such an ideal is given by the Eagon-Northcott complex; as the Betti numbers of a Veronese surface are the same as the Betti numbers of a surface scroll in $\mathbb{P}^5$, we have thus the following result.

Lemma 2.2 *Let $V \subset \mathbb{P}^n$ be a variety of minimal degree and codimension c. Then V has a minimal free resolution of the following shape:*

$$0 \to \oplus R(-c-1)^{\beta_{c-1}} \to \ldots \to \oplus R(-2)^{\beta_0} \to I_V \to 0$$

where $\beta_i = \ \mathrm{rank} \ [Tor_i^R(k, I_V)]_{i+2} = (i+1)\binom{c+1}{i+2}, \quad i = 0, \ldots, c-1.$

Now we are able to compute the graded Betti numbers of certain subschemes of a rational normal curve. This generalizes [2], Proposition 3.1 and [3], Theorem 6.

Proposition 2.3 *Let X be a finite subscheme of $\mathbb{P}^n$ of degree $2n + 1 - p$ where $0 \le p < n$. Suppose that X is a subscheme of a rational normal curve. Then the minimal graded free resolution of I_X has the following form:*

$$0 \to R(-n-2)^{\beta_{n-1}} \to R(-n-1)^{\beta_{n-2}} \oplus R(-n)^{\alpha_{n-2}} \to \ldots$$

$$\to R(-p-3)^{\beta_p} \oplus R(-p-2)^{\alpha_p} \to R(-p-1)^{\alpha_{p-1}} \to$$

$$\to R(-p)^{\alpha_{p-2}} \ldots \to R(-2)^{\alpha_0} \to I_X \to 0$$

where

$$\alpha_i = \begin{cases} (i+1)\binom{n+2}{i+2} - \binom{n}{i} \ deg \ X & if \ 0 \le i \le p \\ (i+1)\binom{n}{i+2} & if \ p \le i \le n-2 \end{cases}$$

and

$$\beta_i = \ \binom{n}{i+1} \ deg \ X - (i+2)\left(\binom{n+2}{i+3} - \binom{n}{i+3}\right) \ for \ p \le i \le n-1 \ .$$

Proof: By [9], Theorem 3.2, X has Hilbert function $1, n + 1, deg \ X, \ldots$. Thus we get (cf., for example, [21], Remark 2.5(v))

$$[Tor_i^R(k, I_X)]_j = 0 \text{ for all } j \ne i + 2, i + 3.$$

E-10

Hence, using the additivity of the rank function on exact sequences (applied here to the minimal fee resolution of R/I_X), as wll as the above description of the Hilbert function of X, we obtain, as in [2], proposition 1.6

$$\text{rank } [Tor_p^R(k, I_X)]_{p+2} - \text{ rank } [Tor_{p-1}^R(k, I_X)]_{p+2} =$$

$$(p+1)\binom{n+2}{p+2} - \binom{n}{p} \deg X.$$

But, from Lemma 2.1 and Lemma 2.2, after some computations, we get

$$\text{rank } [Tor_p^R(k, I_X)]_{p+2} = (p+1)\binom{n}{p+2} = (p+1)\binom{n+2}{p+2} - \binom{n}{p} \deg X.$$

It follows that $[Tor_{p-1}^R(k, I_X)]_{p+2} = 0$. Using, for example, our Duality Theorem we get

$$[Tor_i^R(k, I_X)]_{i+3} = 0 \text{ for all } i \leq p - 1,$$

Thus the claim follows by Lemma 2.2, Lemma 2.1 and [2], Proposition 1.6.

After writing this paper, the preprint of K. Yanagowa [24] came to our attention. He obtains the above result (cf. [24], Corollary 3.4) by completely different means.

3 The length of the linear part of a resolution

One of the most beautiful results in M. Green's paper [13] is the so-called $K_{p.1}$ Theorem. The aim of this section is to show that some of the assumptions for this result in [13] can be relaxed.

In this section we will consider hyperplane sections of projective schemes, so we need to make this notion clear. Let $I \subset R = k[x_0, \ldots, x_n]$ be an homogeneous ideal and let $S = Proj(R/I)$. We denote, as before, the homogeneous ideal of S by I_S. Let $H = Proj(R/lR)$ be a general hyperplane. The geometric hyperplane section $S \cap H$ is $Proj(R/I_S + lR)$ and will always be considered as a subscheme of $Proj(R/lR)$. Its homogeneous ideal $I_{S \cap H}$ is thus the saturation of the ideal $(I_S + lR)/lR$. This latter ideal is called the algebraic hyperplane section of S.

Let $I \subset R$ be a homogeneous ideal with initial degree $t = \min \{s \in \mathbb{Z} : [I]_s \neq 0\}$. Then a nonzero element of $[Tor_i^R(k, I)]_{i+t}$ corresponds to a i-linear syzygy in the sense of [7]. If I is saturated and $S = Proj(R/I)$ then we call the i-linear syzygies of I also i-linear syzygies of S. A linear syzygy of S is an i-linear syzygy for some i. The linear syzygies correspond to a subcomplex of the minimal free resolution. This subcomplex is called the t-linear or simply linear part of the resolution (for more details, cf. [7]).

The following facts show that linear syzygies are easier to study than arbitrary syzygies.

Remark 3.1 a) If I is a saturated ideal and l is a linear form whose residue class modulo I is a non-zero divisor in R/I, then it is well-known that all the syzygies of $I + lR/lR$ are restrictions of the syzygies of I. In particular, the Betti numbers of I as an R-module are the same as the Betti numbers of $I + lR/lR$ as an R/lR-module.

b) If t is the initial degree of I then it is not hard to see (cf. [2]) that

$$[Tor_i^R(k, I)]_{i+t} \cong (\Lambda^i[R]_1 \otimes [I]_t) \cap K_i$$

where K_i is the kernel of the Koszul map $\Lambda^i[R]_1 \otimes [R]_t \longrightarrow \Lambda^{i-1}[R]_1 \otimes [R]_{t+1}$.

c) It follows from b) that if $I \subset J$ are homogeneous ideals with the same initial degree t, then every linear syzygy of I is also a linear syzygy of J; in other words the canonical morphism $[Tor_i^R(k, I)]_{i+t} \to [Tor_i^R(k, J)]_{i+t}$ is injective for all i.

d) Combining a) and c) we see that for a general hyperplane H, linear syzygies of a subscheme S restrict to linear syzygies of $S \cap H$ provided that I_S and $I_{S \cap H}$ have the same initial degree.

For arbitrary subschemes of $\mathbb{P}^n$ there is the following bound for the length of the linear part of the minimal resolution.

Lemma 3.2 *Let $S \subset \mathbb{P}^n$ be a closed subscheme of codimension c and let t be the initial degree of its homogeneous ideal I_S. Let $L \subset \mathbb{P}^n$ be a general linear subspace of dimension c and suppose that $I_{S \cap L}$ has initial degree t too. Then*

$$[Tor_i^R(k, I_S)]_{i+t} = 0 \quad \text{for all } i \geq c.$$

Proof: Suppose $[Tor_i^R(k, I_S)]_{i+t} \neq 0$ for some $i \geq c$. Let $L = Proj(B)$. Then we get from Remark 3.1 d) that $Tor_i^B(k, I_{S \cap L}) \neq 0$. But this contradicts the theorem of Auslander and Buchsbaum since $B/I_{S \cap L}$ is a 1-dimensional Cohen-Macaulay ring.

There are conditions ensuring that the assumption above is satisfied. If $t = 2$ and S has a top-dimensional component S' such that S'_{red} is nondegenerate then $I_{S \cap L}$ has also initial degree 2. This follows by induction because $I_{S'_{red} \cap H}$ is nondegenerate in H for a general hyperplane H by Bertini's Theorem.

If S is an integral curve in $\mathbb{P}^3$ then the assumption of Lemma 3.2 is satisfied if $deg(S) > t^2 + 1$. This result is due to Gruson and Peskine. For some generalizations we refer to [20].

We need some more notation. For a finite set J we write $|J|$ for its cardinality. If $J = \{j_1, \ldots, j_i\} \subset \{0, \ldots, n\}$ we set $e_J = x_{j_1} \wedge \ldots \wedge x_{j_i}$. Thus the e_J form a basis of $\Lambda^i[R]_1$, where J varies in the set of i-tuples $\{j_1, \ldots, j_i\} \subset \{0, \ldots, n\}$ with $j_1 < \cdots < j_i$. Let $0 \neq \alpha \in [Tor_i^R(k, I)]_{i+t}$ for some homogeneous ideal I with initial degree t. By Remark 3.1 b), we can write

$$\alpha = \sum_{|J|=i} e_J \otimes F_J$$

with forms $F_J \in [I]_t$. Let $I(\alpha)$ denote the ideal generated by the F_J, and call it the ideal asssociated to the (linear) syzygy α. By definition, we have that $I(\alpha) \subset I$. Moreover, we set $V(\alpha) = Proj(R/I(\alpha))$ and call it the subscheme associated to α. Note that we do not know a priori if $I(\alpha)$ is saturated. Note, moreover, that $I(\alpha)$ does not depend on the choice of a basis for $\Lambda^i[R]_1$.

In case $t = 2$, the $K_{p.1}$-Theorem in [13] gives a much better description of the length of the linear part of the resolution than Lemma 3.2. The basis for this improvement is the so-called Strong Castelnuovo Lemma. Using Green's ideas this has been refined in [3] and can be stated as follows.

Proposition 3.3 *Let $S \subset \mathbb{P}^n$ be a closed subscheme such that S contains a finite subscheme Y of degree at least $n + 3$. Then S is contained in a rational normal curve C of $\mathbb{P}^n$ if and only if $[Tor_{n-2}^R(k, I_S)]_n \neq 0$ and Y is in linearly general position.*

Moreover, if $0 \neq \alpha \in [Tor_{n-2}^R(k, I_S)]_n$ and if Y is in linear general position, then $I(\alpha)$ is prime and $V(\alpha)$ is the unique rational normal curve of $\mathbb{P}^n$ containing S.

Note that we do not assume that S is zero dimensional. Since only a slightly weaker and less precise version of Proposition 3.3 is proved in [3], we include a proof using the results of [3].

Proof: If $S \subset C$ then we get by Remark 3.1 c) and Lemma 2.2, that $0 \neq [Tor_{n-2}^R(k, I_C)]_n \hookrightarrow [Tor_{n-2}^R(k, I_S)]_n$. Moreover, Y is in linearly general position because every finite scheme of degree at least n on a rational normal curve is in linearly general position. This proves one implication.

To prove the other implication let $0 \neq \alpha \in [Tor_{n-2}^R(k, I_S)]_n$. Since Y is in linearly general position it lies on an unique rational normal curve C by Theorem 1 in [9]. Thus, using Remark 3.1 c) and Lemma 2.1 we get $\alpha \in [Tor_{n-2}^R(k, I_Y)]_n \cong [Tor_{n-2}^R(k, I_C)]_n$. Therefore we obtain, by Remark 3.1 b), that $I(\alpha) \subset I_C$. Now our Lemma 2.2 and Proposition 4 in [3] give that

$$\binom{c}{2} = \text{rank } [I_C]_2 \geq \text{rank } [I(\alpha)]_2 \geq \binom{c}{2}.$$

Since I_C is generated by quadrics it follows that $I(\alpha) = I_C$ completing the proof.

The result above applies, in particular, to an irreducible, nondegenerate subscheme S of positive dimension because on such a scheme S we can find a set of t points in linearly general position for any given positive integer t. Here we use the notion nondegenerate in the following sense.

Definition 3.4 A closed subscheme $S \subset \mathbb{P}^n$ is said to be nondegenerate if S_{red} is not contained in any hyperplane of $\mathbb{P}^n$.

This definition is a bit unusual but useful for our purposes.

We are now ready to state the algebraic analog to Green's $K_{p.1}$-Theorem.

Theorem 3.5 *Let* $S = Proj(R/I_S) \subset \mathbb{P}_k^n$ *be a closed subscheme of dimension* $m > 0$ *and codimension* $c \geq 2$. *Suppose that* S *has a nondegenerate* m-*dimensional component* S'. *Then we have:*

(i) $[Tor_i^R(k, I_S)]_{i+2} = 0$ *for all* $i \geq c$;

(ii) $[Tor_{c-1}^R(k, I_S)]_{c+1} \neq 0$ *if and only if* S *is a variety of minimal degree;*

(iii) *if* $\deg S'_{red} \geq c + 4$ *and either* $char(k) = 0$ *or* S'_{red} *is smooth, then* $[Tor_{c-2}^R(k, I_S)]_c \neq 0$ *if and only if* S *is contained in a variety of minimal degree having dimension* $m + 1$;

(iv) The claim in (iii) is also true if S is a nondegenerate, integral sub-scheme of degree $c + 3$ and either $char(k) = 0$ or S is smooth.

Note that $[Tor^R_{i-1}(k, I_S)]_{i+1} \cong [Tor^R_i(k, R/I_S)]_{i+1}$ and this corresponds in Green's notation to the Koszul homology group $K_{i,1}$ (from which the name of the theorem is derived).

The assumption that S has a nondegenerate top-dimensional component is necessary for Theorem 3.5 (i) and (ii). One need only consider the example of two skew lines in $\mathbb{P}^3$. Moreover, the claim in (iii) fails in general for integral schemes with deg $S = $ codim $S + 2$ as the del Pezzo surface of degree 9 in $\mathbb{P}^9$ shows. This example is due to Green [13].

Part (iii) of the above theorem is the most difficult to prove. We will deduce it from the following more general result.

Proposition 3.6 *Let $S = Proj(R/I_S) \subset \mathbb{P}^n$ be a closed subscheme of codimension $c \geq 2$. Suppose that for a general linear subspace $L \subset \mathbb{P}^n$ of dimension c, $S \cap L$ contains a finite scheme in linearly general position in L of degree at least $c + 4$. Then $[Tor^R_{c-2}(k, I_S)]_c \neq 0$ if and only if S lies on a variety of minimal degree having codimension $c - 1$.*

In particular: If $0 \neq \alpha \in [Tor^R_{c-2}(k, I_S)]_c$ then $I(\alpha)$ is prime and $V(\alpha)$ is a variety of minimal degree having codimension $c - 1$ and containing S.

Proof: If S lies on a variety V of minimal degree having codimension $c - 1$ then, by Lemma 2.2,

$$\text{rank } [Tor^R_{c-2}(k, I_S)]_c \geq \text{ rank } [Tor^R_{c-2}(k, I_V)]_c = c - 1.$$

For the other implication we induct on the dimension $m = n - c$ of S. If $m = 0$ then Proposition 3.3 gives the claim. Suppose $m > 0$. The assumption on $S \cap L$ implies in particular that $I_{S \cap L}$ has initial degree 2. Therefore Remark 3.1 d) applies to all successive general hyperplane sections of S.

Let

$$0 \neq \alpha = \sum_{|J|=c-2} e_J \otimes F_J \in [Tor^R_{c-2}(k, I_S)]_c.$$

Let H be a general hyperplane and l its defining equation. We choose a basis $\{l_0 = l, l_1, \ldots, l_n\}$ of $[R]_1$ and write l_J for $l_{j_1} \wedge \ldots \wedge l_{j_s}$, where $J = \{j_1, \ldots, j_s\}$.

E-15

Then $\{l_J \ : \ |J| = c - 2, J \subset \{0, \ldots, n\}$ with $j_1 < \cdots < j_{c-2}\}$ is a basis for $\Lambda^{c-2}[R]_1$ and we can write α as

$$\alpha = \sum_{|J|=c-2,\ 0\notin J} l_J \otimes G_J + \sum_{|I|=c-3,\ 0\notin I} l \wedge l_I \otimes Q_I \in \Lambda^{c-2}[R]_1 \otimes [I_S]_2.$$

Let $\bar{F}$ denote the image of a form $F \in R$ under the canonical map onto $\bar{R} = R/lR$; we see that the restriction of α to the general hyperplane H is

$$0 \neq \alpha|_H = \sum_{|J|=c-2,\ 0\notin J} l_J \otimes \bar{G}_J \in [Tor^{\bar{R}}_{c-2}(k, I_{S\cap H})]_c.$$

Since H is general we have $\dim S = \dim S \cap H$. Hence we may apply the induction hypothesis and get that $I(\alpha|_H)$ is a prime ideal defining a variety W of minimal degree having codimension $c - 1$ in $H \cong \mathbb{P}^{n-1}$. In particular we have $I(\alpha|_H) = I_W \subset I_{S\cap H}$.

We now want to show that $\bar{Q}_I \in I(\alpha|_H)$ for all Q_I occuring in α. Since α is mapped onto zero under the Koszul map we see that

$$\beta = \sum_{|I|=c-3,\ 0\notin I} l_I \otimes Q_I \in [Tor^{R}_{c-3}(k, I_S)]_{c-1}.$$

Suppose $\beta \neq 0$. Then we get as above

$$0 \neq \beta|_H = \sum_{|I|=c-3} l_I \otimes \bar{Q}_I \in [Tor^{\bar{R}}_{c-3}(k, I_{S\cap H})]_{c-1}.$$

Let $L = L' \cap H = Proj(R')$ be a general linear subspace of dimension c. Since we consider only linear syzygies we get (cf. Remark 3.1)

$$\text{rank } [Tor^{R'}_{c-3}(k, I_{S\cap L})]_{c-1} = \text{rank } [Tor^{R'}_{c-3}(k, I_{S\cap L'\cap H})]_{c-1} \geq$$
$$\text{rank } [Tor^{\bar{R}}_{c-3}(k, I_{S\cap H})]_{c-1} \geq \text{rank } [Tor^{\bar{R}}_{c-3}(k, I_W)]_{c-1} =$$
$$\text{rank } [Tor^{R'}_{c-3}(k, I_{W\cap L'})]_{c-1}.$$

The last equality is true because W, as a variety of minimal degree, is arithmetically Cohen-Macaulay. Since $S \cap L$ lies on the rational normal curve $W \cap L'$, Lemma 2.1 applies, and we conclude that the inequalities above are in fact equalities. Thus we get, in particular,

$$\text{rank } [Tor^{\bar{R}}_{c-3}(k, I_{S\cap H})]_{c-1} = \text{rank } [Tor^{\bar{R}}_{c-3}(k, I_W)]_{c-1}.$$

Hence $I_W \subset I_{S \cap H}$ implies

$$\sum_{|I|=c-3} l_I \otimes \bar{Q}_I \in [Tor_{c-3}^{\bar{R}}(k, I_{S \cap H})]_{c-1} = [Tor_{c-3}^{\bar{R}}(k, I_W)]_{c-1} \subset \Lambda^{c-3}[R]_1 \otimes [I_W]_2.$$

Therefore we have that $\bar{Q}_I \in I(\alpha|_H)$. It follows that

$$I(\alpha) + lR/lR = I(\alpha|_H) = I_W \subset \bar{R}.$$

Since l is a general linear form we get deg $I(\alpha) = $ deg $I_W = c$. Moreover, since I_W is perfect, $I(\alpha)$ is perfect too. Thus $I(\alpha)$ is equidimensional and has only nondegenerate components because I_W is nondegenerate. Since any nondegenerate component of $I(\alpha)$ has degree at least $c = $ deg $I(\alpha)$, $I(\alpha)$ must be prime. This concludes the proof of Proposition 3.6.

We are now ready for the proof of our version of the $K_{p,1}$ theorem.

Proof of Theorem 3.5: By the remarks immediately after the proof of Lemma 3.2, the existence of S' allows us to apply Remark 3.1 and Lemma 3.2. The latter implies claim (i).

By Lemma 2.2 the conditions in (ii) - (iv) are sufficient for the non-vanishing of the appropriate Tor groups. Now we show the reverse implication beginning with (ii).

Let $L = Proj(R') \subset \mathbb{P}^n$ be a general linear subspace of dimension $c + 1$. Suppose that we have $\alpha \neq 0$ in $[Tor_{c-1}^R(k, I_S)]_{c+1}$. Then we get, by Remark 3.1, that $0 \neq \alpha|_L \in [Tor_{c-1}^{R'}(k, I_{S \cap L})]_{c+1}$. Furthermore, $S \cap L$ has a 1-dimensional nondegenerate component coming from S'. Hence Proposition 3.3 applies to $S \cap L$ and we obtain that $I(\alpha|_L) = I_C$, i. e., the 1-dimensional scheme $S \cap L$ is contained in a rational normal curve C. It follows that $S \cap L = C$ and deg $S = $ deg $C = c + 1$. On the other hand, deg $S' \geq c + 1$ because S' is nondegenerate. It follows that S has exactly one top-dimensional component, namely a variety V of minimal degree. It remains to exclude the possibility that S has lower-dimensional components. Assume $I_S = I_V \cap J$ where J is an ideal of dimension $< m$. We have, by Lemma 2.2:

$$\binom{c+1}{2} = \text{rank } [I_V]_2 \geq \text{rank } [I_S]_2.$$

On the other hand we have $I_C = I(\alpha|_L) \subset I(\alpha)R'$. This implies

$$\text{rank } [I_S]_2 \geq \text{rank } [I(\alpha)]_2 \geq \text{rank } [I_C]_2 = \binom{c+1}{2}.$$

E-17

Putting both estimates together we see, in particular, that $[I_V]_2 = [I_S]_2$. It follows that $[I_V]_2 \subset J$. But I_V is generated by quadrics, a fact that implies $I_V \subset J$, a contradiction. Hence $S = V$ and (ii) is shown.

To prove (iii) we first note that the assumptions "$char(k) = 0$" or "S'_{red} smooth" ensure that, for a general linear subspace L of dimension c, $S'_{red} \cap L$ is a set of deg S'_{red} points in linearly general position in L (see [16], p. 197 and [18], Proposition 5). Hence Proposition 3.6 applies and proves (iii).

The proof of (iv) follows an argument of M. Green. We sketch it here for the sake of completeness. Let $0 \neq \alpha \in [Tor^R_{c-2}(k, I_S)]_c$. Let $H_0, \ldots, H_m$ be general hyperplanes. Then we want to show

Claim: $V(\alpha|_{H_0 \cap \ldots \cap \hat{H}_i \cap \ldots \cap H_m}) \cap H_i = V(\alpha|_{H_0 \cap \ldots \cap H_m})$ for all $i = 0, \ldots m$

where $H_0 \cap \ldots \cap \hat{H}_i \cap \ldots \cap H_m$ means that H_i is omitted in the intersection.

Proof of the claim: As in (iii) we have for all i that $S \cap H_0 \cap \ldots \cap \hat{H}_i \cap \ldots \cap H_m$ is a set of $c + 3$ points in linearly general position. Thus $V(\alpha|_{H_0 \cap \ldots \cap \hat{H}_i \cap \ldots \cap H_m})$ is a rational normal curve due to Proposition 3.3 and $V(\alpha|_{H_0 \cap \ldots \cap \hat{H}_i \cap \ldots \cap H_m}) \cap H_i \subset V(\alpha|_{H_0 \cap \ldots \cap H_m})$ is a set of c independent points in a $(c-1)$-plane. Then it follows by [12] that

$$\binom{c}{2} \leq \operatorname{rank} [I(\alpha|_{H_0 \cap \ldots \cap H_m})]_2.$$

On the other hand the ideal of c independent points is generated by $\binom{c}{2}$ quadrics. Thus our claim follows from the containment relation above.

Now we choose pencils of general hyperplanes $\{H_{\lambda_i} : \lambda_i \in \mathbb{P}^1\}$ $(i = 1, \ldots m)$. Then there exist open subsets $U_i \subset \mathbb{P}^1$ such that $S \cap H_{\lambda_1} \cap \ldots \cap H_{\lambda_m}$ is in linearly general position for all $\lambda_i \in U_i$. We put

$$T = \overline{\bigcup_{\lambda_1 \in U_1, \ldots, \lambda_M \in U_m} V(\alpha|_{H_{\lambda_1} \cap \ldots \cap H_{\lambda_m}})}$$

where $^-$ denotes the closure in the Zarisky topology. We want to show that T is the required variety of minimal degree containing S. To clarify ideas we assume $U_i = \mathbb{P}^1$ for all i. The general case follows by using relations like $T \cap L = \overline{\bigcup_{\lambda_1 \in U_1, \ldots, \lambda_m \in U_m} V(\alpha|_{H_{\lambda_1} \cap \ldots \cap H_{\lambda_m}})} \cap L$ for a general hyperplane L.

Under our assumption we obtain

$$T = \overline{\bigcup_{\lambda_1 \in \mathbb{P}^1, \ldots, \lambda_m \in \mathbb{P}^1} V(\alpha|_{H_{\lambda_1} \cap \ldots \cap H_{\lambda_m}})} \supseteq$$
$$\overline{\bigcup_{\lambda_1 \in \mathbb{P}^1, \ldots, \lambda_m \in \mathbb{P}^1} V(\alpha) \cap H_{\lambda_1} \cap \ldots \cap H_{\lambda_m}} = V(\alpha) \supseteq S.$$

Let now $L_1, \ldots, L_m$ be be further general hyperplanes. Then we get by using the claim

$$
\begin{aligned}
T \cap L_1 \cap & \ldots \cap L_m \\
&= \bigcup_{\lambda_1 \in \mathbb{P}^1, \ldots, \lambda_m \in \mathbb{P}^1} V(\alpha|_{H_{\lambda_1} \cap \ldots \cap H_{\lambda_m}}) \cap L_1 \cap \ldots \cap L_m \\
&= \bigcup_{\lambda_1 \in \mathbb{P}^1, \ldots, \lambda_m \in \mathbb{P}^1} V(\alpha|_{H_{\lambda_1} \cap \ldots \cap H_{\lambda_{m-1}}) \cap L_m} \cap L_1 \cap \ldots \cap L_{m-1} \cap H_{\lambda_m} \\
&= \bigcup_{\lambda_1 \in \mathbb{P}^1, \ldots, \lambda_{m-1} \in \mathbb{P}^1} V(\alpha|_{H_{\lambda_1} \cap \ldots \cap H_{\lambda_{m-1}}) \cap L_m} \cap L_1 \cap \ldots \cap L_{m-1} \\
&= \ldots \\
&= V(\alpha|_{L_1 \cap \ldots \cap L_m}).
\end{aligned}
$$

By Proposition 3.3 $V(\alpha|_{L_1 \cap \ldots \cap L_m})$ is a rational normal curve. Then it follows as in the proof of (ii) that T is a variety of minimal degree of dimension $m+1$ concluding the proof of Theorem 3.5.

In [1] D. Bayer and D. Eisenbud have introduced ribbons. A ribbon is a subscheme $S \subset \mathbb{P}^n$ such that the ideal sheaf $\mathcal{I}$ of S_{red} in S has square 0 and the conormal sheaf $\mathcal{I}/\mathcal{I}^2$ is a line bundle on S. By [9], Theorem 3.1, the general hyperplane section of an irreducible ribbon is in linearly general position. Thus we get, from Theorem 3.5(ii) and Proposition 3.6, the following corollary.

Corollary 3.7 *Let* $S \subset \mathbb{P}^n_k$ *be a nondegenerate irreducible ribbon over an algebraically closed field* k *of characteristic zero. Let* $c = codim\ S$. *Then we have*

(i) $[Tor^R_{c-1}(k, I_S)]_{c+1} = 0$;

(ii) $[Tor^R_{c-2}(k, I_S)]_c \neq 0$ *if and only if* S *is contained in a variety of minimal degree and of codimension* $c - 1$.

Another application of Theorem 3.5 is concerned with a problem which arises, for example, in the study of varieties with maximal geometric genus. One wants to know if a scheme is contained in a variety of minimal degree, knowing that its general hyperplane section is contained in such a variety.

Corollary 3.8 *Let* $V \subset \mathbb{P}^n_K$ *be a nondegenerate integral and linearly normal subscheme of codimension* c *and degree at least* $c + 3$. *Suppose that either* $char(K) = 0$ *or* V *is smooth. If the general hyperplane section of* V *is contained in a variety of minimal degree having codimension* $c - 1$ *in the hyperplane, then* V *is contained in a variety of minimal degree having codimension* $c - 1$.

This result is well-known if deg $V \geq 2c + 1$. In this case V lies on the variety of minimal degree cut out by all quadrics containing V (cf. [17]). This fails if deg $V \leq 2c$. Of course, the assumption linearly normal ensures that for all hyperplanes H, all quadrics containing $V \cap H$ lift to quadrics containing V, but the variety cut out by these lifted quadrics depends on H. Thus we do not know a priori its general hyperplane section.

Proof: Let $H = Proj(R')$ be a general hyperplane. Since $V \cap H$ lies on a variety of minimal degree and is nondegenerate by Bertini's Theorem we get, by Remark 3.1 c) and Lemma 2.2, that $[Tor_{c-2}^{R'}(k, I_{V \cap H})]_c \neq 0$. By the linear normality of V, every quadric containing $V \cap H$ lifts to a quadric containing V. Therefore every linear syzygy of $V \cap H$ lifts to syzygy of V. If follows that $[Tor_{c-2}^{R}(k, I_V)]_c \neq 0$. Thus Theorem 3.5 shows the claim.

If the characteristic of the ground field is zero and $V \subset \mathbb{P}^n$ is smooth of dimension $> \frac{2n-3}{3}$ then V is linearly normal according to Zak's solution of the first part of Hartshorne's conjecture on varieties of low codimension.

References

[1] D. Bayer, D. Eisenbud: Ribbons, in preparation.

[2] M. P. Cavaliere, M. E. Rossi, G. Valla: On the resolution of certain graded algebras, Trans. Amer. Math. Soc. 337 (1993), 389 - 409.

[3] M. P. Cavaliere, M. E. Rossi, G. Valla: The strong Castelnuovo lemma for zerodimensional subschemes, Preprint, University of Genova, 1993.

[4] L. Ein, R. Lazarsfeld: Syzygies and Koszul cohomology of smooth projective varieties of arbitrary dimensiom, Invent. Math. 111 (1993), 51 - 67.

[5] D. Eisenbud, J. Koh, M. Stillman: Determinantal equations for curves of high degree, Amer. J. Math. 110 (1988), 513 - 539.

[6] D. Eisenbud, S. Goto: Linear free resolutions and minimal multiplicitiy, J. Algebra 88 (1964), 89 - 133.

[7] D.Eisenbud, J. Koh: Some linear syzygy conjectures, Adv. Math. 90 (1991), 47 - 76.

[8] D. Eisenbud, J. Harris: On varieties of minimal degree (A centennial account), Algebraic Geometry, Bowdoin, 1985, Proc. Sympos. Pure Math., 46, Part 1, Amer. Math. Soc. Providence RI (1987), 3 - 13.

[9] D. Eisenbud, J. Harris: Finite projective schemes in linearly general position, J. Alg. Geom. 1 (1992), 15 - 30.

[10] D. Eisenbud, J. Harris: An intersection bound for rank 1 loci, with applications to Castelnuovo and Clifford theory, J. Alg. Geom. 1 (1992), 31 - 60.

[11] T. Fujita: Defining equations for certain types of polarized variety, in: Complex Analysis and Algebraic Geometry, W.L. Baily, Jr. and T. Shioda, eds. Cambridge Univ. Press (1977), 165 - 173.

[12] M. Green: The canonical ring of a variety of general type, Duke Math. J. 49 (1982), 1087 - 1113.

[13] M. Green: Koszul cohomology and the geometry of projective varieties, J. Diff. Geom. 19 (1984), 125 - 171.

[14] A. Grothendieck: Eléments de géométrie algébrique III, Publ. Math. IHES 11 (1961)

[15] R. Hartshorne: Algebraic Geometry, Springer-Verlag, New-York 1977.

[16] J. Harris: The genus of space curves, Math. Ann. 249 (1980), 191 - 204.

[17] J. Harris: A bound on the geometric genus of projective varieties, Ann. Scuola Norm. Sup. Pisa Cl. Sci. (4) 8 (1981), 36 - 68.

[18] D. Laksov: Indecomposability of restricted tangent bundles, in: Tableaux de Young et functeurs de Schur en algebre et geometry, Asterisque 87 - 88 (1981), 207 - 219.

[19] D. Mumford: Varieties defined by quadratic equations, C.I.M.E. (1969)-III, 29 -100.

[20] E. Mezzetti: Differential-geometric methods for the lifting problem and linear systems on plane curves, Preprint 1993.

[21] U. Nagel: On the equations defining arithmetically Cohen-Macaulay varieties in arbitrary characteristic, Preprint, 1993.

[22] B. Saint-Donat: Sur les équations définissant une courbe algébrique, C.R. Acad. Sc. Paris 274 (1972), 324 - 327.

[23] P. Stückrad, W. Vogel: Buchsbaum Rings and Applications, VEB Deutscher Verlag der Wissenschaften, Berlin, 1986.

[24] K. Yamagawa: Some extensions of Castelnuovo's lemma on zero-dimensional schemes, Preprint, 1993.

F: Powers of Ideals and Growth of the Deficiency Module

C. S. Peterson
Department of Mathematics
University of Notre Dame
Notre Dame, Indiana 46556-5683
U.S.A.

POWERS OF IDEALS AND GROWTH
OF THE DEFICIENCY MODULE

C.S. PETERSON

Introduction.

Throughout this paper, we will work in $\mathbb{P}^3 = \mathbb{P}^3_k$, where k is an algebraically closed field with $\text{char}(k) = 0$. Let $\mathbf{R} := k[w,x,y,z]$ and let a curve be taken to mean a locally Cohen-Macaulay closed subscheme of $\mathbb{P}^3$ of pure dimension one. The Hartshorne-Rao module (or deficiency module), $M(C)$, of a curve, C, is defined

$$M(C) = \bigoplus_{n \in \mathbb{Z}} \mathbf{H}^1(\mathbb{P}^3, \mathfrak{I}_C(n))$$

where $\mathfrak{I}_C$ is the ideal sheaf of C. $M(C)$ is a graded $\mathbf{R}$-module of finite length. Various properties of C can be deduced from the structure of the Hartshorne-Rao module. We can see from the definition that $M(C)$ measures the failure of C to be arithmetically Cohen-Macaulay (i.e. it measures the failure of the linear systems on C, cut out by hypersurfaces, to be complete). Thus, $M(C)$ is equal to zero if and only if C is arithmetically Cohen-Macaulay and "simple" curves tend to have "simple" Hartshorne-Rao modules.

Let $\mathbf{I}$ be a homogeneous ideal in the ring $\mathbf{R}$, let D be the scheme defined by $\mathbf{I}$ and let $\mathfrak{I}_D$ be the associated ideal sheaf. The saturation, $\bar{\mathbf{I}}$, of $\mathbf{I}$ is defined

$$\bar{\mathbf{I}} = \bigoplus_{t \in \mathbb{Z}} \mathbf{H}^0(\mathbb{P}^3, \mathfrak{I}_D(t))$$

$\bar{\mathbf{I}}$ is also called the homogeneous ideal of D. If $\mathbf{J}$ is any other ideal defining the same scheme as $\mathbf{I}$, then $\mathbf{J} \subseteq \bar{\mathbf{I}}$ and $\bar{\mathbf{J}} = \bar{\mathbf{I}}$. We will say $\mathbf{I}$ is saturated if $\mathbf{I} = \bar{\mathbf{I}}$. A theorem of Huneke and Ulrich [HU], when viewed in the context of curves in $\mathbb{P}^3$, tells us that if C is an arithmetically Cohen-Macaulay curve and $\mathbf{I} = \bar{\mathbf{I}}$ is the homogeneous ideal of C with C a generic complete intersection but not a complete intersection then for all n≥2 either $\mathbf{I}^n$ is not saturated or the scheme defined by $\mathbf{I}^n$ is not arithmetically Cohen-Macaulay. This leads to an interesting question: is the theorem of Huneke and Ulrich true if we drop

The author would like to thank the University of Notre Dame for their hospitality

Typeset by $\mathcal{A}\mathcal{M}\mathcal{S}$-TEX

the assumption that C is arithmetically Cohen-Macaulay? We examine this and the related question: what can we say about the nature of $M(C_n)$ where C_n is the scheme defined by $\mathbf{I}^n$?

The paper is divided into four sections. Section 1 is mainly a collection of definitions and theorems related to the notions of "analytic spread" and "symbolic powers" of an ideal. Section 2 describes a theorem from a paper of Migliore [M] and a method for attacking powers of ideals. In section 3 we combine the ideas found in section 1 and section 2 and examine the consequences. Section 4 discusses possible directions of further investigation.

I am very thankful to L. Ein and M.S. Ravi for fruitful discussions in person and by e-mail, to A.V. Geramita for his many questions and suggestions, to M. Johnson for helpful clarifications and discussions, and most especially to J. Migliore for his time and patience. The work for this paper was carried out while I was a visitor of the Department of Mathematics at the University of Notre Dame; I am very grateful for their kind hospitality.

§1. Analytic Spread and Symbolic Powers of Ideals.

In this section we collect some ideas and results from the theory of the analytic spread of an ideal. We also define the symbolic power of an ideal. The theorems and definitions are all stated in the context of a graded ring $\mathbf{R}=k[x_0,...,x_r]$ where k is an algebraically closed field and $\mathrm{char}(k)=0$. The main reference is the paper of Northcott and Rees [NR].

Definition 1.1. *Let $\mathfrak{a}$ and $\mathfrak{b}$ be ideals in the graded ring $\mathbf{R}=k[x_0,...,x_r]$ with $\mathfrak{b} \subseteq \mathfrak{a}$. Then $\mathfrak{b}$ is called a reduction of $\mathfrak{a}$ if $\mathfrak{b} \cdot \mathfrak{a}^n = \mathfrak{a}^{n+1}$ for $n \gg 0$.*

Remark 1.2. *If $\mathfrak{b} \cdot \mathfrak{a}^r = \mathfrak{a}^{r+1}$ then $\mathfrak{b} \cdot \mathfrak{a}^n = \mathfrak{a}^{n+1}$ for all $n \geq r$.*

We illustrate this with an example: let $\mathfrak{a}=(x^2,xy,y^2)$ and let $\mathfrak{b}=(x^2,y^2)$ then $\mathfrak{b} \subseteq \mathfrak{a}$ and $\mathfrak{b} \cdot \mathfrak{a} = (x^2,y^2) \cdot (x^2,xy,y^2) = (x^4,x^3y,x^2y^2,xy^3,y^4) = (x^2,xy,y^2) \cdot (x^2,xy,y^2) = \mathfrak{a} \cdot \mathfrak{a} = \mathfrak{a}^2$ so $\mathfrak{b}$ is a reduction of $\mathfrak{a}$.

Theorem 1.3 [NR]. *If $\mathfrak{a}$ is an ideal and $\phi(s,\mathfrak{a})= \dim_k(\mathfrak{a}^s/\mathfrak{a}^s\mathfrak{m})$ then $\phi(s,\mathfrak{a})$ is a polynomial in s for $s \gg 0$ (here $\mathfrak{m}$ denotes the maximal ideal in $\mathbf{R}$).*

By definition, $\phi(s,\mathfrak{a})$ is the number of elements in a minimal base of $\mathfrak{a}^s$. Since $\phi(s,\mathfrak{a})$ is a polynomial in s for $s \gg 0$ it is natural to consider the polynomial defined by $\phi(s,\mathfrak{a})$. We denote it by $\Phi(s,\mathfrak{a})$.

Definition 1.4. *We let $l(\mathfrak{a})$ denote the analytic spread of the ideal $\mathfrak{a}$ and we define $l(\mathfrak{a}) = degree(\Phi(s,\mathfrak{a}))+1$.*

There is a way to connect the idea of analytic spread of an ideal to the notion of reduction of an ideal. This is accomplished in the following lemma

Lemma 1.5 [NR]. *The analytic spread of an ideal is equal to the analytic spread of any reduction of the ideal.*

Given an ideal $\mathfrak{a} \in \mathbf{R}$ it would be nice to have some bounds on $l(\mathfrak{a})$; the following theorem of Burch gives us much more.

Theorem 1.6 [Bu]. $l(\mathfrak{a}) \leq dim(\mathbf{R})\text{-}min\ \{codim(\mathbf{R}/\mathfrak{a}^n)|n \in \mathbb{N}\}.$

From Theorem 1.6 and Definition 1.4 we see that the homogeneous ideal of a curve in $\mathbb{P}^3$ can have an analytic spread equal to 2, 3, or 4. Let $\nu(\mathfrak{a})$ denote the number of elements in a minimal generating set of $\mathfrak{a}$. Definition 1.4 leads directly to the inequality $l(\mathfrak{a}) \leq \nu(\mathfrak{a})$ so we can conclude that the homogeneous ideal of a complete intersection curve in $\mathbb{P}^3$ has analytic spread 2. A theorem of Cowsik and Nori gives us a nice converse to this statement.

Theorem 1.7 [CN]. *If C is a reduced curve in $\mathbb{P}^3$ and $\mathbf{I}_C$ is the homogeneous ideal of C then $l(\mathbf{I}_C)=2$ implies that C is a complete intersection.*

Now let's examine symbolic powers of ideals and the relationship to analytic spread.

Definition 1.8. *Let $\mathfrak{a}$ be a $\mathfrak{p}$-primary ideal in $\mathbf{R}$. If we look at a primary decomposition of $\mathfrak{a}^n$ then $\mathfrak{p}$ will be a minimal associated prime. The nth symbolic power of $\mathfrak{a}$ is the unique $\mathfrak{p}$-primary component of $\mathfrak{a}^n$ and is denoted $\mathfrak{a}^{(n)}$.*

Let $\mathbf{I}_C$ be the homogeneous ideal of a curve in $\mathbb{P}^3$. $\mathbf{I}_C^{(n)}$ is obtained by saturating the ideal $\mathbf{I}_C^n$ and then removing embedded points. If a curve, C, is a local complete intersection then the scheme defined by $\mathbf{I}_C^n$ has no embedded points [Ma], so for local complete intersection curves in $\mathbb{P}^3$, $\mathbf{I}_C^n = \mathbf{I}_C^{(n)}$ if and only if $\mathbf{I}_C^n$ is saturated. We have the following theorem of Dutta.

Theorem 1.9 [D]. *Let $\mathbf{I}_C$ be the homogeneous ideal of a curve in $\mathbb{P}^3$. Then $\nu(\mathbf{I}_C^{(n)}) \leq Kn^2$ for some constant K.*

If a curve, C, is a local complete intersection and $l(\mathbf{I}_C)=4$ then from the previous remarks and the theorem of Dutta we can conclude that $\mathbf{I}_C^n$ is not saturated for all $n \gg 0$. The following theorem of Brodmann is a useful extension to Theorem 1.6.

Theorem 1.10 [B1, B2]. *The set of associated primes of $\mathfrak{a}^n$ stabilizes and $l(\mathfrak{a}) \leq dim(\mathbf{R})\text{-}codim(\mathbf{R}/\mathfrak{a}^n)$ for $n \gg 0$.*

From Theorem 1.7 and Theorem 1.10 we see that if $\mathbf{I}_C$ is the homogeneous ideal of a reduced curve in $\mathbb{P}^3$ and if $\mathbf{R}/\mathbf{I}_C^n$ is arithmetically Cohen-Macaulay for all $n \gg 0$ then $l(\mathbf{I}_C)=2$ and C is a complete intersection. We can rephrase this as follows: if C is a curve in $\mathbb{P}^3$ which is reduced but not a complete intersection then for some constant k and all $n \geq k$ either $\mathbf{I}_C^n \neq \mathbf{I}_C^{(n)}$ or the scheme defined by $\mathbf{I}_C^n$ is not arithmetically Cohen-Macaulay. The following theorem of Huneke and Ulrich tells us we can let $k=2$ if $\mathbf{I}_C$ is arithmetically Cohen-Macaulay.

Theorem 1.11 [HU]. *Let C be an arithmetically Cohen-Macaulay curve in $\mathbb{P}^3$ which is generically a complete intersection but not a complete intersection. Let $\mathbf{I}_C$ be the homogeneous ideal of C. Then for all $n \geq 2$, $\mathbf{R}/\mathbf{I}^n$ is not Cohen-Macaulay.*

It is an interesting problem to determine when $\mathbf{I}_C^n = \mathbf{I}_C^{(n)}$. From some of the preceeding comments we immediately obtain that $l(\mathbf{I}_C)=2$ implies that $\mathbf{I}_C^n = \mathbf{I}_C^{(n)}$ and that $l(\mathbf{I}_C)=4$ implies that $\mathbf{I}_C^n \neq \mathbf{I}_C^{(n)}$ (for all sufficiently large n). The case of $l(\mathbf{I}_C)=3$ requires a more careful analysis. Here we quote a theorem of Huneke and Huckaba and then give two examples.

Theorem 1.12 [HH]. *Let $\mathbf{I}_C$ be the homogeneous ideal of a local complete intersection curve in $\mathbb{P}^3$; if $l(\mathbf{I}_C)=3$ then $\mathbf{I}_C^n = \mathbf{I}_C^{(n)}$.*

Example 1.13. *Let $\mathbf{I} \subset k[w,x,y,z]$ be the homogeneous ideal of the monomial quartic (i.e. the ideal of the curve defined parametrically by $w = s^4$, $x = s^3 t$, $y = st^3$, $z = t^4$). We can verify (eg. with the computer algebra system Macaulay [Mac]) that $\mathbf{I}= (xy - wz, y^3 - xz^2, x^3 - w^2 y, wy^2 - x^2 z)$. Let $\mathbf{J}= (xy - wz, y^3 - xz^2, x^3 - w^2 y)$; then $\mathbf{J} \subset \mathbf{I}$ and $\mathbf{J} \cdot \mathbf{I} = \mathbf{I}^2$. Since the monomial quartic is a reduced curve and not a complete intersection, we know that $l(\mathbf{I}) \neq 2$. Since $l(\mathbf{I}) = l(\mathbf{J})$ and $l(\mathbf{J}) \leq \nu(\mathbf{J})=3$, we see that $l(\mathbf{I})=3$. The monomial quartic is smooth so by Theorem 1.12 we have $\mathbf{I}^n = \mathbf{I}^{(n)}$.*

Example 1.14. *Let $\mathbf{I} \subset k[w,x,y,z]$ be the homogeneous ideal of the monomial curve defined parametrically by $w = s^5$, $x = s^2 t^3$, $y = st^4$, $z = t^5$. Using Macaulay [Mac], we can verify that $\mathbf{I}=(y^2 - xz, x2y - wz2, x3 - wyz)$. We see that $\mathbf{I}$ has 3 generators so it is not a complete intersection. The ideal is arithmetically Cohen-Macaulay and has analytic spread 3. C is not a local complete intersection at the point $[1:0:0:0]$. $\mathbf{I}^2$ is a saturated ideal with six generators but has the ideal of the point $[1:0:0:0]$ as an embedded prime. $\mathbf{I}^{(2)}$ has four generators, is arithmetically Cohen-Macaulay and has analytic spread 2. This example demonstrates that a curve must be reduced in order to apply the theorem of Cowsik and Nori. From Remark 1.2 it is easy to see that for any ideal and any $n \geq 1$ $l(\mathbf{I})=l(\mathbf{I}^n)$ but here we have $l(\mathbf{I}) \neq l(\mathbf{I}^{(2)})$.*

These two examples were both drawn from the set of "monomial curves" in $\mathbb{P}^3$. A monomial curve will be taken to mean a curve embedded in $\mathbb{P}^3$ via a parametrization of the form $w = s^c$, $x = s^{c-a}t^a$, $y = s^{c-b}t^b$, $z = t^c$ where a,b,c are relatively prime positive integers with $a < b < c$. In recent work of Gimenez, Morales, and Simis [GMS], it was shown that the homogeneous ideal of any monomial curve in $\mathbb{P}^3$ has analytic spread 2 or 3. From results in the paper of Huneke and Huckaba [HH] one can then conclude that symbolic and ordinary powers of the homogeneous ideal of a monomial curve are equal if and only if the curve is a local complete intersection. Using the theory of numerical semigroups, one can determine if a given monomial curve is a local complete intersection [He]. We can construct in this way a large class of homogeneous ideals in $k[w,x,y,z]$ for which symbolic and ordinary powers are equal. Another large class can be constructed with the techniques of liaison: starting with a complete intersection curve in $\mathbb{P}^3$ we can do a "general" link to a smooth curve in $\mathbb{P}^3$ whose saturated ideal has 3 generators. Applying Theorem 1.12 we find that symbolic and ordinary powers are equal for such an ideal.

§2.   Dubreil's Theorem, Migliore's Generalization and Powers of Ideals.

For any homogeneous ideal $\mathbf{I}$ of $\mathbf{R}$ we will let $\alpha(\mathbf{I}) = \min\{\deg(f) | f \in \mathbf{I}\}$ and $\nu(\mathbf{I})$ be as defined in Section 1. We have the following theorem of Dubreil.

Theorem 2.1 [Du,DGM]. *If* $\mathbf{I}$ *is a homogeneous ideal in the ring* $k[x,y]$ *then* $\nu(\mathbf{I}) \leq \alpha(\mathbf{I}) + 1$.

This leads to the following corollary.

Corollary 2.2 [DGM]. *If* C *is a subscheme of* $\mathbb{P}^n$, *is arithmetically Cohen-Macaulay, and has codimension two then* $\nu(\mathbf{I}_C) \leq \alpha(\mathbf{I}_C) + 1$.

A broad generalization of Dubreil's theorem was achieved by Migliore. In order to explain this generalization in the context of curves in $\mathbb{P}^3$ we need some notation. Choose linear forms L_1, L_2 such that they form a complete intersection $\mathbf{A} = (L_1, L_2)$ not meeting a given curve C. Let $M(C)$ be the Hartshorne-Rao module of C (see page one for the definition). Let $K_A(C)$ be the submodule of $M(C)$ annihilated by $\mathbf{A}$. We then have:

Theorem 2.3 [M]. *If* C *is a curve in* $\mathbb{P}^3$ *then* $\nu(\mathbf{I}_C) \leq \alpha(\mathbf{I}_C) + 1 + \nu(K_A(C))$.

If C is arithmetically Cohen-Macaulay then $M(C) = 0$ and we get simply $\nu(\mathbf{I}_C) \leq \alpha(\mathbf{I}_C) + 1$. A curve, C, in $\mathbb{P}^3$ is said to be arithmetically Buchsbaum if the Hartshorne-Rao module of C is annihilated by the maximal ideal. For such a curve we let N denote the dimension of $M(C)$ as a k-vector space. If a curve is arithmetically Cohen-Macaulay then it is also arithmetically Buchsbaum with N=0. In the case that C is a curve in $\mathbb{P}^3$ which is arithmetically Buchsbaum, we obtain a result of Amasaki as a corollary to Theorem 2.3.

Corollary 2.4 [A, GM3]. *If C is an arithmetically Buchsbaum curve in $\mathbb{P}^3$ then $\nu(\mathbf{I}_C) \leq \alpha(\mathbf{I}_C) + 1 + N$.*

Recall that we let C_n denote the scheme defined by $\mathbf{I}^n$. In the situation where $\mathbf{I}^n = \mathbf{I}^{(n)}$ we have C_n is locally Cohen-Macaulay and $\mathbf{I}^n$ is the homogeneous ideal of C_n. If $\mathbf{I}^n = \mathbf{I}^{(n)}$ for all n and if C is not a complete intersection then by the results found in section 1 we can conclude that the analytic spread of $\mathbf{I}$ is 3 and that $\nu(\mathbf{I}^n) \sim rn^2$ (for some $r > 0$). It is easy to see that $\alpha(\mathbf{I}^n) = n\alpha(\mathbf{I})$ and we get

Corollary 2.5. *If C is a reduced locally Cohen-Macaulay curve in $\mathbb{P}^3$ which is not a complete intersection and if $\mathbf{I}_C^n = \mathbf{I}_C^{(n)}$ for all $n \gg 0$ then $\nu(K_A(C_n)) > sn^2$ for some $s > 0$ and all $n \gg 0$.*

Proof. By Theorem 2.3 we have

$$\nu(\mathbf{I}^n) \leq \alpha(\mathbf{I}^n) + 1 + \nu(K_A(C_n))$$
$$= n\alpha(\mathbf{I}) + 1 + \nu(K_A(C_n))$$
$$\Rightarrow \nu(K_A(C_n)) \geq \nu(\mathbf{I}^n) - n\alpha(\mathbf{I}) - 1$$

but we have $\nu(\mathbf{I}^n) \sim rn^2$ so the result follows.

For a general module, one expects $dim(M(C_n))$ to be much larger than $\nu(K_A(C_n))$. Corollary 2.5 shows us that for many curves, $\nu(K_A(C_n))$ grows faster than a quadratic polynomial in n. We can conclude that the Hartshorne-Rao module is growing at least as fast as a quadratic and probably much faster.

We will assume that C is locally Cohen-Macaulay, has at most three generators at every point and has two generators at most points. Let I be a defining ideal for C. We have a method for constructing resolutions of powers of the ideal sheaf $\mathfrak{I}_C$ of C from a resolution of I.

Let $\mathbf{I} = (F_1, F_2, \ldots, F_r)$ be an ideal defining a locally Cohen-Macaulay codimension two variety, C, in $\mathbb{P}^3$. Let $f_i = deg(F_i)$. Write a graded degree zero homomorphism from $\mathbf{R}(-f_1) \oplus \mathbf{R}(-f_2) \oplus \cdots \oplus \mathbf{R}(-f_r)$ to $\mathbf{I}$ by sending the canonical free basis of $\mathbf{R}(-f_1) \oplus \mathbf{R}(-f_2) \oplus \cdots \oplus \mathbf{R}(-f_r)$ to the generators of $\mathbf{I}$. Let K be the kernel of this map; then we have

$$0 \to K \to \bigoplus_{i=1}^{r} \mathbf{R}(-f_i) \to \mathbf{I} \to 0.$$

We can sheafify this short exact sequence and obtain a locally free resolution

$$0 \to \mathcal{E} \to \mathcal{F} \to \mathfrak{I}_C \to 0$$

with $\mathcal{F} = \mathcal{O}(-f_1) \oplus \mathcal{O}(-f_2) \oplus \cdots \oplus \mathcal{O}(-f_r)$ and $\mathcal{E}$ a locally free sheaf of rank $r - 1$. Let $\mathbf{H}^i_*(\mathbb{P}^3, \mathcal{G}) = \bigoplus_{n \in \mathbb{Z}} H^i(\mathbb{P}^3, \mathcal{G}(n))$. Consider the long exact sequence in cohomology associated to the above short exact sequence of sheaves:

$$0 \to \mathbf{H}^0_*(\mathbb{P}^3, \mathcal{E}) \to \mathbf{H}^0_*(\mathbb{P}^3, \mathcal{F}) \to \mathbf{H}^0_*(\mathbb{P}^3, \mathcal{I}_C) \to \mathbf{H}^1_*(\mathbb{P}^3, \mathcal{E}) \to 0.$$

Since $\mathbf{H}^0_*(\mathbb{P}^3, \mathcal{E}) \simeq K$, $\mathbf{H}^0_*(\mathbb{P}^3, \mathcal{F}) \simeq \bigoplus_{i=1}^r \mathbf{R}(-f_i)$, and $\mathbf{H}^0_*(\mathbb{P}^3, \mathcal{I}_C) \simeq \bar{\mathbf{I}}$ we have $\mathbf{H}^1_*(\mathbb{P}^3, \mathcal{E}) \simeq \bar{\mathbf{I}}/\mathbf{I}$. If $\mathbf{I}$ is the homogeneous ideal of C then $\mathbf{I}$ is saturated. The associated locally free resolution of $\mathcal{I}_C$ would then have $rank\mathcal{F} = \nu(\mathbf{I})$, $rank\mathcal{E} = \nu(\mathbf{I}) - 1$, and $\mathbf{H}^1_*(\mathbb{P}^3, \mathcal{E}) = 0$. If $F \twoheadrightarrow I$ then $Sym^n(F) \twoheadrightarrow I^n$. We can sheafify and consider the exact sequence

$$0 \to \mathcal{K} \to Sym^n\mathcal{F} \to \mathcal{I}^n_C \to 0.$$

The associated long exact sequence in cohomology gives

$$0 \to \mathbf{H}^0_*(\mathbb{P}^3, \mathcal{K}) \to \mathbf{H}^0_*(\mathbb{P}^3, Sym^n\mathcal{F}) \to \mathbf{H}^0_*(\mathbb{P}^3, \mathcal{I}^n_C) \to \mathbf{H}^1_*(\mathbb{P}^3, \mathcal{K}) \to 0.$$

From this sequence we conclude that $\mathbf{H}^1_*(\mathbb{P}^3, \mathcal{K}) = \bar{\mathbf{I}}^n/\mathbf{I}^n$. We now recall two definitions from Hartshorne's book [Ha]. If $\mathcal{E}$ is a locally free coherent sheaf on a noetherian scheme X then we define

$$\mathbb{P}(\mathcal{E}) \doteq \mathbf{Proj}(\bigoplus_{d \geq 0} Sym^d\mathcal{E})$$

We call $\mathbb{P}(\mathcal{E})$ the associated projective space bundle of $\mathcal{E}$. If $\mathcal{I}_C$ is a coherent sheaf of ideals on a noetherian scheme X then we define the blowing up, $\tilde{X}$, of X with respect to this sheaf of ideals by

$$\tilde{X} \doteq \mathbf{Proj}(\bigoplus_{d \geq 0} \mathcal{I}^d_C)$$

The surjection $\mathcal{F} \twoheadrightarrow \mathcal{I}_C$ leads to an injection $\tilde{X} \hookrightarrow \mathbb{P}(\mathcal{F})$. We also have the natural projection map $p: \mathbb{P}(\mathcal{F}) \twoheadrightarrow \mathbb{P}^3$ and we obtain the following diagram for curves in $\mathbb{P}^3$:

$$\tilde{X} \hookrightarrow \mathbb{P}(\mathcal{F})$$
$$\downarrow p$$
$$\mathbb{P}^3$$

$\tilde{X}$ can also be seen to be the vanishing locus of the map $p^*\mathcal{E} \to \mathcal{L}$ where $\mathcal{L}$ is the tautological line bundle on $\mathbb{P}(\mathcal{F})$. We look at the koszul resolution of $\mathcal{O}_{\tilde{X}}$ through $\mathcal{O}_{\mathbb{P}(\mathcal{F})}$ modules

$$(*) \qquad \ldots \to \wedge^3 p^*\mathcal{E} \otimes \mathcal{L}^{-3} \to \wedge^2 p^*\mathcal{E} \otimes \mathcal{L}^{-2} \to p^*\mathcal{E} \otimes \mathcal{L}^{-1} \to \mathcal{O}_{\mathbb{P}(\mathcal{F})} \to \mathcal{O}_{\tilde{X}} \to 0$$

If we tensor $(*)$ by $\mathcal{L}^2$ we get

$$(**) \qquad \ldots \to \wedge^3 p^*\mathcal{E} \otimes \mathcal{L}^{-1} \to \wedge^2 p^*\mathcal{E} \to p^*\mathcal{E} \otimes \mathcal{L} \to \mathcal{O}_{\mathbb{P}(\mathcal{F})} \otimes \mathcal{L}^2 \to \mathcal{O}_{\widetilde{X}} \otimes \mathcal{L}^2 \to 0$$

We want to push this sequence down through p into $\mathcal{O}_{\mathbb{P}^3}$. To do this first break up $(**)$ into several short exact sequences

$$\begin{aligned}
&1) \quad 0 \to K_1 \to \mathcal{O}_{\mathbb{P}(\mathcal{F})} \otimes \mathcal{L}^2 \to \mathcal{O}_{\widetilde{X}} \otimes \mathcal{L}^2 \to 0 \\
&2) \quad 0 \to K_2 \to p^*\mathcal{E} \otimes \mathcal{L} \to K_1 \to 0 \\
&3) \quad 0 \to K_3 \to \wedge^2 p^*\mathcal{E} \to K_2 \to 0 \\
&4) \quad 0 \to K_4 \to \wedge^3 p^*\mathcal{E} \otimes \mathcal{L}^{-1} \to K_3 \to 0 \\
&\quad \vdots
\end{aligned}$$

For each of the above short exact sequences we have an associated long exact sequence involving the "right derived functors of the direct image functor" [Ha]. From 1) we get

$$\begin{aligned}
0 \to p_*(K_1) &\to p_*(\mathcal{O}_{\mathbb{P}(\mathcal{F})} \otimes \mathcal{L}^2) \to p_*(\mathcal{O}_{\widetilde{X}} \otimes \mathcal{L}^2) \\
&\to R^1 p_*(K_1) \to R^1 p_*(\mathcal{O}_{\mathbb{P}(\mathcal{F})} \otimes \mathcal{L}^2) \to R^1 p_*(\mathcal{O}_{\widetilde{X}} \otimes \mathcal{L}^2) \\
&\to \ldots
\end{aligned}$$

From the projection formula [Ha] and general properties of projections of the tautological line bundle of a projectivized vector bundle [ACGH,Ha,K] we have

$$p_*(\mathcal{O}_{\mathbb{P}(\mathcal{F})} \otimes \mathcal{L}^2) = Sym^2\mathcal{F}, \quad p_*(\mathcal{O}_{\widetilde{X}} \otimes \mathcal{L}^2) = \mathcal{I}_C^2, \quad and \ R^1 p_*(\mathcal{O}_{\mathbb{P}(\mathcal{F})} \otimes \mathcal{L}^2) = 0.$$

From 2), we get

$$0 \to p_*(K_2) \to p_*(p^*\mathcal{E} \otimes \mathcal{L}) \to p_*(K_1) \to R^1 p_*(K_2) \to R^1 p_*(p^*\mathcal{E} \otimes \mathcal{L}) \to \ldots$$

and we have

$$p_*(p^*\mathcal{E} \otimes \mathcal{L}) = \mathcal{E} \otimes \mathcal{F}, \ R^i p_*(p^*\mathcal{E} \otimes \mathcal{L}) = 0 \ (for \ i > 0), \ R^1 p_*(K_1) = R^2 p_*(K_2).$$

From 3) we get

$$0 \to p_*(K_3) \to p_*(\wedge^2 p^*\mathcal{E}) \to p_*(K_2) \to R^1 p_*(K_3) \to R^1 p_*(\wedge^2 p^*\mathcal{E}) \to \ldots$$

and we have

$$R^i p_*(\wedge^2 p^*\mathcal{E}) = 0 \ (for \ i > 0), \ p_*(\wedge^2 p^*\mathcal{E}) = \wedge^2 \mathcal{E}, \ R^i p_*(K_2) = R^{i+1} p_*(K_3).$$

From 4) we get

$$0 \to p_*(K_4) \to p_*(\wedge^3 p^* \mathcal{E} \otimes \mathcal{L}^{-1}) \to p_*(K_3)$$
$$\to R^1 p_*(K_4) \to R^1 p_*(\wedge^3 p^* \mathcal{E} \otimes \mathcal{L}^{-1}) \to R^1 p_*(K_3)$$
$$\to \cdots$$

and we have

$$R^i(\wedge^3 p^* \mathcal{E} \otimes \mathcal{L}^{-1}) = 0 \ and \ R^i p_*(K_3) = R^{i+1} p_*(K_4).$$

For large enough n we have $\wedge^n p^* \mathcal{E} = 0$, this leads to $R^1 p_*(K_i) = 0 \ \forall i$ (by considering sequence 5, 6, etc.). Putting it all together we have

$$0 \to p_*(K_1) \to Sym^2 \mathcal{F} \to \mathcal{I}_C^2 \to 0$$
$$0 \to p_*(K_2) \to \mathcal{E} \otimes \mathcal{F} \to p_*(K_1) \to 0$$
$$0 \to p_*(K_3) \to \wedge^2 \mathcal{E} \to p_*(K_2) \to 0$$
$$0 \to p_*(K_4) \to 0 \to p_*(K_3) \to 0$$

so $\wedge^2 \mathcal{E} \approx p_*(K_2)$. This leads to $0 \to \wedge^2 \mathcal{E} \to \mathcal{E} \otimes \mathcal{F} \to p_*(K_1) \to 0$ which in turn leads to

Sequence 2.6. $0 \to \wedge^2 \mathcal{E} \to \mathcal{E} \otimes \mathcal{F} \to Sym^2 \mathcal{F} \to \mathcal{I}_C^2 \to 0$

More generally, by tensoring $(*)$ with $\mathcal{L}^n$, we are led to

Sequence 2.7. $0 \to \wedge^n \mathcal{E} \to \wedge^{n-1} \mathcal{E} \otimes \mathcal{F} \to \wedge^{n-2} \mathcal{E} \otimes Sym^2 \mathcal{F} \to \cdots \to$ $\wedge^2 \mathcal{E} \otimes Sym^{n-2} \mathcal{F} \to \mathcal{E} \otimes Sym^{n-1} \mathcal{F} \to Sym^n \mathcal{F} \to \mathcal{I}_C^n \to 0$

The main references for this section are Hartshorne's book on algebraic geometry [Ha], the book by Arbarello, Cornalba, Griffiths, Harris [ACGH], and a paper by Kempf [K]. I wish to thank L. Ein and M.S. Ravi both for bringing this construction to my attention and for explaining to me the steps involved.

§3 Some Consequences.

In this section we combine the ideas of Section 1 and Section 2. We begin by explaining some terminology and definitions. Given a scheme, C, let $\mathbf{I}_C$ denote the homogeneous ideal of C, $\nu(\mathbf{I}_C)$ denote the number of minimal generators of $\mathbf{I}_C$, and $codim(C)$ denote the codimension of C.

Definition 3.1. *A scheme,C, is said to be a scheme theoretic almost complete intersection (STACI) or a quasi complete intersection (QCI) if C is not a complete intersection and if there exists an ideal, $\mathbf{J}$, such that $\bar{\mathbf{J}} = \mathbf{I}_C$ and $\nu(\mathbf{J}) = codim(C) + 1$. C is said to be an almost complete intersection (ACI) if $\nu(\mathbf{I}_C) = codim(C) + 1$.*

Lemma 3.2. *Let C be a complete intersection curve in $\mathbb{P}^3$ with homogeneous ideal $\mathbf{I}_C$. The scheme defined by $\mathbf{I}_C^n$ is arithmetically Cohen-Macaulay and $\mathbf{I}_C^n = \mathbf{I}_C^{(n)}$.*

Proof. Assume the two generators of $\mathbf{I}_C$ have degrees d_1 and d_2. We have the Koszul resolution $\quad 0 \to \mathbf{R}(-d_1 - d_2) \to \mathbf{R}(-d_1) \oplus \mathbf{R}(-d_2) \to \mathbf{I}_C \to 0$. If we sheafify then we have $0 \to \mathcal{O}(-d_1 - d_2) \to \mathcal{O}(-d_1) \oplus \mathcal{O}(-d_2) \to \mathcal{I}_C \to 0$. Sequence 2.7 gives us a short exact sequence, $0 \to \mathcal{E} \to \mathcal{F} \to \mathcal{I}_C^n \to 0$, with $\mathcal{E}$ and $\mathcal{F}$ free. The scheme defined by $\mathbf{I}_C$ is a local complete intersection. This implies that the scheme defined by $\mathbf{I}_C^n$ has no embedded points. $\mathbf{I}_C^n$ is saturated since $\mathbf{I}_C^{\bar{n}}/\mathbf{I}_C^n = \mathbf{H}_*^1(\mathbb{P}^3, \mathcal{E}) = 0$. This gives us $\mathbf{I}_C^n = \mathbf{I}_C^{(n)}$. The scheme defined by $\mathbf{I}_C^n$ is arithmetically Cohen-Macaulay since $\mathbf{H}_*^1(\mathbb{P}^3, \mathcal{I}_C^n) = \mathbf{H}_*^2(\mathbb{P}^3, \mathcal{E}) = 0$.

For the rest of this section, curves will be taken to mean locally Cohen-Macaulay subschemes of pure dimension one. We will also assume that our curves are generic complete intersections with at most three local generators everywhere. The next lemma is well known. We include a proof due to its similarity in style to other proofs in this section.

Lemma 3.3. *For curves in $\mathbb{P}^3$, almost complete intersections are arithmetically Cohen-Macaulay.*

Proof. Since C is locally Cohen-Macaulay and codimension two, we have a resolution $0 \to \mathcal{E} \to \mathcal{F} \to \mathcal{I}_C \to 0$ where $\mathcal{F}$ is free (i.e. a direct sum of line bundles) and $\mathcal{E}$ is locally free with $\mathbf{H}^1(\mathbb{P}^3, \mathcal{E}(n)) = 0 \;\forall n$. Since C is an almost complete intersection, we can choose $\mathcal{F}$ so that it has rank three and $\mathcal{E}$ has rank two. $\mathcal{E}$ is a rank two vector bundle so $\mathcal{E} \approx \mathcal{E}^*(c_1)$ where c_1 is the first chern class of $\mathcal{E}$. By Serre duality $\mathbf{H}^2(\mathbb{P}^3, \mathcal{E}(n)) = 0 \;\forall n$. By the splitting criterion of Horrocks [OSS], $\mathcal{E}$ splits as a direct sum of line bundles. We have $\mathbf{H}_*^1(\mathbb{P}^3, \mathcal{I}_C) \doteq \bigoplus_{n \in \mathbb{Z}} \mathbf{H}^1(\mathbb{P}^3, \mathcal{I}_C(n)) = 0$ and thus C is arithmetically Cohen-Macaulay.

Theorem 3.4. *If C is an almost complete intersection curve in $\mathbb{P}^3$ then we have $\mathbf{I}_C^n = \mathbf{I}_C^{\bar{n}}$.*

Proof. By Lemma 3.3 we have a resolution $0 \to \mathcal{E} \to \mathcal{F} \to \mathcal{I}_C \to 0$ with $\mathcal{E}$ and $\mathcal{F}$ splitting as the direct sum of line bundles. Since the rank of $\mathcal{E}$ is two we have $\wedge^n \mathcal{E} = 0$ for $n > 2$. By Sequence 2.7 we have $0 \to \wedge^2 \mathcal{E} \otimes Sym^{n-2}\mathcal{F} \to \mathcal{E} \otimes Sym^{n-1}\mathcal{F} \to Sym^n \mathcal{F} \to \mathcal{I}_C^n \to 0$. We can write this as two short exact sequences

$$1) \qquad 0 \to \wedge^2 \mathcal{E} \otimes Sym^{n-2}\mathcal{F} \to \mathcal{E} \otimes Sym^{n-1}\mathcal{F} \to K \to 0$$

$$2) \qquad 0 \to K \to Sym^n \mathcal{F} \to \mathcal{I}_C^n \to 0$$

Since $\mathcal{F}$ is a sum of line bundles, we have $Sym^n\mathcal{F}$ is a sum of line bundles as well and this leads to $\mathbf{H}^1_*(\mathbb{P}^3, Sym^n\mathcal{F}) = 0$. Taking the associated long exact sequence in cohomology for 2) we get

$$0 \to \mathbf{H}^0_*(\mathbb{P}^3, K) \to \mathbf{H}^0_*(\mathbb{P}^3, Sym^n\mathcal{F}) \to \mathbf{H}^0_*(\mathbb{P}^3, \mathcal{I}^n_C) \to \mathbf{H}^1_*(\mathbb{P}^3, K) \to 0$$

Since $\bar{I}^n \approx \mathbf{H}^0_*(\mathbb{P}^3, \mathcal{I}^n_C)$ we see that $\mathbf{H}^1_*(\mathbb{P}^3, K) = \bar{I}^n/I^n$ i.e. $\mathbf{H}^1_*(\mathbb{P}^3, K)$ measures the failure of I^n to be saturated. Taking the associated long exact sequence in cohomology for 1) we find that $\mathbf{H}^1_*(\mathbb{P}^3, K) = 0$ (since $\mathcal{E}$ and $\mathcal{F}$ free lead to $\mathbf{H}^1_*(\mathbb{P}^3, \mathcal{E} \otimes Sym^{n-1}\mathcal{F}) = \mathbf{H}^2_*(\mathbb{P}^3, \wedge^2\mathcal{E} \otimes Sym^{n-2}\mathcal{F}) = 0$) hence $I^n = \bar{I}^n$.

Corollary 3.5. If C is a curve in $\mathbb{P}^3$ which is an almost complete intersection and a local complete intersection then $\mathbf{I}^n_C = \mathbf{I}^{(n)}_C$ and $\mathbf{H}^1_*(\mathbb{P}^3, \mathcal{I}^n_C) \neq 0 \ \forall n \geq 2$

Proof. Since C is a local complete intersection, the scheme defined by $\mathbf{I}^n_C$ has no embedded points. Since C is an almost complete intersection, $\mathbf{I}^n_C$ is saturated. We have $\mathbf{I}^n_C$ is saturated and without embedded points hence $\mathbf{I}^n_C = \mathbf{I}^{(n)}_C$. The second statement then follows from Theorem 1.12.

Corollary 3.5 can also be seen to follow entirely from Theorem 1.12 since an ACI local complete intersection must have analytic spread 3.

Theorem 3.6. For a scheme theoretic almost complete intersection (STACI) curve, C, in $\mathbb{P}^3$, $dim\mathbf{H}^1_*(\mathbb{P}^3, \mathcal{I}^n_C) \geq \binom{n+1}{2} \cdot dim\mathbf{H}^1_*(\mathbb{P}^3, \mathcal{I}_C)$.

Proof. Let C be defined scheme theoretically by the ideal $\mathbf{I} = (f_1, f_2, f_3)$. Since C is locally Cohen-Macaulay, we have a short exact sequence $0 \to \mathcal{E} \to \mathcal{F} \to \mathcal{I}_C \to 0$. $\mathcal{E}$ and $\mathcal{F}$ are locally free, $\mathcal{F}$ has rank three and splits as the sum of line bundles and $\mathcal{E}$ has rank two with $\mathbf{H}^1_*(\mathbb{P}^3, \mathcal{E}) = \bar{I}/I$, $\mathbf{H}^2_*(\mathbb{P}^3, \mathcal{E}) = \mathbf{H}^1_*(\mathbb{P}^3, \mathcal{I}_C)$, and $\wedge^n\mathcal{E} = 0$ for $n > 2$. By Sequence 2.7 we have $0 \to \wedge^2\mathcal{E} \otimes Sym^{n-2}\mathcal{F} \to \mathcal{E} \otimes Sym^{n-1}\mathcal{F} \to Sym^n\mathcal{F} \to \mathcal{I}^n_C \to 0$. We can write this as two short exact sequences

$$1) \quad 0 \to \wedge^2\mathcal{E} \otimes Sym^{n-2}\mathcal{F} \to \mathcal{E} \otimes Sym^{n-1}\mathcal{F} \to K \to 0$$
$$2) \quad 0 \to K \to Sym^n\mathcal{F} \to \mathcal{I}^n_C \to 0$$

From equation 2) we can conclude that $\mathbf{H}^1_*(\mathbb{P}^3, \mathcal{I}^n_C) = \mathbf{H}^2_*(\mathbb{P}^3, K)$ and from equation 1) we conclude that $\mathbf{H}^2_*(\mathbb{P}^3, \mathcal{E} \otimes Sym^{n-1}\mathcal{F}) \hookrightarrow \mathbf{H}^2_*(\mathbb{P}^3, K)$. This leads to $dim\mathbf{H}^1_*(\mathbb{P}^3, \mathcal{I}^n_C) = dim\mathbf{H}^2_*(\mathbb{P}^3, K) \geq dim\mathbf{H}^2_*(\mathbb{P}^3, \mathcal{E} \otimes Sym^{n-1}\mathcal{F}) = \binom{n+1}{2} \cdot dim\mathbf{H}^2_*(\mathbb{P}^3, \mathcal{E}) = \binom{n+1}{2} \cdot dim\mathbf{H}^1_*(\mathbb{P}^3, \mathcal{I}_C)$.

Proposition 3.7. *If C is an arithmetically Cohen-Macaulay curve in $\mathbb{P}^3$ then $\mathbf{I}_C^2 = \mathbf{I}_{\bar{C}}^2$.*

Proof. We have $0 \to \mathcal{E} \to \mathcal{F} \to \mathcal{I}_C \to 0$ with $\mathcal{E}$ and $\mathcal{F}$ splitting as sums of line bundles. By Sequence 2.8 we have $0 \to \wedge^2 \mathcal{E} \to \mathcal{E} \otimes \mathcal{F} \to Sym^2\mathcal{F} \to \mathcal{I}_C^2 \to 0$. We can write this as two short exact sequences

$$1) \quad 0 \to \wedge^2\mathcal{E} \to \mathcal{E} \otimes \mathcal{F} \to K \to 0$$

$$2) \quad 0 \to K \to Sym^2\mathcal{F} \to \mathcal{I}_C^2 \to 0$$

By equation 2) we have $\mathbf{H}_*^1(\mathbb{P}^3, K) = \mathbf{I}_{\bar{C}}^2/\mathbf{I}_C^2$ and by equation 1) we have $\mathbf{H}_*^1(\mathbb{P}^3, K) = 0$.

Corollary 3.8. *If C is arithmetically Cohen-Macaulay and a local complete intersection then $\mathbf{H}_*^1(\mathbb{P}^3, \mathcal{I}_C^2) \neq 0$.*

Proof. Follows immediately from Proposition 3.7 and Theorem 1.11

Remark. *For an arithmetically Cohen-Macaulay curve in $\mathbb{P}^3$ with homogeneous ideal $\mathbf{I}_C = (F_1, F_2, \ldots, F_r)$ we have a free resolution $0 \to \mathcal{E} \to \mathcal{F} \to \mathcal{I}_C \to 0$ where $\mathcal{E} = \bigoplus \mathcal{O}_{\mathbb{P}^3}(-e_i)$ and $\mathcal{F} = \bigoplus \mathcal{O}_{\mathbb{P}^3}(-f_i)$. The f_i are the degrees of the minimal generators of $\mathbf{I}_C$ i.e. $deg(F_i) = f_i$ and we are assuming that $f_1 \geq f_2 \geq \cdots \geq f_r$ and that $e_1 \geq e_2 \geq \cdots \geq e_{r-1}$. If $F_1, F_2, \ldots, F_r$ do not share a common component then we have $e_i > f_i$ and $e_2 > f_1$ [DGM, GM1]. We then get, from Sequence 2.6, a direct proof that $\mathbf{H}_*^1(\mathbb{P}^3, \mathcal{I}_C^2) \neq 0$.*

Theorem 3.9. *If $\mathbf{I}_C$ is the homogeneous ideal of C and if $\nu(\mathbf{I}_C) = 4$ then $\mathbf{I}^2 = \mathbf{I}_{\bar{C}}^2$ and $dim\mathbf{H}_*^1(\mathbb{P}^3, \mathcal{I}_C^2) \geq 4dim\mathbf{H}_*^1(\mathbb{P}^3, \mathcal{I}_C)$.*

Proof. We have a locally free resolution $0 \to \mathcal{E} \to \mathcal{F} \to \mathcal{I}_C \to 0$ with $\mathcal{F}$ a sum of line bundles, $\mathbf{H}_*^1(\mathbb{P}^3, \mathcal{E}) = 0$, $\mathbf{H}_*^2(\mathbb{P}^3, \mathcal{E}) = \mathbf{H}_*^1(\mathbb{P}^3, \mathcal{I}_C)$, $rank(\mathcal{F}) = 4$, and $rank(\mathcal{E}) = 3$. Utilizing Sequence 2.6 we can write

$$1) \quad 0 \to \wedge^2\mathcal{E} \to \mathfrak{E} \otimes \mathcal{F} \to K \to 0$$

$$2) \quad 0 \to K \to Sym^2\mathcal{F} \to \mathcal{I}_C^2 \to 0$$

Since $rank(\mathcal{E}) = 3$, we have $\wedge^2\mathcal{E} = \mathcal{E}^*(c_1)$ so by Serre duality we have $\mathbf{H}_*^2(\mathbb{P}^3, \wedge^2\mathcal{E}) = 0$. We have $dim\mathbf{H}_*^1(\mathbb{P}^3, \mathcal{E} \otimes \mathcal{F}) = 4 \cdot dim\mathbf{H}_*^1(\mathbb{P}^3, \mathcal{E}) = 0$ so $\mathbf{H}_*^1(\mathbb{P}^3, \mathcal{E} \otimes \mathcal{F}) = 0$. From equation 1) we then conclude that $\mathbf{H}_*^1(\mathbb{P}^3, K) = 0$. Since $\mathbf{H}_*^1(\mathbb{P}^3, K)$ measures the failure of $\mathbf{I}_C^2$ to be saturated, we get $\mathbf{I}_C^2 = \mathbf{I}_{\bar{C}}^2$. Looking again at equation 1) we have $\mathbf{H}_*^2(\mathbb{P}^3, \mathcal{E} \otimes \mathcal{F}) \hookrightarrow \mathbf{H}_*^2(\mathbb{P}^3, K)$. From equation 2) we have $\mathbf{H}_*^2(\mathbb{P}^3, K) = \mathbf{H}_*^1(\mathbb{P}^3, \mathcal{I}_C^2)$ so $dim\mathbf{H}_*^1(\mathbb{P}^3, \mathcal{I}_C^2) = dim\mathbf{H}_*^2(\mathbb{P}^3, K) \geq dim\mathbf{H}_*^2(\mathbb{P}^3, \mathcal{E} \otimes \mathcal{F}) = 4 \cdot dim\mathbf{H}_*^2(\mathbb{P}^3, \mathcal{E}) = 4 \cdot dim\mathbf{H}_*^1(\mathbb{P}^3, \mathcal{I}_C)$.

For any locally Cohen-Macaulay curve, C, in $\mathbb{P}^3$ we can write $0 \to \mathcal{E} \oplus \mathcal{G} \to \mathcal{F} \to \mathcal{I}_C \to 0$ with $\mathcal{F}$ and $\mathcal{G}$ sums of line bundles, $\mathbf{H}_*^1(\mathbb{P}^3, \mathcal{E}) = 0$, and $\mathbf{H}_*^2(\mathbb{P}^3, \mathcal{E}) = \mathbf{H}_*^1(\mathbb{P}^3, \mathcal{I}_C)$. This leads to the following

Theorem 3.10. *Given a curve, C, in $\mathbb{P}^3$ with homogeneous ideal $\mathbf{I}_C$ we have a locally free resolution as mentioned above and $dim\mathbf{H}^1_*(\mathbb{P}^3, \mathcal{I}^2_C) \geq (rank\mathcal{E} + 1) \cdot dim\mathbf{H}^1_*(\mathbb{P}^3, \mathcal{I}_C) - dim\mathbf{H}^2_*(\mathbb{P}^3, \wedge^2\mathcal{E})$.*

Proof. From $0 \to \mathcal{E} \oplus \mathcal{G} \to \mathcal{F} \to \mathcal{I}_C \to 0$ we get via Sequence 2.6

$$1) \quad 0 \to \wedge^2\mathcal{E} \oplus \mathcal{E} \otimes \mathcal{G} \oplus \wedge^2\mathcal{G} \to \mathcal{E} \otimes \mathcal{F} \oplus \mathcal{G} \otimes \mathcal{F} \to K \to 0$$

$$2) \quad 0 \to K \to Sym^2\mathcal{F} \to \mathcal{I}^2_C \to 0$$

By equation 2) we have $\mathbf{H}^2_*(\mathbb{P}^3, K) = \mathbf{H}^1_*(\mathbb{P}^3, \mathcal{I}^2_C)$ and by equation 1) we have $\mathbf{H}^2_*(\mathbb{P}^3, K) \geq (rank\mathcal{E} + 1) \cdot dim\mathbf{H}^1_*(\mathbb{P}^3, \mathcal{I}_C) - dim\mathbf{H}^2_*(\mathbb{P}^3, \wedge^2\mathcal{E})$. Combining these gives us our result.

Corollary 3.11. *If $rank\mathcal{E} = 3$ then $dim\mathbf{H}^1_*(\mathbb{P}^3, \mathcal{I}^2_C) \geq 4 \cdot dim\mathbf{H}^1_*(\mathbb{P}^3, \mathcal{I}_C)$.*

Theorem 3.10 requires us to find $dim\mathbf{H}^2_*(\mathbb{P}^3, \wedge^2\mathcal{E})$. By the work of Rao [R1] we can use such a result for an entire liaison class. (that is, if we know $(rank\mathcal{E} + 1) \cdot dim\mathbf{H}^1_*(\mathbb{P}^3, \mathcal{I}_C) - dim\mathbf{H}^2_*(\mathbb{P}^3, \wedge^2\mathcal{E}) > t$ then for any curve, D, in the same even liaison class as C we have $dim\mathbf{H}^1_*(\mathbb{P}^3, \mathcal{I}^2_D) > t$).

Using the method of liaison addition [S,GM2] we can construct a curve, C, with resolution $0 \to T_{\mathbb{P}^3}(a) \oplus T_{\mathbb{P}^3}(b) \to \mathfrak{F} \to \mathcal{I}_C \to 0$ where $T_{\mathbb{P}^3}$ is the tangent bundle to $\mathbb{P}^3$. We can then use Macaulay [Mac] to compute $\mathbf{I}^2_C/I^2_C$ and $\mathbf{H}^1_*(\mathbb{P}^3, \mathcal{I}^2_C)$. If we combine this with the information gained from Sequence 2.6 and from the Euler sequence then we can compute $\wedge^2 T_{\mathbb{P}^3}(n)$ and $T_{\mathbb{P}^3} \otimes T_{\mathbb{P}^3}(n)$ for all n. With this information we are able to conclude that for Buchsbaum curves, C, with $dim\mathbf{H}^1_*(\mathbb{P}^3, \mathcal{I}_C) \neq 3$ then either $\mathbf{I}^2_C \neq \bar{\mathbf{I}^2_C}$ or $\mathbf{H}^1_*(\mathbb{P}^3, \mathcal{I}^2_C) \neq 0$ and if $dim\mathbf{H}^1_*(\mathbb{P}^3, \mathcal{I}_C) \geq 4$ then $\mathbf{I}^2_C \neq \bar{\mathbf{I}^2_C}$.

More generally, using the methods of liaison addition combined with information obtained from Sequence 2.7 and with the help of Macaulay, we can often obtain useful information about the cohomology of tensor products and wedge products of vector bundles and then obtain information about the behavior of liaison classes of curves in $\mathbb{P}^3$.

§4 Related Questions and Conjectures.

Much more is left to be said about the growth of the Hartshorne-Rao module. Presently Corollary 3.5 gives us a lower bound on the growth but is almost certainly much too conservative. Knowledge of the liaison class of the curve was probably underused. There are many more "special cases" that should be examined in more detail as well. We have the following questions to investigate further:

Question. What more can we say about the asymptotic growth of $\mathbf{H}^1_*(\mathbb{P}^3, \mathcal{I}^n_C)$?

Question. Do we have $dim\mathbf{H}^1_*(\mathbb{P}^3, \mathfrak{I}^n_C) \leq dim\mathbf{H}^1_*(\mathbb{P}^3, \mathfrak{I}^m_C) \Longleftrightarrow n \leq m$?

Let $A = min\{n|\mathbf{H}^1(\mathbb{P}^3, \mathfrak{I}_C(n)) \neq 0\}$ and $B = max\{n|\mathbf{H}^1(\mathbb{P}^3, \mathfrak{I}_C(n)) \neq 0\}$. The diameter of the Hartshorne-Rao module is defined to be B-A+1. We then have

Question. Do we have $diam(\mathbf{H}^1_*(\mathbb{P}^3, \mathfrak{I}^n_C)) \leq diam(\mathbf{H}^1_*(\mathbb{P}^3, \mathfrak{I}^m_C)) \Longleftrightarrow n \leq m$?

We define $k(n) = min\{\alpha|\mathfrak{m}^\alpha \cdot \mathbf{H}^1_*(\mathbb{P}^3, \mathfrak{I}^n_C) = 0\}$ (where $\mathfrak{m}$ is the maximal ideal in $\mathbf{R}$).

Question. Do we have $k(n) \leq k(m) \Longleftrightarrow n \leq m$? Or does this depend on the curve?

Question. How does the module structure of $\mathbf{H}^1_*(\mathbb{P}^3, \mathfrak{I}_C)$ affect the behavior of $\mathbf{I}^n$? Do we gain more information knowing $\mathbf{H}^1_*(\mathbb{P}^3, \mathfrak{I}_C)$ is cyclic, indecomposable, self-dual? Do we gain more information knowing which powers of the maximal ideal annihilate $\mathbf{H}^1_*(\mathbb{P}^3, \mathfrak{I}_C)$ or knowing the diameter of the module, etc.?

Question. If we know the behavior of $\mathbf{I}^n_C$ and $\mathbf{H}^1_*(\mathbb{P}^3, \mathfrak{I}^n_C)$ for a curve C, what more can we say about the behavior of $\mathbf{I}^n_D$ and $\mathbf{H}^1_*(\mathbb{P}^3, \mathfrak{I}^n_C)$ if D is linked to C? If D is directly linked to C? If D is evenly linked to C?

It should be noted that the construction leading to Sequences 2.6 and 2.7 did not use the fact that we were considering curves in $\mathbb{P}^3$. The argument required a generic complete intersection scheme with a locally free resolution of length two. We could thus derive results similar to those found in section 3 but stated in the context of locally Cohen-Macaulay codimension two subschemes of $\mathbb{P}^n$.

REFERENCES

[A]   M. Amasaki, *On the structure of arithmetically Buchsbaum curves in $\mathbb{P}^3_k$*, Publ RIMS **20** (1984), 793-837.

[ACGH]   E. Arbarello, M. Cornalba, P. Griffiths, J. Harris, *Geometry of Algebraic Curves vol. 1*, Springer-Verlag, New York, 1985.

[B1]   M. Brodmann, *Asymptotic stability of $Ass(M/I^n M)$*, Proc. of the AMS **74** (1979), 16-18.

[B2]   M. Brodmann, *The asymptotic nature of the analytic spread*, Math. Proc. Camb. Phil. Soc. **86** (1979), 35-39.

[BBM]   E. Ballico, G. Bolondi, J. Migliore, *The Lazarsfeld-Rao problem for liaison classes of two-codimensional subschemes of $\mathbb{P}^n$*, American J. of Mathematics **113** (1991), 117-128.

[BEL]   A. Bertram, L. Ein, R. Lazarsfeld, *Vanishing theorems, a theorem of Severi, and the equations defining projective varieties*, J. of the AMS **4, No 3** (1991).

[BM1]   G. Bolondi, J. Migliore, *The structure of an even liaison class*, Trans. of the AMS **316, No 1** (1989).

[BM2]   G. Bolondi, J. Migliore, *Buchsbaum liaison classes*, J. Algebra **123** (1989), 426-456.

[Bu]   L. Burch, *Codimension and analytic spread*, Math. Proc. Camb. Phil. Soc. **72** (1972), 369-373.

[C]   M. Chang, *Characterization of arithmetically Buchsbaum subschemes of codimension 2 in* $\mathbb{P}^n$, J. Diff. Geometry **31** (1990), 323-341.

[CN]   R.C. Cowsik and M.V. Nori, *On the fibres of blowing up*, J. Indian Math. Soc. **40** (1976), 217-222.

[D]   S.P. Dutta, *Symbolic powers, intersection multiplicity, and asymptotic behaviour of Tor*, J. London Math. Soc. **28** (1983), 261-281.

[DGM]   E. Davis, A.V. Geramita, P. Maroscia, *Perfect homogeneous ideals: Dubreil's theorems revisited*, Bull. Soc. Math. France, 2e serie **108** (1984), 143-185.

[Du]   P. Dubreil, *Sur quelques propriétés des systèmes de points dans le plan et des courbes gauches algébriques*, Bull. Soc. Math. France **61** (1933), 258-283.

[EN]   J.A. Eagon and D.G. Northcott, *Ideals defined by matrices and a certain complex associated with them*, Proc. Royal Soc. Ser. A **269** (1962), 188-204.

[GLP]   L. Gruson, R. Lazarsfeld, C. Peskine, *On a theorem of Castelnuovo and the equations defining projective varieties*, Inv. Math. **72** (1983), 491-506.

[GM1]   A.V. Geramita and J.C. Migliore, *Hyperplane sections of a smooth curve in* $\mathbb{P}^3$, Comm. in Algebra **17 (12)** (1989), 3129-3164.

[GM2]   A.V. Geramita and J.C. Migliore, *A generalized liaison addition*, J. Algebra (to appear).

[GM3]   A.V. Geramita and J.C. Migliore, *Generators for the ideal of an arithmetically Buchsbaum curve*, J. Pure and Applied Algebra **58** (1989), 147-167.

[GMS]   Gimenez, Morales, Simis, *preprint* (1993).

[H1]   C. Huneke, *The theory of d-sequences and powers of ideals*, Adv. in Math. **46** (1982), 249-279.

[H2]   C. Huneke, *Criteria for complete intersections*, J. of the LMS (2) **32** (1985), 19-30.

[Ha]   R. Hartshorne, *Algebraic Geometry*, Springer-Verlag, New York, 1977.

[He]   J. Herzog, *Generators and relations of abelian semigroups and semigroup rings*, Manuscripta Math. **3** (1970), 175-193.

[HH]   S. Huckaba and C. Huneke, *Powers of ideals having small analytic spread*, Amer. J. of Math. **114** (1992), 367-403.

[Ho]   M. Hochster, *Criteria for equality of ordinary and symbolic powers of primes*, Math. Z. **133** (1973), 53-65.

[HU]   C. Huneke and B. Ulrich, *Powers of licci ideals*, Commutative algebra (Berkeley, CA, 1987) MSRI Publ. 15, Springer-Verlag, New York, 1989, pp. 339-346.

[K]   G. Kempf, *On the geometry of a theorem of Riemann*, Annals of Math. 2nd series **98** (1973), 178-185.

[LR]   R. Lazarsfeld and P. Rao, *Linkage of general curves of large degree*, Algebraic Geometry-open problems (Ravello 1982) LNM 997, Springer-Verlag, New York, 1983, pp. 267-289.

[M]   J.C. Migliore, *Submodules of the deficiency module*, J. Lond. Math Soc. (to appear).

[Ma]   H. Matsumura, *Commutative Ring Theory*, Cambridge, 1986.

[Mac]   D. Bayer and M. Stillman, *Macaulay: A system for computation in algebraic geometry*.

[MDP]   M. Martin-Deschamps and D. Perrin, *Sur la Classification des Courbes Gauches (Asterisque 184-185)*, 1990.

[NR]   D.G. Northcott and D. Rees, *Reductions of ideals in local rings*, Proc. Camb Phil Soc. **50** (1954).

[OSS]   C. Okonek, M. Schneider, and H. Spindler, *Vector Bundles on Complex Projective Space*, Birkhauser, 1988.

[PS]   C. Peskine and L. Szpiro, *Liaison des varietes algebriques I*, Inv. Math. **26** (1974), 271-302.

[R1]   P. Rao, *Liaison among curves in* $\mathbb{P}^3$, Inv. Math. **50** (1979), 205-217.

[R2]   P. Rao, *Liaison equivalence classes*, Math. Ann. **258** (1981), 169-173.

[S]   P. Schwartau, *Liaison Addition and Monomial Ideals*, Ph.D. thesis, Brandeis University, 1982.

ftp 130.15.100.29 81076235 q